birth of a
psychedelic
culture

Ralph Metzner

Ram Dass and Ralph Metzner

FOREWORD BY JOHN PERRY BARLOW

with Gary Bravo

& commentaries by other contributors

Conversations
about Leary,
the Harvard
Experiments,
Millbrook
and the Sixties

birth of a psychedelic culture

Synergetic Press

Published by Synergetic Press
1 Bluebird Court, Santa Fe, NM 87508

Library of Congress Cataloging-in-Publication Data

Ram Dass.
Birth of a psychedelic culture : conversations about Leary, the Harvard experiments, Millbrook and the sixties / by Ram Dass and Ralph Metzner, with Gary Bravo and commentaries by other contributors.
    p. cm.
Includes bibliographical references.
ISBN 978-0-907791-38-6 (alk. paper)
        1.Hallucinogenic drugs—Research—United States—History—20th century. 2. Hallucinogenic drugs—Psychological aspects. 3. Leary, Timothy, 1920-1996. 4. Ram Dass. 5. Metzner, Ralph. 6. Harvard University. Dept. of Social Relations. 7. Psychology, Experimental—United States—History—20th century. 8. Counterculture—United States—History—20th century. I. Metzner, Ralph. II. Bravo, Gary. III. Title.
    BF209.H34R36 2010
    154.4—dc22
                                          2009020096

Book design: Arlyn Eve Nathan
Editor: Linda Sperling
Cover illustration: "Psychedelic Ocean," Georgios Kollidas
Typesetting: Deborah Parrish Snyder
Typeface: Diotima and Gill Sans Light
Printed by Arizona Lithographers

Contents

Ram Dass, Timothy Leary and Ralph Metzner, Harvard Project Reunion, 1996

Dedication

I would like to acknowledge with deep gratitude and affection my two great mentors from those magical, joyous times of creativity and exploration in the 1960s – Timothy Leary and Richard Alpert (now Ram Dass). They generously shared their gifts of vision, experience and energy and remained my life-long friends.

Ralph Metzner

We all three are profoundly grateful to the fellow explorers and inner space cosmonauts who participated in these journeys and adventures, some of whom are represented in the accounts in this book. To all of them and to the many thousands of others who witnessed and participated in the birth joys and pangs of a new visionary, psychedelic culture – we offer heart-felt salutation and blessings.

Ram Dass, Ralph Metzner and Gary Bravo

Special Thanks
to the Contributors

DARLENE DE SEDLE

DOROTHY FADIMAN

FRANK FERGUSON

LORA FERGUSON

LISA FERGUSON

GRAY HENRY

PEGGY HITCHCOCK

SUSAN HOMER

MICHAEL KAHN

PAUL LEE

GEORGE LITWIN

JEAN McCREEDY

ELSA VON ECKARTSBERG

ROLF VON ECKARTSBERG

GUNTHER WEIL

John Perry Barlow, former Wyoming rancher, lyricist for the Grateful Dead,
cofounder and vice-chair of the Electronic Frontier Foundation

In the Beginning ...

by John Perry Barlow

LSD is a drug that produces fear in people who don't take it. Timothy Leary

It's now almost half a century since that day in September 1961 when a mysterious fellow named Michael Hollingshead made an appointment to meet Professor Timothy Leary over lunch at the Harvard Faculty Club.

When they met in the foyer, Hollingshead was carrying with him a quart jar of sugar paste into which he had infused a gram of Sandoz LSD. He had smeared this goo all over his own increasingly abstract consciousness and it still contained, by his own reckoning, 4,975 strong (200 mcg) doses of LSD. And the mouth of that jar became perhaps the most significant of the fumaroles from which the '60s blew forth.

Everybody who continues to obsess on the hilariously terrifying cultural epoch known as the '60s – which is to say, most everybody from "my ge-ge-generation," the post-War demographic bulge that achieved permanent adolescence during that era – has his or her own sense of when the '60s really began.

There are a lot of candidates: the blossoming pink cloud in the Zapruder film, Mario Savio's first speech in Sproul Plaza, the passage of the Gulf of Tonkin Resolution, the Beatles first appearance on the *The Ed Sullivan Show*, the first Acid Test, the Human Be-In in Golden Gate Park, the release of the song "Good Vibrations," the day Jerry Garcia got kicked out of the army.

But often as not, if you are a Boomer, the '60s began for surreal on the day you dropped acid.

And if that is when the shit hit your personal fan, you may owe a debt of ambiguous gratitude to the appealingly demonic young sociopath who conveyed the Stark Bolt of Chemical Revelation to the nice young gentlemen of the Harvard Psilocybin Project.

The essential tameness of the group that was to become so notorious is only one fascinating feature of discourse to follow between the Project's second and third most celebrated veterans: Ram Dass (who as Richard Alpert, PhD, was Tom Sawyer to Tim Leary's Huckleberry Finn) and Dr. Ralph Metzner (who began as an acolyte and wound up presiding over the remains).

In the fascinating book you're about to read, you will find numerous photographs of members of the Project, taken prior to the arrival of Mr. Hollingshead and his Magic Mayonnaise Jar. In some of these, the learned investigators are actually whacked on psilocybin and yet, their narrow black ties are still neatly knotted, their horn-rimmed glasses are on straight, their earnest civilization is still visibly intact. Consider that Dr. Alpert's first impulse, upon regaining the ability to walk during his first psychedelic experience, was to head off through the snow to his parents' house and start shoveling their driveway. Upon being discovered, his defiant response was to dance a jig. This is truly a rebel without claws.

But a few days after that fateful lunch with Hollingshead, Timothy Leary dropped acid and everything changed. The sober, scientific center of the Harvard Psilocybin Project lost its hold on the centripetal edge. The past started to end and the future started to begin. Their ties loosened and disappeared, along with belief in any such prosaic artifact as objective reality and the social conventions that accompanied it. As Leary later wrote in *High Priest* (p. 256-257):

From the date of this session it was inevitable that we would leave Harvard, that we would leave American society and that we would spend the rest of our lives as mutants, faithfully following the instructions of our internal blueprints, and tenderly, gently disregarding the parochial social inanities.

Ram Dass had a somewhat more alarmed reaction in this book:

When Tim first took LSD, he didn't speak for weeks. I went around saying, "We've lost Timothy, we've lost Timothy." I was warning everybody to not take that drug, because Tim wasn't talking and he was sort of dull … When I took it, I felt it went so far beyond the astral, beyond form, to pure energy. It showed me that in previous psychedelic sessions, I had been screwing around in the astral plane. LSD was no nonsense. If you weren't grounded somewhere, you'd go out on this drug.

They were both right, of course. These were by no means unusual responses to the experience. Thanks in very large part to the subsequent exertions of Drs. Leary, Alpert and Metzner, the experience was one shared over the following decade by tens of millions of Americans, the larger part of whom found it difficult ever after to take seriously the verities that few in Eisenhower's America would have questioned. Our paradigm got fucking well shifted.

At least mine certainly did. And so, I would venture, did that of the United States of America, during the trip we took between 1961 and 1972.

One can make a non-ludicrous case that the most important event in the cultural history of America since the 18'60s was the introduction of LSD. Before acid hit American culture, even the rebels believed, as Thoreau, Emerson and Whitman implicitly did, in something like God-given authority. Authority, all agreed, derived from a system wherein God or Dad (or, more often, both) was on top and you were on the bottom.

And it was no joke.

Whatever else one might think of authority, it was not funny. But after one had rewired one's self with LSD, authority – with its preening pomp, its affection for ridiculous rituals of office, its fulsome grandiloquence, and eventually, and sublimely, its tarantella around Mutually Assured Destruction – became hilarious to us and there wasn't much we could do about it.

No matter how huge and fearsome the puppets, once one's perceptions were wiped clean enough by the psychedelic solvent to behold their strings and the mechanical jerkiness of their behavior, it was hard to suppress the giggles. Though our hilarity has since been leavened with tragedy, loss, and a more appropriate sense of our own foolishness, we're laughing still.

The book you're about to read – and I recommend that you actually do – is a saga of holy heroism. The people you'll meet in it were like the Lewis and Clark of the Mind. But it is also a cautionary tale and contained within it is a lot of the real reason that America had such a visceral immune reaction to our sudden, terrifying and transforming "Otherness" in the middle of its consciousness.

Before delightedly steering the train off its rails, we were given a glimpse of grace and infinity. But like all that is utterly true, the lightning was brief and the thunder rolls still.

In the beginning for me – and for many of us – there was the realization that religion was mostly the creation of God in man's own image. Just as Tim Leary became furious at Catholicism shortly after hitting West Point, I bought a little Honda motorcycle and found that my dopily consoling Mormonism couldn't seem to ride along. Like the maddeningly glib Dick Alpert – and believe me, he was a man of many words in those days – I left monotheism for sex and velocity.

But there had been, even in a book as weird as the one the Angel Moroni purportedly gave Joseph Smith (Mark Twain called it "chloroform in print"), a spark of something. It was not religion, but you could almost see it from there.

I sped around with a longing for the Spirit that seemed inaccessible until sometime in 1964 when I read about the "Good Friday Experiment" in which, on Good Friday of 1962, Walter Pahnke, Tim Leary and the two battle-scarred saints of the Unnamable whose reminiscences you're about to read, had given psilocybin to some divinity students in Boston University's Marsh chapel and – *mirabile dictu!* – they fucking saw God or something like It. And all because somebody gave them a pill.

Like most people raised by hick kids in the mountains, I was a mystic without ever having heard the word. If I could have a direct experience of The Thing Itself, without all that regulatory obligation wrapped around it, I would become whole again. After that, I read everything I could find about mystico-mimetic chemicals: Gordon Wasson's 1957 article for *Life* magazine about magic mushrooms, Aldous Huxley's *Doors of Perception*, Bill Burroughs's *Yage Letters*, etc. I wanted a piece of that communion wafer and so did a lot of other kids raised around the dreary wasteland of American piety.

In the fall of 1965, I entered Wesleyan University where both the man who was to become Ram Dass, as well as the man who sheltered and then spurned the Harvard Psilocybin Project, Dave McClelland, had taught shortly before. I knew about Leary, Alpert and Metzner and had my own copy of *The Psychedelic Experience*. But I thought they were still at Harvard. I was going to go find them.

Before I could get around to that pilgrimage, I found myself at a Vassar mixer one late night in late 1965 and met a strangely luminous Indian Brahmin fellow who stood apart. He asked me if I could give him a ride to the "religious retreat" where he was staying not far from Poughkeepsie and I agreed. So we wheeled around shiny narrow roads to Millbrook in a truly Biblical downpour and the next thing I knew I was looking at the headquarters of the Castalia Foundation.

He invited me in. I didn't know who lived there. Now, at that point, as you will read herein, my heroes had not only been cast out of Harvard, but paradise as well. Inside the house it was not such a pretty sight. The social order had been whupped upside the head too many times already, but that didn't bother me. I had Forrest Gumped my way into the Temple of Delphi. Not long after that, I was fully enrolled in the Eastern Orthodox Church of LSD.

A great deal more could be said about my initiation and the adventures that followed, but this is not about my long, strange trip. Besides, there are better stories in the pages that lie before you about the perception of *mysterium tremendum* and its effect upon mere mortals. (Hell, understanding the legend of Dr. Faustus might not be a bad start either.)

I will say that there was a night in late 1966, I think, when I rode a motorcycle from Millbrook to Middletown during an ice storm and was, because of the acid, convinced that I could no more leave the road than an electron could escape the centerline of a linear accelerator.

I will also say that, by then, I'd switched my academic focus from physics to phenomenology with a particular focus on Medieval Christian mystics like St. Theresa, St. John of the Cross, and Meister Eckhart. I had a sign on my dorm room door displaying the following formula: [picture of me] + [skeletal schematic representation of the LSD-25 molecule] = [picture of the Buddha]. The acid was working.

What I didn't know then was that my best friend from prep school, a kid named Bob Weir, who had been strangely incommunicado since shortly after he worked on my family's ranch, had been right next to another great fumarole of pharmaceutical whacketydoodah, the Acid Tests.

His little band the Grateful Dead had been part of an experiment in mass hallucination which seemed, from our East Coast view, to make Millbrook look like a Trappist monastery. It sounded to me like what these West Coast people were doing was a particularly blasphemous form of drug abuse, the spiritual equivalent of breaking into Chartres Cathedral and getting drunk on the communion wine.

But, while we were looking down our long patrician noses at these barbaric shenanigans, they were apparently producing transformations similar to our own. Five years later, Hunter S. Thompson recalled 1965 and 1966 in San Francisco like this (*Fear and Loathing in Las Vegas*, pg 68):

There was madness in any direction, at any hour … You could strike sparks anywhere. There was a fantastic universal sense that whatever we were doing was right, that we were winning. And that, I think, was the handle – that sense of inevitable victory over the forces of Old and Evil. Not in any mean or military sense; we didn't need that. Our energy would simply prevail.

Yes. That seemed right. Even as we were dismantling the monotheistic model of God as Abusive Father, we were assembling another one – in our own image of course – more personally available through mysticism and generally more immanent than the Previous Dude, but still inclined to lend special sanction to the actions of a particular socio-political cohort. Which, happily, turned out to be ours. God, or Something Like It, was on our side this time.

The fact that God might turn up looking like a fat guy with an elephant head or as an aperture into pure, spirit-scalding Light, or even as Michael Hollingshead on a bad day, didn't matter to us. The Apocalypse was nigh. The Age of Aquarius had dawned, and God was no longer in his Heaven but getting down, right there inside of us and our holy pills.

By spring of 1967, the central characters of this book had already started to feel the arrogance of this premise. All three had gone to India and two had come limping back. Personally, I was still accelerating into the radiant fog, and so was a large percentage of my swollen generational demographic.

The Gathering of the Tribes had taken place in Golden Gate Park in January of that year. Leary and Ginsberg had turned up there along with the international press and the coastal schism in the Church of Acid had been officially healed. Somewhere in there, *Time* magazine ran a cover story on "The Hippies." A more attentive cultural observer than I would have known by that sign that we'd reached our high-water mark.

Whatever my earlier misgivings about the Acid Tests, I had learned by then that my dear Weir had been part of this heresy. I was tickled to hear that the Grateful Dead were going to play their first New York gig at a Bleecker Street disco called the Cafe Au GoGo in June.

Early June 1967 was a mighty time the reverberations of which are now as ubiquitous in American cultural history as is the Big Bang in the rest of the universe. As I remember it, the Dead played on June 6th. The Six Day war had broken out the day before. *Sgt. Pepper's Lonely Hearts Club Band* had been released five days before, as had the Grateful Dead's eponymous first record. I had helped make arrangements to take the Dead up to Millbrook the day after.

After the show, which was kind of forgettable, Weir and I wandered over to Washington Square Arch and were trying to debrief one another. It was steady work. It wasn't obvious that he had entirely passed the Acid Test. His eyes were all pupil, it seemed. He had the longest hair I'd ever seen on a human with a penis. And he'd become a fellow of very few words.

While we were struggling with the acquisition of a common language, a pale green Ford Falcon station wagon leapt the curb fifteen feet away and, like evil clowns emerging in platoon strength from a tiny circus car, some ten Long Island toughs poured out of it and headed toward us. You could see with one eye that they weren't from our side of a culture war that had already gotten ugly in America. Like T cells in jackboots, they took us for antigens and meant us harm.

As they were circling, Weir looked up and said mildly, "You know, I sense violence in you guys, and whenever I feel it in myself, there's a song I like to sing." (And I'm thinking, "??!") All of a sudden he's chanting "Hare Krishna," and what with my wondering ears should I hear but the toughs singing along. For about fifteen seconds. And then they beat the crap out of us.

John Perry Barlow, 1967

So, as I drove my 550 horsepower Chevy Super Sport up the Taconic to Millbrook the next day, both Bobby and I looked like Wiley Coyote after a bad run-in with an Acme product. Also on board was a girl named Bos (over whom I was totally goofy at the time), Phil Lesh and Frank Zappa's star chick singer, a hot number who called herself Uncle Meat.

We listened to war news from the Holy Land on the radio and we had on board a copy of Sgt. Pepper's, which I'd bought on the way out of town and which none of us had heard yet. I was trying to explain to my inamorata Bos, both of whose parents were Jewish psychiatrists, why I felt so moved by St. John of the Cross' *Dark Night of the Soul*.

It was a moment in the '60s, that day was.

When we got to the Hitchcock Mansion, it was pretty clear that whatever else the charming Dr. Leary was trying to tell the world, housekeeping tips were not being integrated into it. Few of the regulars remained. Ralph, Tim, and even Michael Hollingshead had reached a point the year before when they'd found Dr. Alpert's manias so alarming that they'd sent him packing off to India. (Where he was, by this time, already in a dhoti and well on his way to becoming Baba Ram Dass. He dropped the Baba as soon as the wisdom actually kicked in.)

That night we all gathered in the second floor library and, with ecclesiastical ceremony, we put on *Sgt. Pepper's Lonely Hearts Club Band*. Nobody said a word while the record played. Many of us couldn't have if we'd wanted to. I was so high I could taste the music and found the purple notes a little hard to chew. When the London Philharmonic's last cacophonous notes trailed out of "A Day in the Life," there was a portentous silence and … Timmy intoned solemnly, "My work is complete." Little did he know how right and how wrong he was.

I say this because, while he and the rest of us crazy angels had truly delivered some form of apocalypse, it could not actually take effect in a couple of years or even a couple of generations. No revelation so culturally shattering was going to be universally accepted overnight. No generation that called itself Now was going to find lengthy evolution palatable, but that was what was on our plate nonetheless.

Yes, the Beatles had dropped acid and the whole world had noticed but not everyone was pleased. The Empire was about to strike back. Moreover, we had, with our giddy carnival frenzies and darker madnesses soon to come, sown the seeds of our own disaster.

Hell, there was a moment in the fall of 1967 that I myself became convinced, with passionate intensity, that we were that "rough beast" Yeats had described. We were leading society into such a quagmire of narcissistic, self-reaffirming subjectivism that if we continued to "Storm Heaven," as Jay Stevens put it, little of what might be a reasonable basis for polity or even what passes for civilization would survive our self-indulgence.

I went unhinged. I became psychotic and grandiose and decided to become what would have been America's first suicide bomber. I was prepared to sound a warning with my own spattered flesh and that of innocent others. I would be the admonition on the front page of every paper that would slow the juggernaut of hideous Truth. I had the means and the moment. Fortunately, praise Providence, I was found out and stopped forty-five minutes short of my own vile apocalypse. I lived on Thorazine for a while after that.

But my intended mission attracted other willing soldiers. In my stead, we got Charlie Manson and Altamont. We got the behavioral sink of the long autumn that followed the Summer of Love. We got the Chicago Democratic Convention, the Weather Underground, the Symbionese Liberation Front, the communes that turned into rural slums overnight. What we got was the Bill.

Hunter S. Thompson put it very harshly but with some accuracy a few years later in *Fear and Loathing in Las Vegas* (pgs 178-179):

All those pathetically eager acid freaks who thought they could buy Peace and Understanding for three bucks a hit. But their loss and failure is ours, too. What Leary took down with him was the central illusion of a whole life-style that he helped to create ... a generation of permanent cripples, failed seekers, who never understood the essential old-mystic fallacy of the Acid Culture: the desperate assumption that somebody ... or at least some force – is tending the light at the end of the tunnel.

Who can blame the Rotarians of America for being alarmed? We became terrifying enough to scare ourselves. The Babbitry came down with a not-ill-considered immune response that, however draconian its methods, was nevertheless their Apollonian duty just as appropriately as the creation of Dionysian chaos had seemed to be ours.

But perhaps even more unsettling to the Powers That Had Been was the fact that, as I mentioned earlier, in addition to calling into question their version of God-given authority, we now found them amusing.

Since there is nothing authority hates worse than being laughed at, the authorities resolved to make themselves even less funny. The harder the acidheads laughed, the more bellicose, pig-headed, and, well ... authoritarian the Powers became. And thus, instead of a quick abdication by the cultural forces that had been in charge of Western "Civilization" for two thousand years and a peaceful transfer of power to the laughing Aquarians, there commenced the forty year Mexican standoff that I call the War Between the Fifties and the Sixties.

Of course, this conflict had a lot of other names along the way, most of them delicious with the kind of dark irony it takes an acidhead to properly savor. There was the Viet Nam War, the War on Poverty, The War on Terror, both Wars on Iraq, and throughout, interwoven into every inch of American life, there was the War on (Some) Drugs. There was also, implicitly, the War on the Bill of Rights.

Whatever its other depraved social consequences – the millions jailed, the military dead and maimed, the deceit and denial at all levels of American society, particularly within the nuclear family – The War Between The Fifties and The Sixties endowed us with a golden age of irony. If you didn't have a sense of irony, you were missing most of the fun, and, um, ironically, just about the only Americans who did have one were the acidheads. This created yet another badly hung loop as various iterations of "We had to destroy the village in order to save it" concatenated through the culture and, once again, we were the only ones laughing.

And then, lest we forget, throughout much of this period, and scarcely mentioned by anybody, acidhead or Republican Whip, was the greatest surreality of all: the almost universal belief that somewhere and sometime soon, someone would foul up and launch the nuclear storm that would glaze the planet with our elemental constituents. And if you couldn't laugh at that, what could you laugh at?

Now, it seems many of these horrors may be consigned to the history of a future that never happened. While new horrors surely await us, very few still believe we're likely to go "toe-to-toe with the Russkies" in nuclear combat as Slim Pickens put it in one of the most immortal lines of the 1960s.

Better still, the worst of the authoritarian prigs have so magnificently shot their wad during eight long years of Cheney/Bush that only those savagely beaten by their own fathers or the clergy support them now. Aside from the coming kerfuffle over war crimes indictments and ongoing skirmishes along the Mason-Dixon Line, the War Between the Fifties and the Sixties may be finally drawing to an end.

Indeed, as I write these words, the President of the United States, in addition to being black and self-admittedly smart and well-educated, strikes me as a fellow who probably dropped acid at some point. At the least, when asked if he "inhaled," he replied, "I thought that was the point."

Now that the worst of it may be over, perhaps it may become possible for various members of Congress, federal judges, ranked military officers, prominent clergy, and captains of industry – aside from the peculiarly honest Steve Jobs – to do as most of these, had they been brave enough, ought to have done decades ago and say in public:

There was a moment, years ago, when I took LSD. And, whatever the immediate consequences, it made me a different person than I would have been and different in ways I have been grateful for all this time.

That would be a mighty moment. Those who still live are all now older and wiser than we were in those literally heady days, and we may finally be ready to tell such truths without setting off another round of conflict. Ram Dass, whose terse phrases make up less than half the text of this book but the majority of its insights, has come a long way along the path of the profound since when I first met him as the maddeningly manipulative Dick Alpert.

Indeed, at one point some years ago, I was having dinner with him and confessed to a moral dilemma that I was having a hard time teasing apart. I can't even remember what it was now, but he cut through it snickety-snack, like a sword through the Gordian Knot, with a few well-chosen words.

"That's the problem with you, man," I said, and continued with a concession I would not have made even to Baba Ram Dass, who turned up first at Wesleyan when he returned from India, still pretty full of self-promoting nonsense, "You're just a lot wiser than I am."

His eyes narrowed. "Don't you lay that wisdom shit on me, Barlow," he retorted, thereby defeating his own argument with its refutation. But even before then, he had uttered a motto that has been far more important to carrying the essential message of the sixties than "Turn on. Tune in. Drop out" (which was actually coined by Marshall McLuhan and given to Tim Leary since it didn't fit McLuhan's rap).

Ram Dass said, "Be here now."

And here we all are. Now. Ready at last with the patience, forgiveness, contrition and self-amusement necessary to continue the work in earnest. It is a good time to go back to the beginnings of the revolution still underway and take stock.

It is a good time to read this book. Now.

Morning yoga class at Millbrook House

HARVARD UNIVERSITY
DEPARTMENT OF SOCIAL RELATIONS

CENTER FOR RESEARCH IN PERSONALITY
MORTON PRINCE HOUSE

5 DIVINITY AVENUE
CAMBRIDGE 38, MASSACHUSETTS

December 6, 1960

Olympia Press
Paris
France

Gentlemen:

    Would you please send me a copy of <u>Naked Lunch</u> by William Burroughs. This book is needed in connection with research I am doing on drugs and their effect on creativity.

    I am making arrangements with American customs to see that this book can be admitted to the United States.

Sincerely yours,

Timothy Leary

TL:ds

Letter to publisher, Maurice Girodias, Olympia Press

*Professors Timothy Leary (top left) Richard Alpert (top right) visit Copenhagen
with friends during the Congress for Applied Psychology, 1961*

Harvard Professors Timothy Leary and Richard Alpert,
spokesmen for psychedelic research, 1961

Part 1

The Harvard Psilocybin Project 1960 – 1962

Summer, 1960

Timothy Leary takes visionary mushrooms, known to the Aztecs as *Teonanácatl,* in Cuernavaca, Mexico. He returns to Harvard University, and together with fellow faculty members Frank Barron and Richard Alpert and several graduate students, initiates research projects with psilocybin, the psychoactive ingredient of the mushroom, supplied by Sandoz Pharmaceuticals.

Fall, 1960

Aldous Huxley, then visiting lecturer at MIT, and Huston Smith, professor of religion at MIT, become involved with the project as consultants and advisors. Poets Allen Ginsberg and Peter Orlovsky visit, take psilocybin and become allies and supporters of the project. They take Leary to turn on Beatnik novelist Jack Kerouac and adventurer Neal Cassady. Arthur Koestler, author of *Darkness at Noon* and other books, visits Leary and takes psilocybin. He later dismisses the experience as "ersatz mysticism."

Spring, 1961

Richard Alpert and Ralph Metzner each have their first experiences with psilocybin. Studies are conducted giving psilocybin to artists and writers, as well as graduate students and "normal" people (not undergraduates); collecting written accounts and questionnaire responses. First published formulation of the "set and setting" hypothesis, according to which the content of a psychedelic experience is a function of the internal set or intention and the external context or environment.

Leary initiates a research project at Concord State Prison, designed to bring about insight and behavior change in convicts, using psilocybin. Graduate students participating and assisting with this project include Ralph Metzner, Gunther Weil and Ralph Schwitzgebel. Madison Presnell, MD, prison psychiatrist, provides medical supervision.

Fall, 1961

William Burroughs, author of *Naked Lunch* and other books, visits Leary and takes psilocybin. He and Leary present on a panel at the American Psychiatric Association convention in Boston. Burroughs is cynically dismissive of the project's aim.

Walter Houston Clark, Professor of the Psychology of Religion at Andover Newton Theological Seminary, joins the project as an enthusiastic supporter and advisor.

Professor David McClelland, Director of the Center for Research in personality, where the psilocybin project is housed (and Leary and Alpert's boss) circulates a memo questioning the scientific value of the research, and the societal impact of psychedelic drugs in places like India. Michael Hollingshead, English freelance researcher and writer, arrives at Tim's house on Grant Avenue. He provides Leary his first LSD session.

November, 1961

Important turning point session at Alpert's house in Cambridge, around themes of good and evil, ethics and spiritual leadership. Participants include, besides Leary and Alpert, Ralph Metzner, Michael Kahn, George Litwin and his wife, and Gunther Weil; also, musician Maynard Ferguson and his wife Flo.

Spring, 1962

Frederick Swain, American Vedantist monk, arrives to visit the Harvard group; introduces group to his Indian guru Gayatri Devi, of the Bengali lineage of Ramakrishna, who headed Vedanta ashrams on the East and West coasts. Gayatri Devi and Rabbi Zalman Schachter experience psilocybin and become supportive advisors to the project.

At a faculty meeting at the Center for Personality Research, the psilocybin project, and Leary and Alpert personally, are vigorously criticized on both scientific and ethical grounds. Social Psychology professor Herbert Kelman is one of the chief critics, as is experimental psychologist Brendan Maher.

Control of the supply of psilocybin is removed from Tim Leary and put in hands of psychiatrist Dr. Dana Farnsworth, head of the Harvard University Counseling Center. Leary and Alpert are forbidden to give psilocybin to undergraduate students. The Concord Prison Project is completed; other work with psilocybin comes to an end. The results of that and other studies are written up and published in the psychological and psychiatric journals.

Professor David McClelland, Chair of the Center for Personality Research, tells graduate students on the project, including Metzner, Litwin and Weil, that they will not be able to do their PhD thesis on research with psilocybin. Metzner chooses to work under supervision of Walter Mischel on a study in child development, asking what are the factors influencing the capacity of a child to learn to delay gratification. He obtains his PhD in the spring of 1962.

April, 1962 – The last Harvard-sponsored psilocybin study, known as the "Good Friday" study in "experimental mysticism," takes place during an Easter service conducted by renowned preacher Howard Thurman, in Marsh chapel in Boston. Designed and conducted by Walter Pahnke, doctor of medicine and divinity, the study is a double blind placebo controlled examination of psilocybin in the induction of mystical experiences in divinity students.

Timothy Leary

Richard Alpert

Ralph Metzner

Beginnings of the Harvard Psilocybin Project

GB   Let's start by setting the scene for both of you getting to Harvard and meeting Timothy Leary. What were you doing and what were you like at that time? What were your first impressions of Tim Leary before he went to Cuernavaca and took mushrooms?

RD   I got my master's degree at Wesleyan University, where the chairman of the department was David McClelland. He transferred to Harvard to become Director of the Center for Personality Research. McClelland's professor at Yale University was Robert B. Sears, who had become head of the psychology department at Stanford. So, I was recommended to the doctoral psychology program at Stanford University, where I enrolled. But I got Cs in two of my courses and fell behind in the program. Robert Sears wrote me a letter, which I read when I was on a ship to vacation in Hawaii with my parents. The letter said "You are a disappointment and we are taking away your scholarship." I turned myself around. I decided to work nights and sleep during the day. I got high grades and the PhD from Stanford.

RM   So you got your psychology doctorate at Stanford?

RD   Yes, and Stanford invited me to join the faculty, even though I was not doing that well as a graduate student and was a middle of the road researcher. But I was a very good teacher – none of the other faculty wanted to teach Psychology 1. They changed the rules to let me in as a faculty member. That was very funny – all because of my charisma. Later, Dave McClelland wrote to Bob Sears and asked him, "Do you think Dick Alpert knows anything about psychology yet?" Because I had a lot of charisma, I got offered a faculty position at Harvard, as well.

RM   The image that I, as a graduate student, had of you as a faculty member was that you were a golden boy, a rising star.

RD   When Dave McClelland brought me to Harvard in 1958-59, my first job was to work with John M. Whiting, the cultural anthropologist who was doing cross-cultural research on child development. I was his assistant in that project on Child Development, in the Department of Education. I was also working as Research Associate on a project at Stanford, called the SMSG (School Mathematics Study Group). I also had

GB *Gary Bravo*

RD *Ram Dass*
      (Richard Alpert)

RM *Ralph Metzner*

three other appointments at Harvard: At the Center for Personality Research, which was part of Department of Social Relations; at the Psychology Department, where they studied rats; and also at the Health Services department, where I was doing therapy. There were eight psychiatrists and me, the lone psychologist (Laughs).

RM   You were a money magnet apparently. You attracted thousands of dollars in research grants and gave lots of people jobs, including me, when I worked for you at Stanford, in the summer of 1959, my first year of graduate school. It was my first time in California.

RD   I didn't see myself as a money magnet. It's true that I had this grant from the SMSG (School Mathematics Study Group), which was studying the results of teaching the new mathematics. I could do what I wanted and hired people to help me with the research. Our studies showed, among other things, that if you were introduced to math by a woman teacher, you were probably going to hate math.

GB   Even if you were a girl and were introduced to math by a woman teacher?

Richard Alpert, 1962

RD   They still had the math aversion. At the Center for Personality Research, I had the big office at the end of the hall. One day, Dave McClelland said, "Dick, we have a new guy coming. I picked him up in Italy; he was riding a bicycle. His ideas are interesting." Three doors down from my big palatial office was a closet for mops and things like that. Dave said, "Could we put him in there?" "Sure," I said. So Tim Leary got this closet for an office.

RM   It was the most heavily trafficked place. People were going by all the time, and Tim was very genial and would invite them in for conversations.

RD   Tim and I were forced together a little bit because we were both single – he was a widower and I was unmarried. We started spending evenings at the bar or with his kids. Very quickly, faculty colleagues and the students saw Tim as different. They were all impressed that they were even at Harvard University. The only one that wasn't impressed was Tim. I liked the fact that Tim was not starry-eyed about being on the Harvard faculty.

GB   Ram Dass, what was your theoretical orientation in psychology at that time?

RD   You couldn't get into any of these big schools without a commitment to behaviorism. I didn't like behaviorism and Tim rescued me from that, because our research was not behaviorist. That was one of the reasons the other faculty didn't like us.

GB   What was your first impression of Tim, Ralph?

RM   I actually took a course with him, the semester before he took the mushrooms, which has always stuck in my mind. He was talking about what he called his philosophy of "Existential-Transactionalism." Eric Berne's writings on game theory were part of that. He taught a seminar with a small group of students, of which I was one. He was saying that the usual relationships that psychologists have, as psychologists, are either doctor – patient, or experimenter – subject, both of which are artificial, asymmetric power relationships. One person is always superior to the other person, by the nature of the relationship. And he would say "I don't want to do that. There are better ways to relate to people." So we, the graduate students with the instructor, would go into somebody's house who had asked for consultation or help. We would sit around the kitchen table, drink coffee, and say, "Okay, what's the situation and how can we be of help?" Present ourselves as resources, not doctors or authorities. I thought that was very impressive. I liked that. It was very egalitarian.

RD   Who would the people be?

RM   They could be members of a family that had requested help, or a group of some kind. Connecting with people was part of the design of the course. This philosophy of research led to the design of the prison project: Tim said we're not going to go into the prison as experimenters and subjects. Convicts often get offered shorter parole terms in exchange for volunteering for a study by some drug company. Tim said we don't want to do that. It's totally inappropriate for what we're trying to do. His attitude was: "Here are these experiences we have found very interesting. We want to share them with you. In fact, we're going to take them with you." So, there would be this basis of trust right from the beginning. I thought that was really cool, very beautiful.

RD   In fact, that egalitarian attitude in Tim suffused all the way through everyone involved in the projects.

RM   It's very American, isn't it? He placed high value on freedom and equality.

GB   Wasn't there a study where graduates would go into low income housing projects and do this kind of helping, breaking down boundaries?

RM   Yes. As part of his teaching, Tim encouraged different people to take on different projects. One graduate student in our class was working with the nuns in a convent.

GB   Leary wrote that this was already stretching the Harvard psychology paradigm, even before the psilocybin study got started.

RM   Tim Leary and Henry Murray were the two faculty people at the Center for Personality Research who most impressed me by their vision and originality.

RD   And Tim was very impressed with Murray.

RM   Murray had invented a projective test called the Thematic Apperception Test (TAT). You would be shown pictures of people in ambiguous situations and asked to tell stories that were evoked in you. He used this concept of apperception. What is apperception? It's perception with awareness of a larger context: A consciousness of meaning and understanding in addition to perception of certain stimuli. I think now, in retrospect, it's not unlike a description of an expanded state of consciousness, what you get when you take a psychedelic – enhanced awareness of contextual meaning.

GB   Ram Dass, didn't you offer to take Leary on a plane trip to Central America at the time he had his famous first mushroom session in Cuernavaca?

RD   Yes, and Frank Barron, who knew about the mushrooms, gave Tim the idea to try them.

RM   "Hey, Tim, you should try these mushrooms." Two wild Irishmen! Tim always said Frank Barron was his mentor. The two had met at UC Berkeley. Barron had done studies on the origins of creativity, what qualities of mind and personality fostered creativity. In the first year of the Harvard psilocybin study, Barron participated actively. Later, he returned to California and taught for many years at UC Santa Cruz, continuing his studies of creative individuals.

GB   Ram Dass, had you had some experience with marijuana prior to involvement with psilocybin?

RD   I was turned on to pot at Stanford by Vic Lovell, a student who was a therapy patient of mine. I guess he had compassion for me. I was a therapist for a lot of far-out people and they liked marijuana. I was into cocktails – that's who I was.

RM   Well, you were far ahead of the curve as far as drugs were concerned, compared to me. I was as naive as a sheep among wolves. I had no idea that there was a drug that could affect the mind so profoundly in a positive direction. Of course, I also didn't know what the mind was. I knew certain theories from writings – behaviorist learning theory and psychoanalysis. I was just a preprogrammed graduate student robot following along; "This is wrong, this is right, read these books, not those, admire those authors, not these others and so forth."

RD   See, that's what Harvard represents.

RM   Harvard told you how the world works. There's behaviorism and psychoanalysis. Those were the two paradigms in psychology. Psychology had its separate building, where Skinnerian behaviorists studied schedules of reinforcement in rats and pigeons. Personality and Clinical Psychology, which I was studying, was part of the Department of Social Relations, along with Social Psychology, Sociology, and Cultural Anthropology. I liked that interdisciplinary concept. We took seminars with students and faculty in all four of these disciplines. I thought it was a great educational model, especially compared to the rather narrow conceptions of psychology I had encountered as an undergraduate at Oxford University. On the other hand, you, Ram Dass, were a rising star, out of my league completely. Plus, you had an airplane and you had a motorcycle. You were out there in the firmament.

GB   You lived in a railroad car?

Alpert, Leary and Dr. Sidney Cohen at a professional presentation early 1960s

RD   Well, I didn't actually live in a railroad car. I had the use of a private railroad car, very luxurious, because my father was president of the New York, New Haven and Hartford Railroad. I would travel between Boston and New York in that car. Once there was an American Psychological Association meeting in New York, and I had a party in a fabulous suite in Grand Central Station. Then, I took the psychologists one by one and showed them the private railroad car. They were very impressed, which is what I wanted.

GB   Ram Dass, was there ever a rivalry between you and Tim Leary? Or were you friends and colleagues all the way through?

RD   We'd get fairly close, and then we would get too close and we'd pull back. We taught some courses together, for example, on Psychotherapy and Game Theory.

RM   Did you turn Tim on to pot?

GB   In *High Priest* Leary writes that after he told Alpert about his mushroom experience, Alpert said, "Oh it sounds like marijuana." And Tim got depressed, "Oh that's all this is?" Do you remember that?

RD   No, I don't remember that exchange. But it seems to me Tim had a negative attitude toward marijuana. He wanted us to separate ourselves from marijuana. I had come to think of marijuana as wonderful, as a mild psychedelic. Tim felt strongly that psychedelics were in a special category, different from pot, which was associated with the New York music scene.

GB   Was that because Tim wanted to make the distinction between the illegality of marijuana and the legality of psychedelics, as opposed to an experiential distinction?

RD   Yes, I think so.

RM   I think that was probably true for Tim at that point, although later he came to appreciate the valuable sensory-enhancing qualities of pot. In the early days at Harvard, his recreational drug of choice was alcohol. I remember driving home with Tim sometimes from Harvard, and he'd be drinking a martini in the car.

GB   Where were you, Ralph, prior to participating in the Concord Prison Project?

RM   I was a graduate student in the Personality and Clinical Psychology track. It was my second year. I was just following along the pre-programmed path of the graduate student in the Department of Social Relations. Walter Mischel was my advisor.

RD   You hadn't had any experiences with drugs in England?

RM   Oh no, not at all. I took psychology and philosophy at Oxford. The psychology was experimental, and the philosophy was linguistic analysis. Ludwig Wittgenstein was very influential in those circles. My favorite philosophy professor was John Austin, whose specialty was the philosophical analysis of ordinary language. I'm still very much into that. One of the professors in the Psychology Department was J. Anthony Deutsch, who later came to the United States. He had designed and built a robot rat that could learn a maze – to test his theoretical model. So, I was reading all these studies of conditioning and learning in animals. At Harvard, in the Department of Social Relations, we took seminars in behavioral psychology, but also in social psychology and anthropology, sociology and psychoanalysis. At the end of the first year, we were supposed to write a major paper. I wrote on "Learning Theory and the "Therapy of Neurosis" and it was actually published in the *British Journal of Psychology*, as a separate monograph, by Cambridge University Press. It was my first publication and used theories and findings from animal learning studies by people like Dollard and Miller, to understand neuroses as learned behavior; it was part of the field of behavior therapy just then emerging. Henry Murray encouraged this effort; he said it was at the interface of different fields that creativity and innovation happen.

At the end of the first year, we were also expected to do an experimental study and I did a maze learning experiment with rats which turned out to be traumatic for me. I set up this maze with the rats in the basement of one of Harvard's buildings. I did it during the Christmas recess when everybody was gone. The experiment worked out as it was designed to do and I wrote it up in a paper for the course. But, at the end of the experiment I had these rats, and what was I supposed to do with them? I had to clean up the room and get rid of the rats. I remember going around to different professors and asking them how to dispose of the rats. I would get these ghoulish suggestions: "Take them by the tail and hit them on the edge of the table, or hit them with a hammer." I was appalled. I had no idea I was expected to kill the rats. They call it "sacrificing" the animals. I even called professional exterminators. When I told them the rats I wanted killed were in cages, they refused to get involved. We don't do that, they said. Eventually, an older graduate student said: "You need to get some chloroform and put it with the rats in big cylindrical cardboard tubs – you have to gas them."

RD   Oh, do you?

RM   So I had to do that. I put the chloroform in the container with twenty to thirty rats. They were sort of jiggling in the container for a while and then were quiet. When I stood up I hit my head on a steel beam and knocked myself out. I don't know how long I was out. Some years later, when I had come to a shamanistic understanding of the interconnected web of life, I tendered my apologies to the Great Rat Spirit for this transgression. At the time, I only knew I was never going to do any more experiments involving animals. So, I welcomed the idea of working with a drug to help people have insight and to change. It was a liberating alternative vision.

GEORGE LITWIN

I was born in Detroit, and raised in an auto industry and labor union family. My father was a tool and die maker, and both my parents and an uncle were involved in the formation of the United Auto Workers (UAW). I came to the Harvard Department of Social Relations in 1958 from the University of Michigan, where I had become interested in the ceremonial use of peyote by the Navajo. I had been studying with David Aberle, a distinguished anthropologist who explained that these ceremonies were held for important tribal purposes. When I came to graduate school at Harvard, I used the grant money from my NSF fellowship to initiate a research project at the Massachusetts Mental Health Center, giving mescaline to volunteer subjects. My faculty sponsor was Dr. Martin Orne, the well-known psychiatrist-researcher on hypnosis, who didn't believe mescaline had any value, but did believe in supporting research projects that were "outside the box."

George Litwin, c. 1961

When Tim Leary arrived at Harvard in 1959, I was assigned to him as my academic advisor. I met with him weekly in his tiny little office and he would lecture me sternly on the dangers and problems of the use of drugs in psychology. He had a strong position that the primary use of drugs in psychology was to manipulate and control patients, which is certainly true in most mental health settings. He urged me to stop doing this research and turn toward more existential issues that had to do with people coping with their everyday lives. He would say to me, "George, you're a very intelligent young man. You should get off this drug interest, and turn your work to something that would be more practical and will have more long-term merit."

Leary had become very interested and involved in existential psychology. As I listened to his lectures about existentialism as the kind of psychology that has to do with experiencing the moment we are in, not looking back or forward, I was struck by the parallels to what my mescaline subjects were saying. They spoke in the same kind of language about what was happening right now … in the hospital, in the situation they were in, feelings inside themselves, and so forth. They had very little external orientation, and little of the intense hallucinatory phenomena that I had been told to expect. In fact, many of the subjects were quite lucid and very concerned with what was happening right now, in their life right now, and what was coming up about that. I maintained my point of view that the mescaline project had potential, while Leary still preferred existentialism.

When Timothy arrived back in Cambridge in the fall of 1960, returning from his experience with visionary mushrooms in Oaxaca, he had changed. I was in the building when he greeted several people and, grabbing me by both shoulders, pulled me aside. He said "I now understand about these mind-altering drugs. I have experienced what you were talking about. We need to initiate research in this area immediately. Can you help?" I told him that synthetic psilocybin (originally extracted from the psilocybe mushroom) and LSD were developed and manufactured by Sandoz Pharmaceuticals in Switzerland. That very afternoon he and I sat down and wrote a letter on Harvard stationery to Sandoz, at their branch in New Jersey, saying we were Harvard psychologists interested in researching and experimenting with these substances for the possible benefit of people suffering with various kinds of emotional disorders. We expected to receive a long form back that had to be filled out and signed by various people. Instead, what came in the mail was a large bottle of psilocybin pills with a little note that said "Good luck in your research. Let us know your findings." As the senior professor, Timothy took charge of the psilocybin supply, which is perhaps an important event given the development of the story.

First Experiences with Psilocybin

RM   What was your first experience with psilocybin like? I think the first one is really interesting to look at. It's an initiation, isn't it?

RD   It's the one I relate in *Be Here Now.* It was at Tim's house, in Newton, Massachusetts, March 6, 1961. I remember the next Monday I had to teach a class on motivation.

RM   Was it just you and Tim?

RD   No, there was one other person: Tim's 12-year old son Jackie was upstairs hanging out with the dog. The dog came in during the session and didn't seem to be breathing properly. We decided we couldn't tell if something was wrong because our perception was altered and so we called Jackie. We watched Jackie with the dog and it turned out that Jackie realized our predicament. The dog was fine, as it turned out. Then I went into the living room and I had my solo trip.

I had gone off by myself to reflect upon these new feelings and senses. A deep calm pervaded my being. The rug crawled and the pictures smiled, all of which delighted me. Then I saw a figure standing about eight feet away, where a moment before there had been none. I peered into the semi-darkness and recognized none other than myself, in cap and hood, as a professor. It was as if that part of me, which was Harvard professor, had separated or disassociated itself from me.

"How interesting … an external hallucination, "I thought. "Well, I worked hard to get that status but I don't really need it." Again I settled into the cushions, separate now from my professorness, but at that moment the figure changed … now it was that aspect of me who was a social cosmopolite. "Okay, so that goes too, "I thought. Again and again the figure changed and I recognized over there all the different aspects I know to be me … cellist, pilot, lover … With each new presentation, I again and again reassured myself that I didn't need that anyway.

Then I saw the figure become that in me which was Richard Alpert-ness, that is, my basic identity that had always been Richard. I associated the name with myself and my parents called me Richard: "Richard, you're a bad boy." So Richard has badness. Then "Richard, aren't you beautiful!" Then Richard has beauty. Thus develop all these aspects of self.

Sweat broke out on my forehead. I wasn't at all sure I could do without being Richard Alpert. Did that mean I'd have amnesia? Was that what this drug was going to do to me? Would it be permanent? Should I call Tim? Oh, what the hell – so I'll give up being Richard Alpert. I can always get a new social identity. At least I have my body … But I spoke too soon.

As I looked down at my legs for reassurance, I could see nothing below the kneecaps, and slowly, now to my horror, I saw the progressive disappearance of limbs and then torso, until all I could see with my eyes open was the couch on which I had sat … I felt that I must be dying since there was nothing in my universe that led me to believe in life after leaving the body …

The panic mounted, adrenalin shot through my system – my mouth became dry, but along with this, a voice sounded inside – inside what, I don't know – an intimate voice asked very quietly, and rather jocularly, it seemed to me, considering how distraught I was, "… but who's minding the store?"

When I could finally focus on the question, I realized that although everything by which I knew myself, even my body and this life itself, was gone, still I was fully aware! Not only that, but this aware "I" was watching the entire drama, including the panic, with calm compassion.

Instantly, with this recognition, I felt a new kind of calmness – one of a profundity never experienced before. I had just found that "I," that scanning device – that point – that essence – that place beyond. A place where "I" existed independent of social and physical identity. That which was I was beyond Life and Death …

Fear had turned to exaltation. I ran out into the snow laughing as the huge flakes swirled about me. In a moment the house was lost from view, but it was all right because inside I Knew …

Around five in the morning I walked back, plowing through the snow to my parents' home, and I thought, "Wouldn't it be nice; I'll shovel the walk – young tribal buck shovels the walk." So I started slowly to shovel the walk and my parents' faces appeared at the upstairs window.

"Come to bed, you idiot. Nobody shovels snow at five in the morning."

And I looked up at them and I heard the external voice I had been listening to for thirty years, and inside me, something said, "It's all right to shovel snow and it's all right to be happy." (From Be Here Now)

RD   From my first trip I got liberated. I saw my parents and saw that peeved look and how it affected me. And I stopped and I did a jig with the shovel. It was the first time that I experienced an inner thing that was stronger than my social conditioning. I'd always listened to the power. My father taught me to always listen to the power, the authority. It was the first jig I did from hearing what happens inside as predominant over that. They and my teachers and my professors and my bosses taught me the dance. I figured I'm a professor at Harvard, I must know the dance. The Monday after the session, I was teaching my class on human motivation and I noticed the difference between my consciousness Friday night and what I was teaching on Monday. As a result of the psilocybin experience, I felt that the stuff I was teaching about motivation was just nonsense. I was teaching nonsense and they were all writing it down. I had tremendous guilt Monday morning because I was teaching wrong things. I realized that psychologists thought the world was a psychological world and I was sure, after this experience, that there was lot more to it than that.

RM   As regards my first psychedelic experience, I believe we both got turned on to psilocybin around the same time (March 1961). I first got interested by hearing fellow graduate students and friends George Litwin and Gunther Weil talking about experiences they'd had taking psilocybin with Tim. I would be doing statistical calculations on a calculator, adding numbers on a machine, working on some research project or other. The tone of voice they used sounded very different and somehow more alive and vital than usual. Tim was always so enthusiastic – he talked about "turning convicts into Buddhas." A change in the recidivism rate was the perfect behavioral criterion for inner change. I thought it sounded interesting and the Harvard research administration would approve since they liked things to be measurable. I believed in the importance of that. Plus, knowing Tim's philosophy of direct participation, I realized I'd be taking the substance too, as part of the project. So I went to him and asked if I could be his assistant on the prison project. He's written in his autobiography, that he was dubious at first. He thought I was too "intellectual, dainty and British" to mix it up with hardened criminals. But it all worked out okay. Gunther Weil and I spent a summer combing through the archives of the Massachusetts Department of Corrections to

Susan Homer & Gunther Weil, 1962

establish the recidivism base-rate, to which we would later compare the hopefully changed recidivism rate of our project participants.

My first experience occurred as preparation for the Concord Prison Project. It involved Gunther Weil, his wife Karen, the prison psychiatrist and his wife, and another graduate student friend Lynn K. It took place at Tim's house in Newton on March 13, 1961. Here's an extract of my account of that session, which I told Tim was the "most amazing experience of my life."

Tim Leary and Karen Weil, 1962

My first reaction was lassitude … I lay down on the floor and stretched out, feeling very relaxed and yet very alert. My body seemed for a while to be in a strange sort of limbo … All of a sudden I found myself in a completely new and magical world. The little green strands of the shag rug were writhing and undulating, like a mass of worms, yet in a most delightful way. The lights reflecting off the glass coffee table top sparkled with a kind of moist luminescence. The furniture, the walls, the floor, were all pulsing and undulating in slow waves, as if the whole room was breathing. I felt like I was inside a living structure, like a vast cell. The rate of the waving motion seemed to be coordinated with my breathing.

When I closed my eyes, fantastically beautiful and intricate geometric depth patterns were interweaving behind my eyelids, washing, colliding, streaming by at great speed. Occasionally, there would be images of precious stones or different parts of bodies, but nothing stood still long enough to congeal into anything definite. It felt as if my eyes were giving off a white-hot radiance; my mouth and the sense organs in my face and the rest of the body were glowing, flashing, oozing with liquid light, my nerve fibers crackling with white lightning; my blood stream felt like a seething stream of lava. My skin was embracing me, enwrapping me, in a kind of alternately wet and dry, hot and cool almost unendurably pleasurable embrace …

A moment of panic occurred that illustrated the fantastic amplifying power of the psychedelic. When I looked at the faces of the others, they were bright and strong and clear. I thought "this is how archangels look." They were somehow naked, shed of a fog of dissimulations, anxieties, and hypocrisies. Everyone was true to their own selves and not ashamed. I looked at them without shyness and with frank admiration. At one time all the faces were suffused with a soft greenish light. I looked at Karin across the room and told her she was beautiful. She just looked back without saying anything. Then she got up and started to leave the room (probably to go to the bathroom). I began to panic. I implored her not to leave, that dreadful things would happen if she did. Lynn who was sitting next to me, said it would be all right, but I got more and more upset and terrified, pleading with her not to leave. Karin said she would be back, but I said, "No, no, don't leave." She asked, "What will happen if I leave?" I replied, in a tone of desperation, "Something terrible will happen ... the music will stop." At that point she got up and walked through the door, and somehow that action became identified with all feelings of abandonment and loss I had ever experienced – there was a moment of acute anguish. And then she was gone, and I felt fine, amazed and relieved. I said to Lynn, "She left, and it was all right." And Lynn said, "Yes, it was all right."

Then, holding Lynn close, I suddenly felt myself shrinking in size ... I was very rapidly regressing back into childhood consciousness. I actually felt for brief moments what I had felt as an infant, even to the feel of a baby bottle in my mouth. And then, just as rapidly, I was shuttled back to my adult awareness.

At a certain point I noticed that the intensity of the experiences began to diminish, like a slow gliding down. The body felt very warm and relaxed. I understood how my normal perception of the world was constricted and limited by many prohibitions I had somehow accepted. For example, I went outside and on the porch was a box. I looked inside and saw that it had a garbage can and turned away. Then I realized I didn't have to turn away, that it was okay to look at it, that I had a choice and was not bound by a set of rules regarding what could or could not be experienced and perceived.

This was to me perhaps the most significant revelation of this experience: that I was basically in charge of what I could perceive and think about, that I was not bound by external forces but rather made choices that determined the extent and quality of my awareness. To exercise my newfound freedom, I made some snowballs and threw them at the screened window of the room in which the group was sitting. I felt greatly exhilarated. Tim must have sensed my expansive mood and thoughts, because with a grin on his face, he picked up some small orange pillows and tossed them gently at the window from the inside towards me. The brief interchange had an edge of freshness and spontaneous clarity that made me feel superbly happy.

(From Timothy Leary's *Outside Looking In*, edited by Robert Forte)

RM   Ram Dass, I wanted to ask you your impression of Allen Ginsberg. I only knew him slightly.

RD   At that stage, I only knew him slightly also. He liked Lenny Bruce. And he became obsessed with law and politics.

RM   The politics of Left and Right.

RD   Yes. He had files on everything, in his little apartment on the Lower East Side in New York. Files on the CIA, files on drug busts, on sexual persecution. He was part of an organization of writers that took positions on political issues.

GB   In fact, didn't he bring his files to Harvard when he visited Leary?

RD   Yes. Later, Allen and I became better friends and worked on various projects together. I got to play my cello as the drone for his poetry chanting at a concert in Albuquerque, thus realizing one of my childhood fantasies of performing music for thousands.

RM   The one story that I remember Tim telling about Allen's psilocybin session (that he wrote about in *High Priest*) was that Allen decided that Khrushchev and Kennedy (world leaders at the time) would have to take this and he wanted to telephone them right away. Psilocybin would also help Allen's myopia; he took off his glasses and his clothes and wandered around the house naked.

GB   What was it like in those early days when all these famous artists and philosophers were coming through? People like Aldous Huxley? Arthur Koestler? William Burroughs? What was it like for the two of you?

RM   At Harvard, I wasn't part of that loop. I didn't come to sessions with Allen Ginsberg or Arthur Koestler or Aldous Huxley. I was a lowly graduate student. Regretfully, I never even met Huxley; although in later years I came to know Laura Huxley quite well.

RD   I remember there was a party at Tim's house. There was Aldous Huxley and his friend the philosopher Gerald Heard. They were sitting in two chairs and I was sitting at their feet. I couldn't believe it: Me sitting there. Most of those people were Tim's friends, they weren't my friends. Tim was a beatnik, a Harvard beatnik, and a creative writer. Sometime later, there was an incident when Tim and Bill Burroughs and I took psilocybin together in London. We were walking in the street, very high, and were trying to decide whether we should leave a street corner. There we

Allen Ginsberg, Peggy Hitchcock, Tim Leary & Lawrence Ferlinghetti, 1963

were, the Harvard professors and the famous writer, having a deep philosophical discussion about a seemingly trivial choice.

RM   Tim wrote about that session with Burroughs in *High Priest*. He had a fantastic gift for words. His descriptions of his psychedelic experiences, like his first mushroom experience, are unparalleled. The only other person I know who comes close, a generation later, is Terence McKenna, another Irishman. Paul Lee once said to Tim, how did you teach your cells to write? I later met a former colleague of Tim's from his days at Berkeley, and he remarked how Tim always seemed to be enthusiastic about particular writers: James Joyce always, and before that D.H. Lawrence. He also had a great gift for satire, like those great Irish satirists Jonathan Swift and G.B. Shaw. After the psilocybin projects got under way, I would sometimes accompany Tim on talks to various groups of people, like the divinity students and others. He would start to talk about experiences of ecstatic expanded consciousness, and sometimes there would be a sudden change that would come in his voice, or intonation, something that seemed to charge up the whole energy of the room to another level of intensity. It was a combination of the spiritual and the poetic. Later again, I would sometimes see it happen in a talk to a group of hundreds, or even thousands. He was a silver-tongued orator at those moments, he had them hanging on his every word.

Later Experiences with Psilocybin and LSD

RM   In the first two years or so at Harvard, doing the prison project, studies on psilocybin in a supportive environment, the Good Friday study and others, we worked exclusively with psilocybin. The graduate students working with the project, Litwin, Weil and I, and sometimes Michael Kahn, would also do sessions among ourselves and with friends. We collected experience reports from the participants and they always involved some objective study of some kind as well; for example, we did studies on changes in the perception of time. We would have these sessions that were very interpersonal. Nowadays I wouldn't do a session that way. We would sit and take psilocybin and keep talking, whatever was going on. Sometimes it would be funny and we'd laugh a lot. We weren't using it to go inside and do meditative explorations; we didn't know how to do that. Sometimes there would be insights into relationship dynamics. I remember we called it the "love drug"– much as MDA was called in the late 1960s and early 1970s in San Francisco, and then MDMA in the 1980s. It could open up communication between people at tremendous depth. I remember a group of us did one session with psilocybin out by the ocean on Cape Cod. We camped out on the beach and took psilocybin at night, with a fire. Everybody bonded so much that we couldn't end the session. We went to have breakfast, and we said we should all get married to each other. Let's see, let's start with the two of you, and the two of us. It was that bonding.

RD   That was a very social drug, extremely social.

RM   I'd say that was the intention or set we brought to it and the kind of setting we created, the way we used the drugs.

RD   The way that we used them, yes.

RM   I think nowadays, people that use mushrooms for consciousness expansion probably would not use it in that way. Also, traditional Mazatec shamans and the ancient Aztecs, as far as we can tell, did not use them that way. They used them for divination and healing. If you want to get the real lessons of the mushrooms, you have to stop talking and start listening to what's coming through from within.

RD   The mushroom gives you a shift in the point of perception.

RM   There was a psilocybin session that was very significant for me, that I've always wanted to talk with you about. It was November 1961, a cold winter night, at your house in Newton. It involved Tim, you and me, George Litwin, Gunther Weil and Michael Kahn. Maynard and Flo Ferguson also came a bit later in the evening. I think our intention was to take stock of where we were after a year of working together. We all took psilocybin, except Tim who may have taken a low dose of LSD with some people in New York and then come up. Is this ringing any bells?

RD   It's ringing very, very remote bells.

RM   On the way driving to the session, Michael Kahn had raised this question about the Catholic Church's teaching concerning the sin against the Holy Ghost. This was the worst sin, the one unforgiveable sin, because it denied the very possibility of forgiveness and denied the reality of the Holy Spirit. Michael said it was like a projective test in the Middle Ages, for your worst imaginable sin, the unforgiveable sin. There was intense discussion going on among the four of us, Michael, George, Gunther and me, about sin and good and evil and so forth, as the effect of the psilocybin came on. At one point George Litwin asked, "Well, what about marginal cases? How did the Church decide marginal cases? Like what if I'm this guy who takes these pills and meets God; and I talk to God and we have this great conversation. And after I come back people say I'm bad, or evil – what then? What would the Church say to something like that?" He was asking this question of Tim and Tim was completely speechless; he didn't know what to say. I can imagine, in retrospect, he probably thought: "Why is he asking me this question?"

I had become caught up in this theological issue and added to the tension by saying, "Yes, Tim, what would they say, the Church, in a situation like that?" And of course Tim still couldn't or wouldn't say anything. I remember having this realization that we were confronting the issue of whether what we were doing was good or bad, or even worse, whether it was taboo, and whether we would be or were being judged.

Then Gunther started attacking Tim for getting involved in a New York drug scene that he, Gunther, knew was sinister and decadent. He said,

"You know Tim, there was a time that I idolized you, I thought you were great. But now I don't know; I see you getting involved in these bad drug scenes, I think I may leave." More silence from Tim and everyone. Then Gunther said, "You know Tim, only a Jew and a Catholic could have a conversation like this."

George Litwin spoke up and said, in a ringing voice, "Now wait a minute, guys, I'm neither Jew nor Catholic, so I think I can speak here with some impartiality. There's this old tradition of putting some people up and then killing them or tearing them down. We don't have to do that anymore. You know there's another tradition – that of the Declaration of Independence, which says all beings are created equal and should treat each other as equals." It was magnificent. Everybody heaved a profound sigh of relief, Maynard and Flo cheered, and it was like a fog was lifted. A fog of religious bigotry had entered the room and through George's statement, it was completely dissipated.

RD   Far out!

RM   Tim later said that during that scene he couldn't figure out what was going on, and felt like a figment of George Litwin's imagination, and that he, Tim, didn't really exist. I think that experience made us all much more sensitive to and careful about the power of projections and idealizations and how they could be enormously magnified in a psychedelic session. For Tim, it reinforced his rejection of any kind of spiritual leadership role. He was determined not to play the "guru game." He'd get quite pissed off when he felt that someone was projecting that on him. His model was that of a baseball team, and he'd be temporarily the captain or coach, but those were just temporary roles in the game.

RD   That whole session was Michael Kahn's trip, I think.

RM   Yeah, he initiated the whole thing, with the conversation about the sin against the Holy Ghost in the car driving up. He used to do similar things in several of the small group psilocybin sessions we had. You know, he was an actor before he became a psychologist, and he had this loud booming voice and commanding presence. So, he'd announce, at the beginning of the session, that we were all characters in some play, say T.S. Eliot's *The Cocktail Party*, and give us different roles; which he'd then have to describe, since none of us knew the play. I remember one time feeling stuck in one his play roles for a couple of weeks after a session. He was that persuasive.

RD   He liked raps about good and evil. He really reveled in them.

RM   Yes, he probably played Mephistopheles in Dr. Faustus. He'd be perfect for it. And you (RD) apparently felt at the time that that was not a game in which you particularly wanted to participate.

GB   In his writings, Tim makes a big distinction between LSD and psilocybin. His first LSD trip was apparently quite profound. I was wondering if either of you remember your first LSD trip and what you might say about the difference.

RD   When Tim first took LSD, he didn't speak for weeks. I went around saying, "We've lost Timothy, we've lost Timothy." I was warning everybody to not take that drug, because Tim wasn't talking and he was sort of dull. It was the Englishman Michael Hollingshead who had come up from New York, with a huge supply of LSD in liquid form. I guess Tim's first LSD trip was with Michael Hollingshead, and Maynard and Flo Ferguson; I was looking on. When I took it, I felt it went so far beyond the astral, beyond form, to pure energy. It showed me that in previous psychedelic sessions, I had been screwing around in the astral plane. LSD was no nonsense. If you weren't grounded somewhere, you'd go out on this drug.

RM   Also, it's very important to realize that the effects of LSD last much longer, six to eight hours, than psilocybin, which typically lasts three to four hours. And sometimes, unpredictably, LSD could last for 24 hours or more. I think many bad trips in the 1960s happened because of people not knowing the possibility of prolonged effects.

GB   Was it Hollingshead who introduced LSD to the Harvard scene?

RM   John Beresford, a New York doctor, and Michael Hollingshead had obtained a rather large quantity of LSD from Sandoz, ostensibly for research on amoeba and bacteria. They slipped into taking it themselves, in very large doses. Michael came up to Newton Center and introduced himself and then LSD, to Leary. Tim said his first LSD experience was "the most shattering experience of his life." Because Hollingshead had been the initiator of this experience, Tim regarded him as some kind of "wise alien trickster," an "agent of higher intelligence who could spin a million realities a minute." He followed Michael around, seeking clues to his mastery of space-time scenarios. This behavior of Tim's scared the rest of us.

RD   Yes, he was talking about his children and others as puppets.

RM   I remember driving with Tim in his car, in the days after he had taken LSD, and he was telling me about this puppet world, this vision he had under LSD, where he saw the mechanical puppetry of everything. He would go home and see his daughter Susan as playing the perfect teenager-puppet game. The way that I would understand that now, in retrospect, is that the games of human life, disconnected from spirit and interrelatedness, seem robotic, like puppetry. At the time, hearing Tim talk like that scared the daylights out of me.

RD   Speaking of this puppetry vision reminds me of a story of Neem Karoli Baba. One day, we were in the mountains and he looked up and said that an Indian woman of their acquaintance had just died. He had merriment while saying this. One of his followers asked, "How can you be happy, when she just died?" Maharaj replied, "Do you want me to act like one of the puppets?" Meaning, do you want me to act like all the rest of us do?

RM   Yes, the puppetry vision is not a put-down or disparagement. It's seeing the mechanical conditioning of human behavior. Gurdjieff said the same thing: people are like walking automatons until they wake up. They're sleep walking, somnambulating through life. Consciousness has to be developed or earned through conscious practice; it doesn't get handed to you. Tim Leary came to understand it as an extension of game theory, seeing all of human behavior as game-like.

Leary's definition of a game: *A game is a temporary social arrangement of interactive behavior with clearly defined and agreed upon goals, roles, rules, rituals, values, strategies, and space-time characteristics, all of which are subject to revision by agreement.* (From Castalia Foundation workshop hand-outs).

In time, Tim Leary came to argue that you play the game, but you try to play it consciously and have fun doing it. And remember that you're playing a game. Take time off, in meditative or psychedelic non-game states, to remember that you're playing it and avoid getting caught in it.

Tim was my assigned faculty advisor when I began my graduate studies at Harvard in the fall of 1960. That summer I had just returned from a year in Europe where I had been studying linguistic philosophy and psychology on a Fulbright Fellowship and began working as a graduate assistant with Harry Murray on some Thematic Apperception Test research. I remember being greeted enthusiastically by Tim as I entered his tiny office at the Center for Personality Research to discuss my graduate studies program. He displayed a keen interest in my philosophical leanings, particularly my growing interest in metaphysics and then shared with me some of the insights that he had received in Cuernavaca, Mexico from his psilocybin mushroom experience, and how this had led to his desire to initiate a research program to integrate this deep transactional understanding of altered consciousness into clinical psychology and therapy. Although I did not really understand what he was talking about, my experiences with marijuana in the late 1950's bebop jazz scene prompted my curiosity. Tim invited me to join the research team and I immediately accepted. Two weeks later Karen and I were married and I also had my first psilocybin session at Tim's home in Newton, Massachusetts. One of the most striking memories of this experience was to hear Tim quoting verbatim passages from James Joyce's *Finnegan's Wake*. He was totally inside the character and completely conversant with the cadence and meter and meaning. I was astounded and this certainly reinforced my interest in further exploration.

A striking memory for me of the session in November 1961, which included Tim, Richard, Ralph Metzner, George Litwin and Michael Kahn, was the sense that we were re-enacting a contemporary version of the "The Last Supper" and a harbinger of the events that followed in the coming years. A sub-text, if not a primary theme, of our work with psychedelics was that we were transforming the very basis of society through a transformation of consciousness. Tim, of course was Christ; Dick Alpert was Peter and we all had our roles as disciples of a revolutionary spirituality. I remember the dialogue with Tim that Ralph describes and feeling that in expressing my dismay (and Jewish guilt) with the momentum of our direction, I had cast myself in the role of Judas. This was both saddening and frightening. This probably prompted my first out-of-body experience. To this day, over forty years later, I vividly recall looking down at my body from the ceiling and musing on whether I would or could re-inhabit it. It occurred to me that I might just end up in what would be perceived by others as a permanent catatonic state and simply carried off to a chronic psychiatric ward. Strangely enough, I felt no fear, just a bit of morbid curiosity as to the outcome.

MICHAEL KAHN

I always suspected that Tim must have been a really good therapist, and I had that confirmed the night of the "Sin against the Holy Ghost" session. That was just the first confirmation. I had many after that. Gunther, a musician, arrived late at that session from a gig he had been playing. He came in full of a very engaging, manic energy and regaled us with stories of the gig, mostly stories about the drummer, whom he called a "jive motherfucker." He described the drummer as charming and talented, but infuriatingly dominating, leaving little room for anybody else. Later in the evening, he began the sharp criticism of Tim that Ralph and Richard have reported. Tim listened with interest, leaning forward so as to hear everything Gunther said. His expression was sweet and loving. When Gunther had finished, the room was silent. Tim still had the same sweet expression on his face. After a time he said, very kindly, "Gunther, would you mind telling us again the story about the drummer?" Gunther was delighted to oblige and told the entire story again. Tim listened with interest, the same sweet expression on his face. When Gunther had finished, Tim said, "Thank you, Gunther." We were all quiet for a time. Nothing more was said about the drummer or about Gunther's attack on Tim. I knew I was in the presence of a master therapist.

RD   But sometimes the games that are played in order to get into the non-game state can themselves become captivating.

RM   I believe that's what Chogyam Trungpa called spiritual materialism, getting caught up in the methodology of the spiritual practice, feeling superior because you're meditating.

GB   Ralph, what about your first LSD experience?

RM   My first experience with LSD didn't occur until we were in Zihuatanejo, the first summer (1962), working on adapting the *Tibetan Book of the Dead* as a manual for psychedelic experiences. We wanted to test that model of conducting a session. But I'd say some of the high dose psilocybin sessions we had got into had the same intensity range. I remember a particularly powerful one, in which I became psychotic and suicidal, but also learned a tremendous amount about such extreme experiences.

We had decided to take a very high dose of psilocybin. I took 60 milligrams and George Litwin took 80 milligrams. George Litwin's wife Corky and Gunther Weil were also there. Pushing the edges, trying to see what it's like. Of course, we didn't have a clue. Kind of a foolhardy thing to do, in retrospect. But that's the way we were. The first perceptual change I noticed was flowing energy field lines which I recognized from previous sessions with psilocybin. Delicate flowing lines, very beautiful and sparkly. But then, as I had also experienced before, if you start to become anxious or uptight about something, the energy lines start to freeze up, become ugly instead of beautiful, stiff and rigid, and not moving. These energy bands started to change because I was afraid, because I had taken such a large dose. I had in-built fear about what was going to happen to me. So the sparkling energy lines started to turn malignant, instead of being embracing. It became like a cage or a net, metallic gray or purple-gray. It was freezing up on me and I felt trapped in a kind of deadly mechanical spider's web. Everything stopped moving. I seemingly couldn't move, or think and wondered if I was dead or alive?

The Harvard psilocybin projects got underway and my work with mescaline at Massachusetts Mental Health continued through 1960-61. One day, late in 1961, a fateful letter arrived. I was sitting in Timothy's office when he opened a handwritten letter from Michael Hollingshead. Michael reported in his letter that he had experimented with LSD in New York with the aid of a physician, John Beresford, and that he had brought some of the material with him. He said in the letter he was overwhelmed by the experiences he had, that he couldn't find any order to his life, and he really wanted contact with other people who might understand what was happening with him.

Timothy and I discussed it for a few minutes; he got many crank letters at that point and it was hard to respond to all of them. In this case he said to me, "This man seems to have experimented in the area that we are working in and has come to some difficulty. I just do not feel we can leave him in some lonely apartment in Cambridge. As researchers in this field, it is up to us to look into cases like this where circumstances have caused a certain effect, as well as to conduct experimental studies." As fate would have it, Hollingshead's address was quite near to where I lived. I offered to stop by and see Michael, see if he was OK, and would connect him to Timothy if appropriate. I brought Michael over to our home in Cambridge where we could relax in a family setting. We talked through half of the night about LSD, psilocybin and the deeper experiences that are hard to explain in words and that do not fit into our social model. Michael Hollingshead seemed very intelligent even though he kept wandering off the subject. But perhaps these were understandable effects from taking LSD for at least three days in a row. I decided he was not mentally ill but was suffering from the effects of drugs which he did not fully understand, but which he wanted to offer to others. I thought it would be dangerous for him to go around Cambridge spreading LSD, and that he would do better working within the framework of the project we had established. So I got Hollingshead into my car and drove him over to Timothy's house and introduced him to Timothy. This was the introduction of LSD into the psilocybin project at Harvard. Michael brought quite a lot of LSD with him from London, and was fairly generous about giving it to people who asked, and even to some who didn't ask.

LSD changed the paradigm of the Psilocybin Project at Harvard. It might be said that what was formerly the "love" project changed in character. The "love" aspect of psilocybin was in part due to the relatively small doses (six to eight milligrams) that we generally used in our studies. The psilocybin experiences were reasonably mild; there were very few extreme reactions. Largely, people felt a softening and melting of their ego boundaries; they came closer together in the group. They spoke (when they did feel they wished to speak, there was a lot of silence) about the closeness they felt, the oneness, the unity of all people and all mankind. They were fully aware of their names, their situations, but their experiences of themselves were changing as the drug had an effect. It must be noted that psilocybin has an active period of only three or four hours, so Harvard experiments could be conducted in an afternoon or evening and people could go home to rest. It was "ego softening."

But the LSD provided by Michael Hollingshead represented another dimension of human experience entirely. Taking the doses Michael suggested (perhaps up to two hundred and fifty micrograms) led to more dramatic inhibition of the mechanisms that control everyday sensory perception and cognition. I think it is appropriate to think of these high-level LSD experiences as representing a kind of "ego death." That is, there is a period of hours when you probably do not remember your name or where you are, or how you got there. You are floating out in a free space of consciousness, without the anchor you have always had – the ego that you built up from early childhood to protect and nurture you. This experience, without doubt, can be much more disturbing; if there is any underlying pathology, it is liable to emerge in the absence of the various inhibitors which LSD disconnects. LSD also lasted much longer. Through this "ego death" experience, it was hoped that people would have a chance to see the world beyond themselves and then be reborn back into this world. The Harvard project found that successful rebirth and "reassembly" of the ego depended so much on the expectations subjects came in with, their underlying life experiences, particularly the presence of various unconscious fears. I want to emphasize that Timothy's collaboration with Michael Hollingshead, and the adoption of LSD into the project was a charitable gesture on Timothy's part – there was no malice or intent of harm, nor was it wild and irresponsible behavior. Rather, Timothy was concerned about a fellow human being who was suffering, and he asked that I help him with a charitable gesture.

Richard Alpert, 1962

RM   In retrospect, only many years later, in the 1970s when I read Stanislav Grof's writings based on his LSD therapy work, did I understand that experience in terms of Grof's model of the four stages of the birth process. In what he calls Basic Perinatal Matrix Number Two (BPM II), the contractions have started but the cervix hasn't opened, so no movement takes place. Grof says that the memory of being stuck there and squeezed with tremendous force, is translated in later psychedelic sessions as experiences of being trapped, stuck, bound, caught, imprisoned, buried alive, no exit and so on. There may be (quite justifiable) fear of dying, or feelings of numbness, due to the effect of anesthesia on the fetus. At the time, of course, I had no idea of any of this. I remember feeling – what is real? Psychiatrists call that "derealization." Not knowing who or what I was – that's called "depersonalization."

RD   That's far out.

RM   Understanding the experience later, in terms of Grof's model, was very liberating. Nothing in ordinary psychology could prepare you for this. The Tibetan Buddhist language is too strange and alien for most Westerners, although the basic underlying teachings are very helpful of course. But again, at the time, we hadn't really begun to use that model either.

GB   Did the other people in that session feel the same type of energy?

RM   It looked to me as if everyone else was also trapped in the same metallic spider's web. But in terms of their subjective experience, I wouldn't know. I was too out of it.

RD   I think not because they came and told me Ralph had flipped out.

RM   Well, in the midst of this hellish state, I somehow got the idea I should ask Tim to help me figure out what was real and what not. So I said, "I've got to go and telephone Tim" (he was not in the session). I remember Gunther Weil came along to help me with the phoning; he was sympathetic with my quest to get some reality. We dialed Tim's number. I said to him, "Tim I want to ask you something" and he said, "Okay." "Tell me something that's real. Can you tell me something that's real?" He got it right away and said, "Ah okay. We're here sitting in the kitchen, and Jack's eating a hamburger, Susan's doing her homework and I'm having a beer." I said, "Thank you, that's great. I feel better already. It feels more real. Could you please come over?" So he said, "Sure I'll come over." I sort of felt he was going to save me from this awful dungeon realm of not knowing reality. When he walked in the door, he walked into this fibrous static network that was holding everybody trapped. He came into it and at first he was moving freely and I thought "Great!" But then, in a very short time he too became trapped in it, another fly in the spider's sticky web. My despair deepened. There was no exit from this hell hallucination, see. Then I thought, "I can't tell what my sensory experience is. So maybe if I cause some pain, it will cause me to feel real and be real." I took a candle, tried to burn my leg, have a real sensation. That didn't do any good. (Again, on reflection, this may be an underlying motivation of people that cut themselves.) The session was in a house near a train track. Every now and again this thundering train would pass by, making the whole house vibrate. I remember thinking, "I wish that train would barrel through the house and kill me, so I would be dead. It would be over with; I would be out of this hell." I said to George Litwin, "I don't see why I should continue to live, I should just kill myself." He said, "Would you live if I ask you to?" And I said, "Yes."

RD   Live for the rest of us.

GB   You wrote that that experience was the closest you ever came to suicide. What would you say helped you get over it?

RM   The turning point was George asking me that question. It was like very slightly tipping the balance in favor of staying alive. Then I also remembered I had taken this drug, as the intensity started to diminish. Many (twenty) years later, I was in a situation with a woman friend in Germany who was on a DMT trip, and who had a soothing voice in her head telling her she didn't need to breathe. I got scared because she stopped breathing. When I asked her to breathe, she said she didn't see why she should. I remembered my conversation with George, and said, "If not for yourself, would you breathe for me? " She said, "Sure," and came back from the brink. I was glad I remembered the magic words for breaking the suicide spell.

GB   How did that experience inform your subsequent research in giving psychedelics to subjects?

RM   It made me, and all of us I think, be much more aware of the need for some kind of framework for understanding what happens to people in these experiences so we can help them navigate through difficult quasi-psychotic states.

RD   Like Stan Grof's model?

RM   Yes, but we didn't even know about his model until several years later. At the time, I felt the need for an explanation, for a greater understanding of these states, of what can go wrong, and how to talk with somebody who is confused and terrified. All we could do at the time was to lay a person on the bed and tell him to hope for the best and relax. Stick around and make sure he didn't doing anything rash. Which most of the time worked. I thought it was a wonderful lesson, it was beautiful. I had no regrets at all about going through that experience. I learned so much from it and it motivated me to learn more. But it was definitely humbling.

GB   Had the *Tibetan Book of the Dead* been circulating at that point?

RD   I think not, because we were having difficult experiences like that before we got into the *Tibetan Book of the Dead*.

RM   That's right, the experiences with high doses of psilocybin could produce the kind of ego-death terror experiences that can occur with LSD, and that the *Tibetan Book of the Dead* manual specifically addresses. With that model, you have some additional resources. They do talk about the visions of "wrathful deities" and "peaceful deities" that you can encounter in the after-death bardo states. Hellish and heavenly visions. Their advice is: Remember they all come from within you, your own mind, and have no reality apart from that. If you could remind the voyager of those teachings, as Aldous Huxley had said, you would be able to get through the hard parts and not be deluded and distracted by the pleasurable ones.

End of the Harvard Psilocybin Project

GB   What led to the demise of the Harvard Project, in your view?

RM   One factor, I think, was the envy of the other faculty. Some other faculty members at that Center for Personality Research became envious because the psilocybin project got so many good graduate students. The professors all had graduate students, whom they paid as research assistants out of grants that they received. The more grants and assistants you had, obviously the bigger you were. And they were losing research assistant students and were pissed off.

RD   Brendan Maher and the others were pissed off because Tim and I had so many of the graduate students. And the scientists around us complained because we were taking drugs ourselves as part of our experimenting. But actually the data we were collecting were our own internal stuff.

RM   Yes, from the point of view of the behaviorist science game, taking a drug that produces an inner experience violates the paradigm.

RD   We were finding that the feedback from our own experiences offered the data that we were going to use in describing these drugs. We recognized how personality, or set, as well as setting, affects the experience. We were proceeding with tremendous thought in designing our studies.

GB   You were doing systematic naturalistic studies, observing things and people in their own natural environment. But that went against the behaviorist paradigm of psychology at the time. Although your critics would have said the opposite, right? That this wasn't systematic, that it was sloppy and unscientific and not objective. Isn't that what they were saying about you?

RD   Yes.

GB   That it was just parties where drugs were given.

RD   We were giving it to artists, to musicians, to philosophers and creative people who could tell us what these drug experiences meant.

It was 1961, and my wife Charlene and I had just returned from my father-in-law's funeral in Milwaukee. There was a message waiting for us about a meeting at Huston Smith's house with Timothy Leary. I was teaching assistant to Paul Tillich and I had filled in for Huston Smith at MIT when he was on sabbatical, and was then hired for a three year stint to teach philosophy of religion. There was Tim in all of his Irish charm and bosh, extolling the virtues of psilocybin and LSD. He was recruiting some theologians to try it and to consult on his mystico-mimetic model to supplant the psychotomimetic model, in which psychedelics were seen as a training psychosis for psychiatrists. The language for consciousness was very unstable. Behaviorism, the chief trend, had eliminated consciousness in favor of stimulus response mechanisms. Mystical experience seemed like an upgrade from psychosis and no one could figure out what hallucinogen meant. I remember I was the first to raise my hand, which shot up as though by its own accord, when Tim asked who wanted to try some.

We gathered some days later in a room at Huston Smith's house and LSD was passed around by George Litwin. After half an hour we were gone. I mostly re-member going and coming back and wondering where I had been and why it had taken so long, – like the twinkling of an eye, and then going and coming back again. Wagner was played, ye gods, the Flight of the Fucking Valkyries of all things, and the fireplace backed up and smoke filled the room, which seemed oddly ap-propriate, although it made someone vomit. Not the best set and setting. There was a psychologist there (whose name I will withhold) who took umbrage with his wife, who was prone on the floor next to him – and he thought her head was a pumpkin that he wanted to smash. He raised his arm in a menacing chop and struck the floor about an inch from her head. This was registered as disturbing and untoward behavior, and some question was raised in our minds about something he seemed to have been repressing about his marriage. I was in bliss. My wife kept asking for the "anecdote" (instead of "antidote") which I thought was funny even years later, and she kept looking under my shirt for the lock of hair she had placed on the corpse of her father. Why would she think I was her dead father? Huston Smith was prone on the floor next to me and would sit up every once in a while and look me in the eye and intone: "Woonnndderfullll, Paul! Woonnnd-derfulll!" and then drop down again for another round. George Litwin came around and examined us and said I looked great and did I want another hit.

I thought – another hit – is he kidding? I had already skied the Matterhorn and I didn't even know how to ski. My wife outdid herself looking at George and saying: "Oh, you poor little ugly dwarf!" I thought that was unkind. Anyhow, we survived and I was an initiate. My wife didn't like it because as a doctor's daughter she had a scruple against drugs. Hell, I was a doctor's son and I liked it. It was no Parmenidean chariot ride to the vision of Being but it was sure some version of it.

So I joined the Leary project and became one of the editors of the *Psychedelic Review* along with Ralph Metzner and Rolf von Eckartsberg. I always wanted German friends. I didn't contribute much but my smiling and sunny personality, though I did find a quote from Plato's *Laws* for the first issue, about whether there could ever be a drug that would teach us what to fear and what not to fear – so I deferred to Metzner who was much smarter than me. He had published a fancy scholarly monograph that was very impressive.

PSYCHEDELIC REVIEW

Issue Number 1
SUMMER 1963
$1.50

Psychedelic Review
Issue #1, 1963
Issue #5, 1965

PSYCHEDELIC REVIEW

NUMBER 5
1965 / $2.00

GURDJIEFF / Terry Winter Owens / Suzanne D. Smith

EXPECTATION, MOOD & PSILOCYBIN

RALPH METZNER
GEORGE LITWIN
GUNTHER M. WEIL

TWO PSYCHEDELIC EXPERIENCES   René Daumal & William James

● ZEN BUDDHISM / Edward Maupin   ● OUR SECOND YEAR / The Editors
● REBIRTH WITHOUT FEAR / Gerald Heard

PSYCHEDELIC METAPHYSICS / David Drake

RM The studies at Harvard were naturalistic – it was not a laboratory, and not a clinic – they were done in someone's home – in what we called a "supportive environment." But they were systematic, in that we systematically gathered data on questionnaires and reports. We analyzed and published the results in the psychological and psychiatric journals. Besides the prison project, we had this group of friends, graduate students and their friends, my girlfriend and we would go to the beach at Cape Cod and other places. We would do all night sessions under the stars by the ocean, it was amazing. Or we would do indoor sessions too, where I would do my thing with psychology experiments, experiments on changes in the perception of time. I'd have people estimate how much time had elapsed. See how time stretches or expands. We were always collecting written accounts from people as well. My brother Ken, a physicist who was at MIT at the time, also participated in some of these experiments.

GB What was David McClelland's attitude toward your project?

RM McClelland, the Director of the Center, was a puritanical Quaker, whose main research focus was on the need for achievement and how you develop it. It seemed to me he was generally disapproving of mind-altering drugs, didn't think anything useful for science or society could come from them. Of course, he never tried them himself, with that kind of prejudice. All of us graduate students working on the psilocybin projects, Gunther Weil, George Litwin, myself, were told by McClelland that we would not be allowed to do our thesis research with psilocybin.

RD Did Dave McClelland say you couldn't?

RM Yes, you didn't know that? Walter Pahnke did his research with psilocybin, the Good Friday study, in the following year; but he was not in that department, so therefore not under McClelland's authority. He was getting his PhD in the Philosophy of Religion, I think. Plus he already was an MD and had a Masters of Divinity degree. I decided to choose an easy topic and get it done as quickly as possible, so I could get back to the psychedelic research which most interested me. So that's what I did. I had been working with Walter Mischel on his research on delay of gratification: I did my thesis study on what factors influence the learned capacity to delay gratification. No doubt it's symbolic of my character neurosis. I finished it by June 1962, prior to the first retreat in Zihuatanejo, that summer.

I remember one time later in the fall of 1962, George and Gunther and I were having this conversation with McClelland, arguing about scientific methodology, trying to persuade him that you could be scientific about inner states. He was just incensed. At one point, he was so frustrated with my way of thinking, that he actually said if you're thinking like that, we shouldn't have given you the PhD degree. I said, well, it's too late, you already did. He couldn't believe it. He seemed to take it as a personal affront that we were not committed to the same paradigm as he was – the only correct one in his mind, the only way to look at it.

RD   You see that was Tim Leary's influence. He was inspiring us all to give up the prevailing paradigm.

RM   Yes, and take an independent perspective. Frank Barron would say the same thing. His studies on the personality correlates of creativity showed one of the key factors is independent thinking. Don't take anything for granted. Keep your wits about you. Re-think your assumptions. I think it's a good strategy. I'm all for it. The more consciousness the better. Think for yourself.

GB   In your research at Harvard, did you stick with psilocybin throughout?

RM   In the Harvard-sponsored research projects, yes, we used psilocybin, which was sent by the American branch of Sandoz, in New Jersey, free of charge, for research purposes. After the Harvard projects were discontinued by the administration, we were still living in the area, for another year in Newton Center, a community housing arrangement. Leary and Alpert were still teaching, and I had a post-doctoral fellowship at the Harvard Medical School. At that point, we started to work with LSD, DMT and various other tools. But there was no more psilocybin.

I remember there was one final, highly symbolic confrontation with the Harvard academic authorities. There was supposed to be a last shipment of psilocybin, in two milligram tablets, fifty tablets in each bottle, a case of twenty bottles. We were living in Newton Center. This shipment was going to be delivered to the Center for Research in Personality, and I was supposed to pick it up on a Saturday. I remember waiting there in the office. But Brendan Maher, one of our main critics and enemies, had also found out that we were getting a last shipment, and decided to send his graduate assistant to confiscate it. The other graduate research assistant and I both had our hands on the package. I grabbed it and he grabbed it. We looked at each other - he was frightened, I was determined. He said, "We're supposed to keep it." I said, "You have no right to it, it's addressed to us." So he had to let it go. But that was the last one. I've not had any psilocybin since those Harvard studies more than forty years ago. Mushrooms yes, many times, but no psilocybin. I don't think any of us have.

Trying to develop a research program using psychedelic substances did not fit into any of the psychological or psychotherapeutic models known to the Harvard psychologists. There was little place in the medical profession, which is primarily concerned with identification and treatment of disease, for ecstasy or spiritual exploration. The psychologist team decided the most likely opportunity for these psychedelic experiences to be used for the possible benefit of mankind was in the field of religion and the study of divinity. Accordingly, Tim Leary made several trips to the Harvard Divinity School, spoke about psychedelic experiences, and enlisted a number of divinity school faculty and graduate students who were interested trying out this experience. A number of sessions were run for people in that field, including Walter Houston Clark, Paul Lee, Huston Smith and others who became involved in the psychedelic research program, and continued to support and advocate the use of this work as an adjunct to the study of divinity. Tim used to comment that the program involved two very different things: One was the study of divinity as it is written about in history and religious texts, in custom and culture; the other was the direct experience of God.

I recall one psychedelic session with divinity school people that I hosted at my house. We had, a divinity graduate student; Paul's wife, Charlene; Gene Nemesh, who was a psychologist at Brandeis University and several others whose names I cannot remember. Someone whose presence I certainly recall was Huston Smith, a professor of world religion at MIT, who had spent many years in a Buddhist monastery prior to undertaking his work in the teaching of world religions. Huston Smith sat like a Buddha, glowing, with an energy that you could feel halfway across the room; shining with eyes closed, not moving, just smiling; a person, as far as one could see, in a state of enlightenment. On the other hand, there was another person in the room (I will not identify him) who found the experience very disturbing, became angry at himself and others and was the first person I ever experienced who turned violent in a psychedelic session. It took two of us to restrain him and get him to sit down and relax a little bit. We explained to him that no violence was necessary, that he was safe and that he would come out of this feeling fine and OK about himself. Paul Lee was in the middle, looking very wide-eyed. There was Huston in his enlightened Buddha state and this other person with his anger and violence. We were seeing the enormous contrast between two people – one highly trained in meditation, ready to accept the fact that there was a world beyond his ego and enjoying experiencing that world and another in the same room with the same dose, slaying demons of fear and buried anger that were brought to the surface without the usual inhibitions. I remember being surprised at the extremely different reactions to LSD that two people could have. Knowing them both in everyday life, they both seemed like good and decent people; although Huston had a gentleness which was very distinctive.

In conclusion, I want to point out that Tim Leary did not conduct these sessions to create some radical change, or to cause any difficulties with the University, but rather in response to requests by divinity school professors and students to better understand the religious experience and how it related to their study of divinity. He gave of his time, of his home, of himself to help others experience what he had experienced. He was a generous person in every way.

PEGGY HITCHCOCK

Peggy Hitchcock, 1962

I first took mescaline in the summer of 1961 in my apartment in New York City with a painter friend, Sven Lukin. I am a "trust fund baby," meaning I did not have to earn my own living. I found myself very bored with my "nice" upper class milieu. My friends at that time were mostly artists and musicians, with whom I felt much more at home. Psychedelics were starting to appear, at least among the folks I knew. I had read Aldous Huxley's *The Doors of Perception*, and thought mescaline would be an extremely interesting experience. It was.

At that time, I was doing individual and group therapy with a wonderful woman, Asya Kadis. I had recently finished a long-term relationship with a musician whom I'd nearly married, and who was a cyclical junkie. After that relationship ended, I thought to myself, "Something is wrong here, and I need to consider why I would get so seriously involved with someone who had such a difficult problem." Asya, my therapist, was an amazing human being. She was one of the people who started group therapy in America. I continued to work with her during the years when I was most actively involved with psychedelics. She was very supportive of my explorations of consciousness.

I first heard of Tim Leary through my friend Van Wolff, an entrepreneur and entertainment agent, who loved to gather different kinds of people together at his apartment, like a salon. Van told me about these two guys who were teaching psychology at Harvard and who were offering to give people psilocybin if they would document their experiences in writing. I was very interested to meet them. Because they had psychological credentials, I thought that to experience psychedelics with their assistance would enhance my therapy and my journey of self-discovery. I first met Tim at a coffee house in Cambridge, Massachusetts and my first impressions were that he was extremely charming, witty and bright. I believe we met socially several times after that in New York City, at Van Wolff's apartment and my own. This was in the winter of 1961–62. At that time, we arranged that I would take psilocybin with Richard Alpert at his Harvard office, which I did, and it was the beginning of an entirely new perspective on my life.

I no longer remember the specifics of my first psilocybin experience. To me it seemed more powerful than mescaline, which was visually beautiful, but lacked much emotional content. I felt that psilocybin could be a truly life-changing experience. The "set and setting" for my psilocybin experience were far different from those when I took mescaline. I was with a trained psychologist, who was acting as my guide and my intent was specifically to gather insights into my life patterns. With mescaline, I had no program in mind. Later, I also took psilocybin with Tim and several friends at Maynard and Flo Ferguson's house in Riverdale in the spring of 1962.

My first experience with LSD also occurred at the Ferguson's house in 1962, with Tim, Flo and Maynard, and my friend Van Wolff. Tim brought Michael Hollingshead to their house and he had introduced LSD to Tim. Michael was a truly unique and bizarre human being. It seems to me that Michael had set himself up as a guru, dispensing LSD to the world. I found him to be ridiculous. I remember laughing hysterically at him during the session; it was impossible to take him seriously. He was very funny, but he was also very pretentious. He wasn't malicious, but I would never trust his judgment, as he was lacking in common sense. The LSD experience was far more powerful and longer lasting than with psilocybin. I felt an enormously heightened awareness of everything and everybody. I could see into people's minds and touch their feelings. Every being and object was vibrating with light and color. I knew without any doubt that I was a part of this incredible vibrant tapestry. It was a most exciting and reassuring experience. I remember experiencing an after-effect of physical depletion. I always felt like I needed extra protein and vitamins the next day after taking LSD because of the tremendous acceleration of brain activity.

Elsa von Eckartsberg,
Harvard, 1962

Freshly imported from Germany, in my first years as a graduate student at Radcliffe/Harvard, I found myself suddenly immersed in a flood of mind-altering experiences, guided there by my husband Rolf, who was a close friend of Timothy Leary and was in the same graduate psychology program as Ralph Metzner. I vividly remember a mysterious trap-door in one of the buildings (in Newton Center) that would lead us into some strange "underworld" where the psychology graduate students were performing their world-shaking "experiments". I liked the upper world better and had my first psilocybin "trip" in my bedroom in Cambridge. And what a literal trip this became, one that opened up whole new vistas of freedom to me.

At the time I was just then finishing my dissertation on the French Symbolist poet Arthur Rimbaud, and working really hard on that, when psilocybin lifted me rocket-like out of all my stress, literally into outer space, where I remained, floating free, laughing all the way, for the entire time of the trip. It seemed I was born to be a mind-astronaut! There was no let-down to the exultation I experienced. I don't remember how I ever got back to earth, yet landed somehow peacefully in my bed. I realized that on this trip I had become a "particle of light," or rather a "wave of light," flowing without the resistance of matter through vastest spaces of the cosmos.

This was a truly great experience that had a very relaxing, yet tonic effect on me. Soon thereafter I could finish my dissertation with ease, thinking what "illuminations" Rimbaud would have written down had psilocybin been available to him and other French Symbolists at that earlier time. This experience made me into the "psychedelic" poet I became ever after, taking more trips over the next two decades, mostly together with Rolf or a group of other friends. In my first volume of poetry entitled *Liquid Light – Journeys through Outer & Inner Space* I was already making the equation of outer space and consciousness, both forming one "psychocosm," as I termed it later. On subsequent trips, I was drawn into the sphere of our sister-planet Venus, leading to an almost total identification with that planet. I wrote a poetry book called *Venus Rising* and a novel *Venus Notebooks*. Yet, I never lost touch with life on this planet, taught my own courses at Harvard, sent three children into this world, and was ecstatic most of the time.

Later on, on a visit we took to Millbrook, I took a very special LSD trip. I remember it clearly, because half way through the experience, I suddenly thought I had found the absolute and unfailing solution to all the problems that plague mankind on this earth I could hardly speak, I was so excited; then "it" vanished from my mind. Only years later it dawned on me what "it" was and I wrote my futuristic, psychedelic novel *Christa Astralis*, published in Germany in 2004.

The High Tower on beach in Zihuatanejo, Mexico

Part 2

First Zihuatanejo Retreat Summer 1962 to Psychedelic Training Program Summer 1963

Summer, 1962

Six-week retreat at the Hotel Catalina, Zihuatanejo, Guerrero, Mexico. Besides Leary, Alpert and Metzner, participants included about a dozen graduate students and people working on the project, as well as spouses or partners. Work starts on adapting the *Tibetan Book of the Dead* as a psychedelic session manual, testing the model and developing best practices for conducting high dose LSD sessions.

Fall, 1962

Ralph receives NIMH postdoctoral fellowship to study psychopharmacology at Harvard Medical School. This eventually results in a lengthy review article of chemical and biochemical research studies with psychedelics, published in the first issue of the *Psychedelic Review.*

A core group establishes communal living situation in a large house in Newton Center. The group includes Leary with his two teenage children Susan and Jack; Peggy Hitchcock; Richard Alpert; Ralph Metzner and fiancée Susan Homer; Frank Ferguson, Wesleyan graduate and Leary's assistant; former Harvard student Foster Dunlap, his wife Barbara and child Alexander; Michael Hollingshead and, later, his girlfriend; and an African-American Boston area musician-entrepreneur named Buster. The artist Bruce Conner, noted for his experimental work with collages, assemblages and film, lives here for a while. Graduate students involved to varying degrees with the psychedelic projects (including Gunther Weil, George Litwin, Rolf von Eckartsberg and Paul Lee) are regular visitors, while finishing work on their doctorates at Harvard. George and Corky Litwin, together with Gunther and Karen Weil, Richard and Max Katz, Alan Cohen and Dave Kolb, set up a second communal living situation on Greycliff Road in Newton Center.

Newlyweds Ralph & Susan Metzner

Ralph and Susan get married. Huston Smith performs wedding ceremony.

The Newton Center House is remodeled to build a hidden chamber, accessible only from the basement, to be used for meditations and psychedelic explorations. Research begins with DMT, a short-acting injectable psychedelic. With help from behaviorist psychologist Ogden Lindsley, Leary designs the Experiential Typewriter, a measuring device for continuously coding varieties of inner experiences. This is used in experiments with DMT.

Winter, 1963

Visitors to the Newton Center house include philosopher Alan Watts; poet Allen Ginsberg,; novelist William Burroughs; psychologist and dream researcher Stanley Krippner; philosopher-anthropologist Jean Houston; jazz musician Charles Mingus; hypnosis researcher Martin Orne; Canadian entrepreneur and pioneer of LSD alcoholism therapy Al Hubbard; and Robert Thurman, Harvard (graduated) student who later enters a Mongolian Buddhist monastery in New Jersey, to study under Geshe Wangyal.

A group of neighbors in Newton Center sues the group for unlawfully accommodating several families in a single-family dwelling. George Alpert, Richard's attorney father and businessman, successfully defends the group, arguing they are living "as one family."

The International Federation for Internal Freedom (IFIF) is established as a non-profit educational and research organization dedicated to psychedelic research, independent of Harvard University. The Board of Directors included Leary, Alpert, Metzner, Walter Clark, Huston Smith, Rolf von Eckartsberg, Paul Lee, George Litwin, Gunther Weil and Alan Watts. IFIF launches the *Psychedelic Review*, under the joint editorship of Ralph Metzner, Paul Lee and Rolf von Eckartsberg, later also Gunther Weil. IFIF plans to supply a network of independent research groups with the (at that time) legal substance LSD, along with instructional manuals for its optimal use. An attempted purchase of one million doses of LSD from Sandoz Pharmaceuticals in Basel, Switzerland, comes to naught when Harvard gets wind of the plan and opposes it; and the $10,000 check that was sent bounces due to insufficient funds.

Spring, 1963

Leary is let go from the Harvard faculty for being absent from his classes – he had already moved to Mexico. Shortly afterwards, Alpert is dismissed from the faculty for violating the agreement not to give psychedelic drugs to undergraduates. Sensationalist newspaper and magazine articles about psychedelics, the Harvard Project and other drug- taking activities, increase dramatically.

Summer, 1963

A four week training program in the responsible use of LSD and other psychedelics is established at the Hotel Catalina in Zihuatanejo; over a hundred people sign up. While Leary, Ralph and Susan Metzner and others start running the sessions, Alpert remains in the Newton Center house to see to the administration of the project, signing up applicants and preparing publication of the *Psychedelic Review*. After two weeks, the Mexican training program is closed by the Federales, and staff and attendees are expelled from Mexico amidst chaos. Attempts are made to salvage the training program by setting it up in the Caribbean islands of first Dominica, then Antigua. Both attempts fail due to resistance by local authorities. The financially and emotionally battered group retreats back to the U.S. and a private estate in Millbrook, New York.

Tim Leary, Richard Alpert & Peggy Hitchcock, Zihuatanejo, c. 1962

Tim Leary, Zihuatanejo, Mexico, c. 1962

First Zihuatanejo Retreat – Summer 1962

RM   The Mexican LSD sessions were strikingly different from the Harvard psilocybin psychodramas. Zihuatanejo, at that time, was still a small, sleepy fishing village with gorgeous beaches on a curving bay on the Pacific Ocean. Here the setting was the exuberant lushness of jungle flora and fauna, the ceaseless rhythmic pounding of the surf, extravagantly beautiful sunsets, silent lightning storms over the Pacific Ocean, tropical heat and balmy air currents, mysterious sounds of night insects, and the sweet aromas of exotic flowers. The women often transformed mythically into sea nymphs or mermaids; the men into Aztec warrior chieftains or jungle shamans.

At the suggestion of Aldous Huxley and Gerald Heard, we began using the *Bardo Thödol* (*The Tibetan Book of the Dead*) as a guide to psychedelic sessions. Tibetan Buddhists talked about three phases of experience on the "intermediate planes" (bardos) between death and rebirth. We translated this to refer to the death and rebirth of the ego, or ordinary personality. Stripped of the elaborate Tibetan symbolism and transposed into Western psychological concepts, the text described visionary sequences remarkably parallel to our experiences.

The *Bardo Thödol* describes the first phase, the first bardo, as a state of complete transcendence, of pure radiant light, that occurs immediately after death; they tell us it can be maintained only by those with high yogic training, who are able to remain undistracted. This first phase usually quickly dissipates into the second bardo, the longest phase of hallucinations and visions of peaceful and wrathful deities, heavenly or hellish experiences. The third bardo was the phase of re-birth, or re-entry as we called it, in which you returned to your ordinary personality. It quickly became obvious that this sequence was not to be taken as a literal description of a typical LSD session. Rather, it provided a general framework for understanding and navigating through inner space.

The basic advice of the Tibetan yogis was always the same: Remain detached and centered within yourself, don't become attracted to the pleasant visions or repelled by the painful ones. Remember they are all in your mind. Accept them and float downstream. During rebirth, or re-entry, don't rush, stay balanced, maintain the light for as long as possible. This ancient text – which before our experience with psychedelics would have seemed to us as so much gibberish – contained in uncanny detail descriptions of many aspects of the voyages we had been taking. Reading beyond the specifics of the Tibetan Buddhist iconography, one could discern vivid descriptions of inner states. The texts made it clear that these were realms that were recognizable and real, regardless of the method used to get to them. Suddenly we were no longer a crazed bunch of psychologists, recklessly plunging into completely uncharted terrain. There had been previous explorations. There was a history, a tradition. There were maps and guidebooks. Leary (and I think all of us really) felt affirmed in our spiritual approach to psychedelic experiences by the discovery of these ancient writings. Leary started to work on the adaptation in Mexico, and later he and I divided up the sections between us. Our initial work on this text was later developed and published as *The Psychedelic Experience: A Manual Based on the Tibetan Book of the Dead.*

RD   They, Tim and Ralph, wrote the *Tibetan Book of the Dead* manual. I didn't. I took care of the children and I cooked.

RM   But you knew about the *Tibetan Book of the Dead*, and were in accord with its teachings, weren't you?

RD   Yes, but I was in the wrong category. I'm not the person to ask about the research or things like that.

RM   Did you feel bad about that? Not participating more?

RD   No. I felt like I was in the right role. I took care of the kids. I took care of the budget. I took care of relations with Harvard. I was sort of Mr. Charisma. I was nice, I was a team person. I was in the kitchen, making bread.

RM   I always felt you were equally part of the writing project, even though not as directly involved; just as I was equally part of the Harvard situation, even though less in the front lines than you. I'm sure that's why Tim said all three of our names should be on the book as co-authors; and I never had the slightest reservation about it being that way. We were doing these projects together, as a group; authorship credit

Richard Alpert, Newton Center, 1962

or any other kind of credit was never the point. I also think that we all realized that the communicative impact of a book authored by three PhDs would be much greater than if it was just one, or two.

GB   Ralph, do you remember your first LSD trip? Was it in Zihuatanejo?

RM   Well, I had heard Tim talk about his first LSD trip with Michael Hollingshead, in Newton Center, and it freaked me out – all his talk about the "plastic doll world." It sounded insane and I wasn't sure I even wanted to go there at all. It was way beyond anything I had come to really value and appreciate about the psilocybin sessions – the openness, the loving connections with others. So then in Zihuatanejo, a much more serene and relaxed setting than Massachusetts, and after studying the Tibetan Buddhist model a bit, I asked him to guide me in an LSD session; we agreed to test the model, and the manual. We used our "session room" with a balcony facing the jungle, the ocean surf roaring below. We agreed that if I felt fear I would say so, rather than struggling with it myself.

We started off in silence. Tim read some passages from our new "manual." For about an hour nothing happened. I was restless and annoyed at myself for not being able to let go. I was thinking too much and too hard. Tim said he'd found focusing on sensory awareness had helped him get out of obsessive thinking. He lit a candle, opened a cool bottle of beer (which I simply touched) and encouraged me just to focus on pure sense perception. This seemed to cut through the excessive mentation like a knife through butter. I suddenly felt released from a heavy fog of restless and pointless thinking.

I looked at Tim's face, and to my amazement it became the face of a god-like Being, radiating light. Then, as I continued gazing at it, it changed and half of his face looked ugly and demonic. Simultaneously with this visual outer perception, I felt subjectively like a piece of protoplasmic jelly stuck to a rock. The part of me that was floating free in the ocean saw Tim's face as radiant and divine; the part of me that was still stuck to the rock saw it as ugly and cold. At times, my mind felt like it was cradled in a beautiful, clear, empty space, but then I would slip back into fear and distress.

Tim got up and sat by the door. I lay down on the floor, closed my eyes, and again tried to reach that state of ecstatic weightlessness by emptying my mind. I couldn't do it and got discouraged. I thought I could only reach it with his or somebody's help. I started to hallucinate – the peaceful and wrathful visions of the second bardo phase. When I saw fearful images, I remembered the admonition of the Bardo Thödol that they were in my mind only, so I told them to go away. To my immense surprise, they did.

Then, with an electrifying shock of insight, I realized that I could do this not only with these relatively trivial demons, but with all my fears. I thought about a friend, actually it was Foster Dunlap, whose outrageous behavior sometimes scared me. Then I thought how absurd it was that I should let fear feelings that were inside of me interfere with the relationship I had with someone outside of me. That was the message of the Tibetan Book of the Dead *– recognize that it's all inside of you. At that moment, I realized that not only my fear of him, but all my emotional reactions, positive and negative, toward him and towards anyone or anything, were all within me. In that moment my whole head opened up spherically in every direction simultaneously, 360 degrees, and I felt both serene and exhilarated as never before in my life. It was incredibly liberating.*

(Excerpted from *Timothy Leary: Outside Looking In*, edited by Robert Forte)

RD   That's a great image.

RM   Then I sat up and looked at Tim. He took one look at my face and said, "You made it." I told him about the fear insight and he added: "Not only the fear of that person, but the love for them is within you too. The point is you have to know your own mental machinery, otherwise it scares the shit out of you." We talked for a while about possible ways to maintain this state, where everything you looked at was pulsing and glowing with divine radiance, and the difficulties of living permanently at that level of consciousness. We finally agreed that "in order to live at that level ... you have to live at that level." For about two or three hours I had no problem maintaining that state of spherical openness. It was effortless. I knew I was in my body, but I had no identity in it. My identity and awareness seemed to be spread throughout the room and even beyond into the forest outside. This meant when somebody came into the room, it was if they were walking into "me." I felt freer than I have ever felt before. Gradually and gently, over a long period of time, "I" returned back to my usual personality and body-self. The memory of the state of consciousness experienced remained with extreme lucidity.

GB Ram Dass, you mentioned that you had a bummer LSD trip in Zihuatanejo.

RD Yes, the big, big one. I had the question of whether I was living or dying. The frightening ones for me were in Zihuatanejo. Because of the jungle.

RM Was that in the first year? There were two years. The first summer was just a group of about twenty or twenty-five. Just experiencing. Then the second summer was a whole program for the public.

RD Yes, we would take a trip and we always had a spotter or ground controller, someone always watching out for you. I was high in the ocean, and I no longer was seeing the ground control person. I felt that they had forgotten about me. I had an image in the ocean: all the stars were out and the ocean was filled with phosphorescent sparks. I couldn't tell which was which, or differentiate up from down. And the waves were coming in. I was afraid. I was afraid of dying. I was not functional and I felt I was going to drown. I was going to die in the ocean and the repercussions of that filled the whole universe. I was going to cease to exist. Then this vision came up of a little girl, way down the road in time, holding a picture of me up to her mother, asking, "Mommy, who is this man?" And Mommy said, "I forget." And nobody would know. I was going to fall from people's minds.

RM That was a classic near-death vision, where you are convinced that you are dead. You could no longer see the ground control folks and that confirmed you in the thought that you were dying.

Ralph measuring out doses, Zihuatanejo, 1963

RD Well, then I was lying on the beach, I was panting and two people found me and they picked me up from the flotsam and the seaweed. I was saying intensely how bad we were and how irresponsible we were by fooling around with this stuff. I mean, I've just finished dying, you know, and we're fooling around. Tim came along and I ran to him, white faced, and I shook him. I said, "This is dangerous, we've got to do something." I was furious that nobody wanted to take me seriously. Tim said "You're just paranoid and keep quiet" and he got me a cup of tea.

GB How did you feel about what Tim said?

RD You know, I was paranoid. It was the terror of ceasing to exist.

I was going to be an embarrassment to the whole psychedelic movement because I'd gone too far. I was always afraid we were going too far.

GB   One common thread I hear in both yours and Ralph's bummer stories is that you looked to Tim Leary as the leader, the savior and the stable one.

RD   The stable one? Ha, ha, ha.

GB   The one who could keep it together in these far out states?

RM   We knew he also had horror trips, because he would tell us. But at those times when we freaked out, he hadn't taken anything, so he was more grounded.

RD   He was the one that was stable, because he was there, when we became frightened. So you could look at Tim as stability, but it was spiritual stability. He was, in that sense, our guru. I consider him my guru, my *upaguru*.

RM   Would you say it that way now? Looking back at that time? Would you consider him your guru even now?

RD   Upaguru. You have a number of *upagurus* along the way until your *sat guru*. Trungpa Rinpoche and Muktananda were also *upaguru* for me. Neem Karoli Baba is my *sat guru*.

RM   So other teachers could teach you something on your spiritual path, but not necessarily for the rest of your life, just for that period in your life? But of course, you know Tim hated the concept of guru. He would get quite annoyed when anyone called him that, or even hinted at it, like in that psilocybin session with Michael Kahn and Gunther and George Litwin. His preferred model was captain of a team, or leader of an expedition, or the baseball coach – coach of the game of life.

PEGGY HITCHCOCK

I went down to Mexico with Tim and Richard to explore Zihuatanejo, which Richard had seen from his plane on an earlier trip. At that time, Zihuatanejo was a sleepy little coastal town on the Pacific, accessible only by dirt road or airplane. There was only one hotel able to accommodate our group, Hotel Catalina, owned by a rather grumpy, sad Swiss man. He was very happy to rent the hotel during the summer, as that was the rainy season and normally few people visited.

I was very excited about the opportunity to experience psychedelics in a nurturing environment. I remember one particularly amazing LSD session when I came out of the sea as an amphibian, transforming into a four-legged, then a two-legged being. Tim would always ask us what insights we had gained. I remember thinking how simple everything was: That in order for positive change to occur, the cosmic timing had to be right. I shared this insight with him and I could see that he thought it trivial. I still believe that timing is a most important factor in effecting change. I could feel the interrelationship of everything in my life, and I knew that if the timing was not right, change was not going to happen for me or for anybody. I don't believe that Tim ever really got that point.

Peggy Hitchcock, 1962

I never spent a night in the high tower at the beach, but I did spend a whole night on the beach during an LSD session. I remember one very weird scene when I was in an altered state of consciousness and went down to the beach for a late night swim alone. A drunken man from the town emerged from the shadows to confront me with a knife. One of our friends, Buster (who was a pot dealer from Boston and very street savvy) suddenly and magically materialized by my side to disarm him; perfect timing, for which I was most grateful!

The baseball game which Tim organized, Harvard versus the Zihuatanejo home team, was definitely the grand finale of our stay. Timothy was a great fan of baseball, which was the most popular game in Zihuatanejo. We all agreed that by ending the summer with a baseball game, we would end our stay on a high note. Our Harvard team all took LSD (unbeknownst, of course, to our opponents). Our team's sense of timing was greatly enhanced, and to our dismay, we started winning. We did not want to win, of course, since our goal was to generate a feeling of good will with the town. As I remember I only played one or two innings. Almost everyone else somehow managed to play out what seemed like a very long nine innings. The home team of Zihuatanejo won, to everyone's delight.

Peggy Hitchcock,
Newton Center, 1962

As the summer ended and I became more involved with Tim, we decided that I would be part of a new community which had evolved from our summer experiences. Richard, Tim, Ralph and Susan, Foster and Barbara Dunlap and her daughter, would all share a house in Newton Center, Massachusetts. I had my own room there, but also kept my apartment in New York City. I was a commuting member of the community, spending at least half of my time there. One memory I have about the house at Newton Center is the weekend I came up to find Tim in a frenzy of deconstruction, knocking down walls to make the kitchen area bigger. As I remember, someone else did the reconstruction. Tim was very good at knocking walls down but not that interested in building them back up.

Tim and I had "a swinging door relationship." Looking back, I doubt that Tim was ever truly in love with me. He was certainly intrigued, interested and loved my spirit of adventure. We had a very strong connection, probably a karmic one. I fell in love with him during that summer in Zihuatanejo. To me, he was the most fascinating person I had ever met. I loved the way his mind worked and his enormous sense of fun and adventure, which was totally contagious. My partnership with Tim evolved as we became close friends and lovers.

Fortunately, I had not yet gone down to Zihuatanejo the second summer when the training course was expelled from Mexico, nor was I part of the Caribbean caper, for which I am most grateful, as I have not heard a single thing about that experience that wasn't really dark. Somehow I always managed to be absent when legal complications arose, good karma perhaps. I was never financially involved in the project other than paying towards my room and helping to pay for groceries when I was there. I think many people assumed I was much more financially involved with Tim than I was. Tim was not bothered by going into debt. He was a very proud Irishman. He never asked me for money. I think he felt he had to make it on his own, which was, in a larger context, rather sad. He never included me in a discussion where he would say, "Here is what we need in terms of resources. Is there a way you can help?" Perhaps he also had a cultural bias because I was a woman with whom he was involved and he would not feel comfortable asking me for money. Much later, after Tim's Laredo marijuana bust, I pitched in along with many other people, giving and raising money to pay his huge legal fees.

When Tim and his party were all kicked out of the Caribbean, and had to leave Antigua, the question was where would they go (or rather we, since I was part of the group even though I had not been there). We were running out of places.

Luckily, my twin brothers, Billy and Tommy, who had just turned twenty-one, had come into considerable money. They had decided to invest in a large thousand-acre property, in Millbrook, New York, where they could raise cattle and take a large tax deduction for this activity. Several houses already existed on the property. One of them was a very large, turreted, rambling Victorian home in which Mr. Dietrich had lived, but which had not been inhabited for some time. My brothers decided to occupy the newer, more comfortable mansion, known as the cottage, which Dietrich had built for his son. I was aware that the large Victorian home existed, so Richard and I went down to check it out. We thought it was perfect. I spoke to my brothers and they happily agreed to rent it to our community for a dollar a year. This seemed to us like the perfect solution to the immediate housing problem for our experimental community.

I have a life-long memory of an extraordinary session with DMT, which was brought to Newton Center by a friend, Rolf von Eckartsberg, and given by injection. I had an aversion to needles, partly from having lived with a junkie, and I thought this was a perfect opportunity to overcome my fear. The experience was one of total dissolution into molecular particles. "I" no longer existed. It was utterly blissful, an experience of emptiness. I remember vividly not wanting to come back. I also knew that I would not want to do it again. I have a life-long eating disorder, which is something that is always present somewhere in my psyche. When I was in therapy in the sixties, I never even mentioned it, as there was so much shame involved. Part of me was not happy to be present.

Psychedelics helped me enormously by expanding the horizons of my being and by strengthening and confirming my spiritual focus. They did not help with grounding myself and with learning how to be here on this earth, which has been a major issue for me in this lifetime. Psychedelics opened up for me a world of endless possibilities. Then, okay, I still had to come back and take out the garbage. For many people, as for me, perhaps Buddhism has provided the container for what we had experienced during psychedelic experiences. Buddhist teachings have helped to integrate those experiences. For me, the great thing about Tibetan Buddhism is that, as a belief system, it is very expansive and yet is very grounded and pragmatic.

Newton Center Commune and IFIF

Newton Center studies, Frank Ferguson (middle) and Barbara Dunlap (right)

RM Going over these stories, Ram Dass, makes me feel affectionate towards you. I like to remember them. Who was living at Newton Center then, after we came back from Zihuatanejo?

RD Before Zihuatanejo, Tim lived on Grant Avenue in Newton Center and I lived on Harvard Street in Cambridge. Then I took that big green house in Newton Center, that Tim, his children, and you and Susan, and the others came into. Foster and Barbara Dunlap and their son, and Buster, lived there.

RM Buster Brown, local pot dealer, from across the river. African-American. He was very cool; he could roll a joint while driving his car through traffic. He came to the first Zihuatanejo retreat.

GB So it wasn't all academic folks?

RM No, not at all. Michael Hollingshead was there. He helped with the house and the children. The craziest man, but a good babysitter. He actually took care of the kids, he never endangered them, he was kind to them, he helped them. Later, his blonde Swedish girlfriend Brita also moved in; and Frank Ferguson, a brilliant Wesleyan graduate, who had started helping Tim with correspondence, telephone and all kinds of work at his office at Harvard. You and Tim still had teaching jobs at Harvard; I started work on my post-doc in psychopharmacology.

GB Ralph, you and Susan got married that fall?

RM Yes, Susan Homer was a Reed College drop-out, whom I met at Harvard. She came to Zihuatanejo with me. She and I and Rolf von Eckartsberg drove to Mexico from Massachusetts in a Land Rover. I proposed to her on a mescaline trip, during the first summer in Zihuatanejo. We decided we were meant for each other. I tried to remember later, when things got difficult, that it was a high state of consciousness in which the contract was made. We set a date in the fall, and Huston Smith agreed to conduct the wedding ceremony which was held at her mother's family country home in Massachusetts. A week before the due date, she got totally depressed and catatonic. She refused to get out of bed. So I asked you, Richard, if you would talk her into taking the fateful step. What else could I do? It was somebody's script; I was just following it as best as I could. You succeeded. What was it you said that got her to change her mind?

RD   He isn't a bad guy.

RM   Somehow I don't think that impressed her. That prospect could be more boring than staying depressed.

RD   She just needed emotional support.

RM   Right, it didn't really matter what you said. The fact that you were willing to sit with her and hold her hand and tell her it would be alright.

GB   So you did get married?

RM   We did get married. Then I got a new red car, a Triumph convertible, and we drove to Maine for our honeymoon. After our wedding night, it was my turn to get depressed. It was the classic story: what have I done, who is this person? But we eventually became good friends and partners. She and I conducted many of the sessions in the psychedelic training program in the summer of 1963 and she moved to Millbrook with us.

GB   So who was Foster Dunlap?

RM   Foster Dunlap was an undergraduate at Harvard, that Richard first met and then I did; a most unusual young man. He turned me on to pot and the underground drug scene in the Boston area.

RD   He was a hippie undergraduate, of which there weren't many at Harvard. And he was a smart, smart fellow. He was married to Barbara. She was a little older than he was and they had a three or four-year old son Alexander.

RM   She had a seven-year old daughter, Lisa, from a previous marriage. She had been a psychiatric aide.

RD   He had been a psychiatric patient.

RM   Did we know that at the time?

RD   No.

Barbara & Foster Dunlap, Mexico, 1962

Susan Homer on her wedding day, 1962

I had met Ralph Metzner through Foster Dunlap. Barbara and Foster were my next-door neighbors on Hayes Street in Cambridge. I had been hearing about Tim Leary and the others and the psilocybin project from Foster. I went with him to Ralph's one spring evening – I don't know why we went. From outside, through a window, we could hear music playing and see Ralph dancing by himself, which I found a little sad but also appealing; he was a kind of shy dancing guy.

My first LSD session was in Newton Center, in the summer before we went to Zihuatanejo, in that house that Tim had on Grant Avenue. Ralph and I had the room on the third floor. One evening, I was up there with Buster, who had gotten hold of a brown glass jar of LSD – the sugary paste. I wanted to try it and so joined Buster – I remember we stuck our fingers in, pulled out big dabs, with no idea of how much we'd be getting. Then, somehow, others realized that Buster and I had turned on and others – Tim, Richard, Ralph and others joined us. One highlight I remember from that first LSD incredible session of mine, was dashing water in Richard's face, with the intent of providing a little playful shock. My impression is that it wasn't received that way.

When we went on our honeymoon in October 1962, the Cuban Missile Crisis was going on; we tuned in the radio to find out if we were going to be blasted off the coast of Maine. I don't know why I agreed to go to Maine at that time of year – it was cold, dreary, grey, and wet. We took a small amount of LSD one night and were like two lost kids without the grown ups (Tim and Dick) around to make sure we were safe. I read the Twenty-Third Psalm from the motel Bible in the bedside table, something we had recited at bedtime when our father put us to bed as children; it didn't reassure me, it just made me feel like a child in need of a parent. I was too scared to let Ralph know how scared I was.

RM   But you found out later that he'd been hospitalized before? I didn't know that, until this minute. What was he hospitalized for?

RD   I think schizophrenia.

RM   He was an amazing person. One of the most unusual minds I've ever met. Compared to the rest of us, it was like we operated on one brain hemisphere and he on another one. Or, like he had a third one. He would assume various roles, he was an impressionist. He would take on someone else's identity, act like you're acting. Create a caricature of you with his gestures and his voice. Really spooky kind of stuff done with such incredible brilliance, I would be astounded; he was like a magician. He would say it was completely unconscious, he had no idea what he was doing. And Barbara was a really funny, warm, loving person, who had been on both sides of the mental health system, and had great insight and compassion. Quite an amazing couple.

Many years later, in the 1970s, when I had my son Ari, and was living in California, and she and Foster had split up, she and her son Alexander moved in with me as house-keeper and childcare-helper, for a while.

RD   I had picked Foster up and given him a job. Tim didn't like him at all, because he didn't climb into Tim's trip. Foster was my assistant. There was a conference session of a division of the American Psychological Association, organized by Henry Murray and myself. Foster was supposed to deliver the program schedule to the APA, but they never got it. One of Murray's friends and colleagues, an important person who was head of some government thing, who normally commanded a large audience, got up to give a talk and there were only three or four people there. Foster had not followed through, and I felt it was my fault. Henry Murray and I never spoke to each other again.

RM   Did you fire Foster?

RD   No.

RM   You were close to him. You liked him a lot.

RD   I liked him a lot.

RM   Maybe you were in love with him.

RD   Maybe.

GB   So what happened in Newton Center with Foster?

RM   We did several sessions with him, sometimes with Barbara and also some other friends of his. I think Buster came to the house through him. And there was another friend of his, a guy who also came in – a younger, muscle man, who was into karate. He'd take psychedelics and do karate moves. I enjoyed being around Foster, he was always fascinating, though some of the things he did had a strange, eerie quality to them. In one session he hallucinated that he had turned into an insect and I was the entomologist studying him. I could never tell whether he really believed these hallucinations, or whether he could tell the difference. I guess that's one of the signs of schizophrenia, isn't it? Not being able to tell the difference between fantasy and perception of reality. Over time, in the Newton Center commune, he became crazier. He started talking about burning the house down. It became serious. We had house meetings. One of us intends to burn the house down, what do we do? This had never happened before. His parents came to visit, and Tim said to his parents, "Well, what is it with you two; you produced this very unusual son? What do you think of him?" I don't remember what they said.

RD   I don't remember them.

RM   Do you remember the crisis about burning the house down?

RD   Yes.

RM   So how was that resolved? I was just freaking out on the sidelines basically.

RD   I remember telling him he shouldn't.

RM   That was good advice. He took it too. He didn't actually do it. But he threatened to do it. Kept everybody hopping for quite a while. He just set that whole thing up to manipulate the entire situation. Have everybody centered on him – what's he going to do next? What crazy thing do we have to watch out for? He had a phenomenal gift, too bad it was so wasted. He could have been a great actor. He was unusual looking too: his face was classically handsome, chiseled features, and his head was enormous, seemingly larger than normal.

Susan Homer, Richard, Tim and Peggy, Newton Center, 1963

RD   The house became a situation similar to the kind R.D. Laing was setting up in England, where psychiatrists and their patients would live together in the same house, turning it into a kind of therapeutic community.

RM   Yes, but our situation wasn't planned that way. We didn't want that, we wanted to be spiritual explorers, on a collaborative journey. Tim and I were writing this article on Hermann Hesse's books (*Journey to the East* and *Steppenwolf*) for the *Psychedelic Review.* We were interpreting them as coded accounts of psychedelic explorations. Foster didn't fit into that paradigm – he didn't fit any paradigm really. Though, often he would seem quite normal and kind and sweet. I never saw him do anything violent to any one or anything. I don't remember for sure, but after the fire thing blew over, we probably made him leave.

Tim recuperating with Barbara Dunlap, Newton Center, 1963

GB   What happened to Foster Dunlap?

RM   While we were preparing the final proofs of this book, I happened to hear from Alexander Dunlap, Barbara and Foster's son, via Facebook. Now in his forties, he lives on the East Coast with his family and works as a psychiatric nurse. His mother Barbara is alive and well, but his father Foster died fourteen years ago, in a boarding house for the mentally ill. "After many years on the street and resisting the well-intentioned Community Mental Health systems to treat him, he dropped in. Why Foster finally decided to start taking meds and going to his outpatient program, is unknown to me but that's what he did. After a time he began to volunteer at the library and became increasingly involved in his community. Foster seemed to have been liberated in part of whatever had been torturing him for many years. Gone was the tinge of fear that had characterized the impressions of so many in the past. In the end (there was) a certain monk like quality of life in the asceticism and simple joy in life he seems to have achieved." A beautiful ending to the story of an amazingly gifted and troubled man.

GB   Is there anything else about your communal living at Newton Center that either of you want to talk about?

RM   I think the way that situation started, was that after the first summer in Mexico, because we were spending so much time with one another, talking about our experiences and planning other sessions, it

Ralph with Alexander Dunlap,
Newton Center, 1963

seemed natural to want to live together, rather than spend all this time and energy driving back and forth to each other's houses.

RD   We had our house, and then, because our house was so successful, George Litwin started another commune house in Cambridge with some of his friends. Our house was a single family house in a single family neighborhood. After some months, because we had a black man and Foster was acting strange, the neighbors began to be concerned. They called a meeting with other neighbors and went to the city council to get us removed. My father, George Alpert, a prominent Boston attorney as well as president of the New York-New Haven Railroad, took on our case. My father is a showman – he had the vest with the gold chain, he looked like Clarence Darrow. He said we were the "family of man." We were a single family; we were the family of man.

RM   He argued that a "family" was defined not by blood lines, but by the sharing of a household. And he won the case. The Newton Center commune was the scene of many new and different kinds of psychedelic research. We carried out experiments in which we deliberately invoked problem situations for an individual, who in the expanded state of consciousness, would attempt to see through his blind spots. We also performed experiments in language learning, where a person under the psychedelic would listen to recordings of a foreign language being spoken, in order to imprint her brain with the sounds and inflections of that language. One room in the house was set up as a meditation and session room. It was a converted closet, remodeled in such a way that it could only be reached from the basement – you had to go downstairs and then up a ladder. Inside, the walls and ceiling were hung with India print cloth and luxuriantly colored pillows covered the floor.

RD   It was a secret room in the downstairs.

RM   You could only get to it from below, using a ladder from the basement to come up.

RD   A person could come into the house and not know that that room existed. I've got a story about that room. I was taking LSD. You had to come down to the cellar and then come up to go to the kitchen.

There was a woman in the kitchen that had arrived at the house the day before. She'd come up from the South by bus, to get a job in the North; she had come to our house and was thinking of working there. She was sitting in the kitchen, drinking a cup of coffee, when I came up from the basement. She took one look at me, and whatever it was she saw must have blown her mind, because the coffee cup went flying and she came running over and fell at my feet. Well, that completely freaked me – I mean, here was this woman, in her fifties, very solid, straight, conservative-looking, kneeling at my feet; it drove me running out of the room. Later, she told me that when I came up the stairs from the basement, all she saw was a radiant, golden light.

(From *Paths to God: Living the Bhagavad Gita*, p. 100)

Jack Leary and Susan Homer, Newton Center, 1962

RM   We used that room for DMT (Dimethyltryptamine) and other intensive exploration sessions.

GB   How did you come to start working with DMT?

RD   Tim and I got it from a research group in Los Angeles. As Harvard professors doing research, we requested it. I was carrying it and as we were crossing the street, Tim said, "If you drop that I am going to be very angry."

RM   I went to Arthur D. Little, a scientific consulting company in Cambridge, and asked them to convert the crystalline powder into an injectable form. It's not orally active so it has to be injected intramuscularly. It was a new thing for us, but we learned to do it. Always to my discomfort.

GB   How was the effect different from LSD or psilocybin?

RM   For one thing it only lasted forty minutes, compared to four hours for psilocybin and six to eight hours for LSD. But at 60 mg it could produce an incredibly intense forty minute experience. Later, in Millbrook, some of us had some experiences with DMT in smokable form. When smoked, it's over in just a few minutes, which is an advantage in case you screw up and land in a hell realm – you don't have to be in hell for forty minutes. I was always scared of it, it was too intense for me; but Tim seemed to really enjoy it and you too, apparently.

RD   Yes, I loved it. Also, you could ask it questions and get answers.

Alpert monitoring Metzner on the Experiential Typewriter, at the Newton Center

RM   Tim, still the inventive research psychologist (at this time of his life), started a collaborative project with Ogden Lindsley, a behavioral scientist who was an associate of B.F. Skinner. Lindsley had pioneered objective continuous recording of the physical behavior of psychotics in a mental hospital. He designed, at Tim's request, a device that looked like a typewriter, with two keyboards, with ten keys for each hand that activated strip-chart recordings, each key representing an experiential category. Tim called it the Experiential Typewriter. The idea was that the person during a session, who might be unable to talk quickly enough to describe his ever-changing experiences, could code them with the push of a button in a few basic categories. Categories could be such things as "body sensations," "cellular memories," "thought patterns."

We used this device in experiments with DMT. In one experiment, described in *High Priest*, Tim was the subject and Susan and I were the guides. Every two minutes one of us would ask Tim to indicate which of the twenty keys on the typewriter best represented his current state of consciousness. I felt the device was a remarkably effective aid in the attempt to objectify internal states. Here's a passage from *High Priest*, describing the experience from the voyager's point of view, and how the programming situation was incorporated into his hallucinatory universe:

MINUTE 2. TIM, WHERE ARE YOU NOW? Ralph's voice, stately, precise, scientific, kind ... what? where? you? ... open eyes ... there squatting next to me are two magnificent insects ... skin burnished, glowing metallic, with hammered jewels inlaid ... richly costumed researchers, they looked at me sweetly ... dear, radiant Venusian crickets ... one has a pad in his lap and is holding out a gem-encrusted box with undulating trapezoidal glowing sections ... questioning look ... incredible ... and next to him Mrs. Diamond Cricket softly slides into a latticework of vibrations ... Dr. Ruby Emerald Cricket smiles ... TIM WHERE ARE YOU NOW ... Moves box towards me ... oh yes ... try to tell them ... where ... Body ... I am swimming in tissue tidelands ... BODY CONSCIOUSNESS ... use mind ... explain ... look down at undulating boxes ... struggle to focus ...

(Timothy Leary, *High Priest*. 1968, World Publishing, p. 270)

GB   Can you say more about Michael Hollingshead, and his role in the Newton Center commune? He later wrote a memoir called *The Man Who Turned On the World.*

RM   Since the termination of the Harvard sponsored research projects in the spring of 1962, we had no more access to psilocybin, and increasingly were starting to work with LSD, mescaline, DMT and various other psychedelic substances (for example, the seeds of certain species of Morning Glory, which contained LSD-like alkaloids). LSD was introduced to us by Michael Hollingshead, an eccentric Englishman, who had arrived one day at the offices of the Harvard Project, broke, depressed and suicidal. He had endeared himself to Tim because of his knowledge of the LSD worlds, and was living in the Newton Center house as a kind of an all-around assistant. He also had an extraordinary sense of humor, as a consummate story-teller and was a genial, good-natured fellow.

Tim had jokingly developed a three or four point rating scale of moral reprehensiveness that went from rascal to rogue to scoundrel and beyond; he and Michael would engage in teasing banter about where he was placed on this scale. I always found Michael's descriptions of his psychedelic experiences completely baffling. I could not relate to what he was describing. He completely shattered all our assumptions and premises. Instead of following our code of openness, trust, sharing and sincerity, Michael made use of the awesome suggestibility of the LSD state to confuse, bewilder, astound, and manipulate awareness and perception. Yet, when confronted, he would deny it stoutly, and protest his innocence in such a guileless, humorous, friendly manner, that it was impossible not to like the man.

Michael used to take a fairly large, though indeterminate, dose of LSD every day, while he still had the supply. He had it made up into a kind of paste, like peanut butter, and would spoon it out of a jar. He thought of it as a kind of daily consciousness vitamin. Often he would, while on the trip, mix himself a drink, like scotch, and then watch TV. I remember walking in to the kitchen while he was there in that state, and he would say, "You watch it for a few minutes, and then something quite incredible appears on the TV." And I'd have to admit that he was right – it was incredible.

Michael's approach to psychedelics was much more like that of the later hippie "acid freaks," Ken Kesey and his Merry Pranksters: not growth, not spiritual experience, not insight or learning, just freak out, go as far as possible to the outermost edge of the hitherto experienced and beyond, blow the mind and yet stay cool and in control, keep up the game.

GB   Any other impressions of Michael Hollingshead, Ram Dass?

RD   He later lived with us in Millbrook, and was part of the Bowling Alley, "stay-high-all-the-time" experiment I created with Arnie and others, while Tim and Ralph were in India,

RM   Yes, Michael Hollingshead was there when we left for India and his little daughter too, a nine year old. He was a very strange man, spooky in a way, but also likeable – at least I liked him.

RD   Very strange

RM   I kept vacillating between being charmed by him, laughing at his outrageous stories and quirky comments, and being spooked by stuff he did.

PAUL LEE

I remember taking psilocybin once at the communal house in Newton Center, in the session room which you entered from the basement up a ladder through a hole in the floor. Paisley curtains festooned the room, of course, and we were on a cruise trip of a lifetime, with Elsa Von Eckartsberg in charge of entertainment, which consisted almost exclusively of her laughter for which we have the word "peals," as in high pitched church bells. We all laughed in unison. I hallucinated cruise hats on everyone. Talk about unbounded gaiety. Tim Leary stuck his head up through the floor opening at one point and I laughed and said I had it figured out, and he was it, and then I fixated on his nose hairs which seemed electrical and functioned as antennae for his consciousness. Oh, those were the days.

Paul Lee, early 1970s

In that same basement room I also took DMT. Marsha Pressman had come to town as Tim's girlfriend. She lay down next to me and caressed me as Tim shot me up with DMT and I watched amoeba film loops projected on a screen while Miles Davis was playing *Sketches of Spain.* I forgot to mention that Marsha was a spitting image of Sophia Loren, or I should say salivating image. She was a goddess. Bob Thurman was in the kitchen, just back from India, and when I walked up to introduce myself, I fell into his eye socket, as he had his patch off. Fortunately, I had hold of my ankles.

I had taken DMT once before in front of two visiting psychologists who sat and watched. When the drug took effect, I thought I had become the broiler in an electric oven and was about to fry. I've always liked crispy things. I felt bad about burning up as Tim would have to dispose of me in front of these visitors and then my daemon said: "Why don't you see what it's like to be an electric oven on broil?" and I willingly and quickly said: "O.K.!" Then I opened my eyes and boy was there ever a phantasmagoria of dots and stuff in the atmosphere not unlike a quantum vacuum illustrated by Euclid. Half an hour later, we were back in the trenches.

These memories live in me like icons. I could have gone on at length about the session in Millbrook, when I hit a psychoanalytic moment about why I went into theology to make up to my mother about the loss of her father, and Metzner, whom I must have been boring half to death, yelled very loudly in my face to shut up right in the middle of the most self-illuminating sentence. It took me into a long spin on nonverbal experience with which I had a hard time as you might imagine. Leary and Alpert got bounced from Harvard and we all feared for our academic careers; not wanting to go the guru route I ducked under the radar and went to Santa Cruz and the new campus of the University of California which I was happy to find out was opened expressly to give students a chance to take psychedelics in the redwoods overlooking Monterey Bay. I had a good time there, too.

I was proud of my identification of students as "oceans of desire" and also my critical reaction to the negative side of psychedelics in what I called "the tyranny of being hip."

One thing psychedelics did for me: They prepared me for the physicalist/vitalist conflict in the system of the sciences, which starting an organic garden opened up for me, and I found out that scientists, by and large at the time, thought organic meant "artificial synthesis" as in organic chemistry. The artificial synthesis of urea (1828) became the smoking gun in the undermining of organic nature, preparing the way for the physicalist take–over and establishing the foundation for the rise of industrial society now in its late stage of self-destruction.

I remember teasing Tim about having been a behaviorist and he took umbrage, though he never repudiated his physicalist past in his transition to vitalism. He was finally honored by the American Psychological Association for his behaviorism prior to the psychedelic period which they took pains to ignore. I took Tim to be the one who re-introduced consciousness into psychology after its elimination by behaviorism. How can there be a psychology without the psyche? Tim overcame the lapse. Neo-vitalism superseded existentialism and re-affirmed the integrity of organic nature, against its physicalistic reduction, spawning the environmental and ecology movements.

I am grateful for these insights into our historical crisis.

RD   He was a sociopath.

RM   I never knew anybody like that. One time I was describing being in Switzerland having Christmas with my family. And he said "Ya, I've been there (in that tiny village), I know that place." And I'd say "Now come on Michael, give me a break, you're putting me on." But he would insist, to the point I'd get a little irritated. Then, later when we took LSD, and I was very suggestible, he came back to this and started describing in great detail various features of the place, repeating that he'd been there; suddenly I'd think that he was telling the truth, and it made me question my own rationality, like a Zen koan mental pop – I actually flipped out, and went semi-unconscious. When I "came to," he was just sitting there, grinning like the Cheshire cat. It was like a kind of mental ju-jitsu maneuver. But what was the point of all that?

RD   He was a very captivating fellow.

RM   I think "mind fucking" is the technical term for that kind of behavior. Your friend Arnie was like that too. But, compared to Michael, Arnie was a beginner and Michael was a master. It's a tricksterish element, which seems completely amoral. On the other hand he was actually kind, I never saw him be cruel. He took care of the kids. He was responsible in that way. He could charm the pants off authorities and intellectuals.

GB   You didn't get the sense that he was a crazy wisdom teacher?

RD   No, no.

RM   More emphasis on the crazy than on the wisdom. Sometimes there was insight, fantastic verbal skill, and cleverness.

RD   I didn't think he was clever.

The International Federation for Internal Freedom

GB   Can you talk about how the IFIF organization came into existence?

RM   When it became clear that Harvard University did not want to sponsor any more psychedelic research of the kind we were interested in doing, Tim came up with the idea of an independent non-profit research organization that would be a kind of institutional umbrella for our work. This was while we were still at Harvard, you and Tim still had teaching appointments and I had the post-doctoral fellowship. The organization was founded in January 1963.

RD   We had an office and an office manager, Lisa Bieberman. A little office in Harvard Square, at first, and then we moved to a medical building in Boston, across the Charles River.

RM   Lisa edited a newsletter. We had to move our office because once the landlords found out what we wanted to do – promote research into psychedelic drugs – they would refuse to rent to us. We kept having to move our furniture from one place to another.

GB   Who were the directors and what was the purpose of IFIF?

RM   The founding directors were Timothy Leary, Richard Alpert, Walter Clark, Ralph Metzner, Huston Smith, Rolf von Eckartsberg, George Litwin, Paul Lee, Gunther Weil; five of them PhDs. Alan Watts was honorary director; Frank Ferguson was Executive Secretary. The statement of purpose spoke about a historical tradition of mystics and visionaries who questioned the prevailing views of reality, and used various methods to expand awareness. New chemical means of doing so were now available and much was being learned about set and setting and how to make use of these tools.

Rolf von Eckartsberg, 1962

To implement the preceding points, there is need for an organization to encourage, support and protect research on psychedelic substances … We are fully aware that institutions, however libertarian their purpose, tend to restrict and inhibit the development of spiritual freedom. They often end in external control of internal freedom. This danger we seek to avoid. This paradoxical tension we recognize and accept.

(From the Statement of Purpose, IFIF)

Statement of Purpose of the

INTERNATIONAL FEDERATION

FOR

INTERNAL FREEDOM

I. THE SITUATION

As long as men have reflected about their world — which is to say, for about 3000 years — a basic issue has divided them. There have been those who regard man's normal conceptual models as straightforward mirror reflections of the way things actually are. Over against them have been men who suspect that these models are more like reducing-valves imposed by finite consciousness upon an infinite, evolving reality to reduce it to manageable proportions. The issue is whether the world of normal sense is unqualifiedly real and, indeed, the only reality, or whether reality is far more than mind and sense disclose — not only quantitatively, but qualitatively as well. That things are what they seem, and that they aren't — this has been the great divide that has separated men since they first became philosophers.

What induced those in the second group to fly in the face of sense evidence and assert that things are in truth dramatically different from the way they appear? Reason doubtless played a part, but its speculations must have appeared pale compared with the full-bodied testament of direct experience. For as far back as men have left records, there have been some who reported visions and theophanies in which the veils were lowered, the masks of God removed, and reality disclosed with startling force.

It may be that all these telltale rents in the fabric of normal awareness involved alterations in brain chemistry, however effected. What we know is that experiences strikingly like those reported by mystics, seers, and visionaries of the past can be induced by chemical means. This puts us in the position of being able for the first time to explore experimentally the momentous question of the absoluteness versus the relativity of our sense perceptions and the prevailing conceptual schemes which order our experience.

Another prospect emerges if we approach the mind psychologically rather than epistemologically. Until the last century the West has equated the mind with its conscious manifestations. With Freud, Jung, and their immediate forerunners, there broke upon the West the realization that not only the mind but also much of what within it is most important for our lives, lies below the level of self-awareness. Our ability to change the chemistry

International Federation for Internal Freedom brochure

of the brain gives us a device for reaching this unexplored material dramatically faster and more fully than was possible before.

The issue arises in a third form, namely socially. Some accept prevailing institutions as God-given and inviolable. Others see them as conventions which can block freedom, stifle creativity, and stunt lives as readily as they can support these and make them possible. One need think only of current patterns of racial discrimination, and prejudice against the mentally ill, for examples. Insofar as our prevailing institutions and attitudes do inhibit the full release of man's potentials, the added awareness that indole substances engender is likely to make this fact more evident. Concern to reform the debilitating institutions should naturally follow, as should attempts to develop new ones.

For the past two and a half years a group of Harvard University research psychologists has been studying these issues. Five research projects on the effects of consciousness-changing drugs have been completed. Their results, supplmented by study of other available data, have led the researchers in question to the following provisional conclusions:

1. Man at present may be using only a fraction (perhaps less than one percent) of his available brain capacity.

2. The politics of the nervous system — psychophysical processes involving censoring, alerting, discriminating, selecting, and evaluating — may be responsible for this restricted use of brain potential.

3. Prevailing patterns of stimulus censorship can be relaxed, thereby admitting to consciousness stimuli otherwise debarred. As a result of this admission, consciousness is expanded — possibly in an absolute sense, but at least in the sense that the mind becomes aware of factors heretofore unknown. Indole substances (LSD, mescaline, psilocybin, etc.) are the most powerful agents yet discovered for opening the mind to new data.

4. *Set* and *setting* control what data are admitted and how they are experienced. *Set* denotes the personality structure of the individual, including his beliefs and mood at the time. *Setting* is physical (weather, feel of the room), social (feelings of persons present toward one another) and cultural (prevailing views as to what is real).

5. Insights gained through the new indole substances appear likely to require innovations in at least the following areas:

    a. *Language.* A new vocabulary is needed to describe experiences which are not only new but different in kind. Beyond this, to experience in areas where vocabulary is lacking and syntax inapposite is to gain new perspective on the role and function of language generally.

b. *Self-understanding*. What does it mean to be a self, a person, a human being?

c. *Metaphysics*. What is real, what unreal?

6. New social institutions are indicated. In particular, it may be important that experimental communities based on new perspectives which indole substances produce be established both to provide support for these perspectives and to test their validity.

7. There is special need to see if indole substances can alter the self-and-reality models of those who are receiving minimum returns from those models they currently possess: criminals, psychotics, delinquents, and the like. Those who see the limitations of their present models — mystics, artists, housewives, the rebellious young — would, for their part, seem to be exceptionally promising candidates for breakthroughs into new outlooks.

8. It is vitally important that responsible research on consciousness-change proceed vigorously; that research institutions not be panicked by unfounded rumors and fears which always seem to spring up around the word "drug"; and that, in view of the importance of *setting* on experience in this area (see point 4 above), research not become the monopoly of a single school of thought on the ultimate significance of the substances in question.

II. ORGANIZATION

To implement the preceding points, there is need for an organization to encourage, support and protect research on psychedelic substances and which will be willing and able to take responsibility for serious studies in the area.

We are fully aware that institutions, however libertarian their purpose, tend to restrict and inhibit the development of spiritual freedom. They often end in external control of internal freedom. This danger we seek to avoid. This paradoxical tension we recognize and accept. It can be a stimulating and fruitful force.

We have formed a Massachusetts non-profit corporation, the *International Federation for Internal Freedom* (IFIF). Its present Board of Directors consist of:

Richard Alpert, Ph.D.   Ralph Metzner, Ph.D.
Walter Clark, Ph.D.   Huston Smith, Ph.D.
Rolf von Eckartsberg   Gunther Weil
Timothy Leary, Ph.D.   Alan Watts, D.D., S.T.M.
Paul A. Lee   (Honorary Director)
George Litwin

The basic units of IFIF are small research groups — assemblages of six to ten persons who share the general goal of consciousness exploration and who are involved in a common research project.

The immediate functions of IFIF are:

1. To encourage persons to band together in such research groups for systematic exploration of consciousness.

    The specific research goals are determined by the members of the individual research group. It is understood that the goals of such subgroups would not contradict principles of IFIF. Among those who have already applied for affiliation are groups made up of ministers, educators, psychologists, and persons involved in the field of behavior change and rehabilitation.

2. To act as a local research center, collecting and disseminating the knowledge gained by each research group.

3. To maintain offices to be used as research centers.

4. To offer advice, medical and legal services, and financial and other support to the research groups.

5. To raise funds necessary to support the research, publication and educational programs of the Federation.

6. To obtain drugs and to make them available (*in conformance with existing laws*) to the research groups. This may mean the purchase and development of actual plant facilities to produce consciousness-expanding drugs and to sponsor needed pharmacological and biochemical research.

7. To establish and support two new journals which will publish scientific and literary articles about consciousness-expansion. A detailed description of this project is available on request. (The first issue of *The Psychedelic Review* appears in June, 1963. Address: P.O. Box 9, Cambridge 40, Mass.)

8. To sponsor the publication of instruction manuals which present a very wide variety of methods and objectives for consciousness-expanding experience.

9. To encourage and assist the development of centers for research in internal freedom in other cities and countries.

The IFIF headquarters office is located at 14 Story Street, Cambridge 38, Massachusetts. (Phone: 617: 547-7244. Cable: IFIFREE — Cambridge.) The Executive Secretary of IFIF is Mr. Frank Ferguson. You are invited to write or visit the IFIF office.

This statement was prepared and distributed by the Chartered Board of Directors of IFIF.

January 24, 1963

Originally, the idea was that there would be small research groups, six to ten persons, who would band together for the purpose of consciousness expansion. IFIF would supply them with consciousness drugs and information manuals on how best to use them. Remember that there was nothing illegal about any of this. LSD was not a "controlled substance" at that time. And, the IFIF proposal specified that distribution of drugs was to be "in conformance with existing laws."

The first part of that purpose never came to pass. A purchase order of 100 grams of LSD, enough for one million doses (100 micrograms each) was submitted on Harvard University letterhead with a $10, 000 check to Sandoz Pharmaceuticals in Basel, Switzerland. When Sandoz checked with Harvard University officials about this order, the University nixed it. The money wasn't there to cover the check anyway so that part never worked out. Media fear-mongering and prohibitionist ideology overtook our plans. But IFIF did start publishing the *Psychedelic Review*, started an information center and sponsored the Summer Training Program in Mexico the following summer.

GB   Could you comment on the religious aspect of psychedelic experience?

RM   Taking LSD made the religious dimensions of psychedelic experience inescapable. You were plunged into realms where all hitherto accepted belief systems and identity structures were suspended, as everything you called "you" dissolved in pearly streams of liquid color, or in pulsing waves of ecstatic sensations. As you returned from these experiences of pure content-less energy, the world of images and categories in which we live our normal lives did indeed seem like a "plastic doll world." People came out of these sessions reeling with awe, overwhelmed by experiences of oneness with God and all other beings, shaken to the depths of their nature by the grandeur and power of the divine life-energy-processes going on within their own consciousness.

We had turned to religious professionals for help. Huston Smith, Professor of Philosophy at MIT, and author of the best-selling book, *The Religions of Man,* friend of Aldous Huxley, was one of the first to join our project. He remarked that his experiences confirmed and validated what he had been writing about for years. In 2000, he published a book called *Cleansing the Doors of Perception – The Religious Significance of Entheogenic Plants and Chemicals.* So his views on their significance have remained consistent over the course of the last forty years, based largely on these few experiences in the 1960s. Some of his students came and joined our project. Walter Huston Clark, Dean of the Theological Seminary at Andover-Newton, a kindly, distinguished older gentleman, became, much to our surprise, an enthusiastic advocate of the potentials of psychedelics.

We ran a series of sessions for ministers, priests, rabbis, and theology students. Some of these were more dramatic and violent than any we'd ever experienced at the prison with hardened criminals. Some got caught up in hell-fire and judgment visions; others wanted to immediately force everyone around to convert, confess, and turn to Jesus; some forgot about God and turned to their wives for solace; some left the ministry; some were deeply confirmed in their calling.

One theology graduate student, a huge, red-haired bear of a man, wrestled with some nameless monsters in his unconscious for hours, sweating and groaning and finally finding release and peace. However, the next day he announced that he didn't see any value to it, that it wouldn't help him write his thesis, or help America beat the Russians, and therefore he didn't want any more of it – an attitude I found frankly bizarre.

Walter Pahnke arrived and began his famous "Good Friday" study, the first (and to this date the only) controlled, double blind, bona fide experimental study of mystical experience. Walter was an MD from the Midwest and an ordained Minister, who was getting his PhD in the History of Religion at Harvard. His idea was to give a group of divinity students psilocybin, during a Good Friday service in a chapel. He understood the set and setting hypothesis, and wanted to maximize every factor to produce religious experiences. A control group would be given placebo, at the same time and same place, and neither subject nor experimenter would know who had the drug and who had the active placebo. Dean Howard Thurman of Boston University Divinity School agreed to the use of Marsh Chapel for the service. Andover-Newton Seminary, through Walter Clark, provided volunteer subjects, who were highly motivated, pre-tested, and screened. Harvard University, through our psilocybin project, provided the trained guides, who would work with the twenty subjects in small groups. Huston Smith of MIT, was on his doctoral committee. Both Huston and I were in the small groups as assistant-observers.

The experiment was a complete success. Walter had culled nine criteria from the literature on religious experience: in terms of these criteria, the psilocybin subjects experienced states and levels of consciousness indistinguishable from classic mystical experience, whereas the control group did not. The study became famous through psychological and religious circles and was widely written up in the media. Walter got his PhD.

Despite successes such as Walter Pahnke's experiment, the political pressures at Harvard University continued to mount. Professor McClelland announced that students who participated in the drug work would be dropped from the PhD program. Newspapers played up the sensational angles with abandon: "HARVARD EATS THE HOLY MUSHROOM. RELIGIOUS VISIONS PRODUCED BY DANGEROUS BRAIN DRUGS. AWESOME NEW DRUGS CAN SET BRAINS AFIRE."

Increasing Degrees of Separation from Harvard

GB   What were your responses to the increasing notoriety of the project and drugs at Harvard and all the headlines?

RM   I kept it at bay, especially in the early days. We were having too much fun, exploring, doing sessions, learning. The newspaper sensationalism was amusing. The outer turmoil in society became less and less important, the more we became involved in the exploration of inner space. Especially since so much of the opposition was prejudice based on fear and often didn't involve any direct experience. As Leary sometimes said, "LSD is a strange drug that produces fear in people who don't take it."

RD   I think that's right. We didn't notice the political turmoil. What we noticed was our own inner processes and our own psychological effects on each other. We were a cult turned inward.

GB   You were accused of cult-like behavior, at the time, by several people and David McClelland was one of them.

RM   Yes, and Tim would answer that, if you look up the definition of a cult, it's a group of people strongly dedicated or devoted to a cause or principle. And that's true of us, he said. There's another definition of a cult, which emphasizes its exclusivity, the strict boundaries between in-group and out-group. I know that kind of cult from my later involvement, in the 1970s, with a meditation school called the School of Actualism, which became a cult, though it wasn't one originally. But our group of psychedelic seekers and searchers was not exclusive. Anyone could join in who wanted to. Strangely, we were being attacked by people who didn't want to participate in mind-altering drug experiences and who didn't want us to have them either. There should be a different name than cult for that kind of behavior; I think it's called "prohibition." And it wasn't like we were trying to turn everybody on; we just wanted to be left alone to explore these things with our friends and colleagues so that we could learn from each other. At the same time, especially in these early years, we were paying our dues as academics and psychologists: We were writing papers, having them published, publishing a journal, talking at conferences, giving lectures, etc. playing the scholarly and scientific game the way it's supposed to be played so that you can be taken seriously. It was as if we were being blamed for the fact that other people found our discoveries interesting. What is that?

GB   At the same time you saw yourselves as something beyond scientific researchers, as a group of seekers on a kind of spiritual "Journey to the East."

RM   Seekers, yes, searchers, explorers. Always searching for new possibilities of human life together that was caring and mutually supportive, not exploitative or focused on material consumption and egoic accomplishment. That's the vision that always excited me, and still does, and that I would bet is true for most, if not all, the people with whom we came into contact. This would go far beyond finding a new tool for psychotherapy, although that, in itself, would also be a good thing.

RD   It always surprised me that Harvard University would not be pushing that kind of thing. Here was a pseudopod of society going out exploring new possibilities.

RM   It surprised you that Harvard wasn't more supportive? Tim's line was: "I don't resent Harvard for making us leave. Universities are the guardians of tradition, especially knowledge traditions and principles, that's their job. They're supposed to keep the traditional academic system going." He'd say, you know, expecting Harvard to fund or support research on mind-expanding drugs is like expecting the Vatican to sponsor research on aphrodisiacs. Their function is the opposite: – instead of mind expansion, they want mind continuation. But – you felt they should have been more supportive?

RD   Yeah, I was surprised. I thought they were a bigger institution than they were.

RM   You thought they should have had more guts. Is that what you thought?

RD   As scientists, yes. I said so at the faculty meeting where they accused us of not being scientists. Tim had said that our methods of evaluating expanded states of consciousness were scientific and objective, in the tradition of William James and the introspectionist school. And I said, when I think about it, you would count me as not a scientist, I'm the datum.

GB   Could you explain?

RD   Well, I was a datum because I was a straight young researcher and I took this drug. They could study me and they could do some good research. I wasn't going to stay in the role of researcher; I was going to be whoever I was. But I was being cute.

GB   You weren't trying to show them up, you were just stating a fact.

RD   Yes, I was breaking out of the science game.

RM   And you said that in the meeting with the Harvard faculty!

GB   Were there any faculty at Harvard who supported you, or spoke out in your favor?

RM   The early supporters had left by the end of the first year. Henry Murray had retired. Frank Barron had married and moved back to California, to UC Berkeley. Others were at best neutral.

RD   David McClelland was on the fence. He had brought us both in, giving us jobs.

Vol. 1, Number 4, Summer 1963

RM   You were both his protégées. His reputation was at stake. Tim writes in *Flashbacks* that he had been told by sympathetic faculty that the attack meeting was a power move by Maher and Kelman to embarrass McClelland, to make him look like a bumbling administrator. It sounded bad in the press: "DRUG PROFS ATTACKED BY COLLEAGUES." At the same time, all the criticisms were ideological; no one suggested that anyone had been harmed by our experiments, no one had complained of a bad trip or being abused or anything like that.

RD   David McClelland didn't like Tim and I took offense at that. I responded to Dave, saying "Stay away from me. You're hurting my friend Timothy."

GB   But didn't David hire Timothy to come in and do innovative research?

RM   Yes, but Tim's drug research was too radical an innovation for McClelland. He was freaked out by that. He may also have been experiencing heat about the drug research from his superiors in the Harvard administration.

RD   There was a twenty year anniversary of our expulsion from Harvard. And Dave was the moderator and that was far out. He was on the stage with us and he was friendly and congenial.

RM   Did he apologize for throwing you out?

RD   No. He changed his mind, and that's pretty apologetic.

GB   How did he change his mind?

RD   McClelland found a spiritual teacher in Switzerland. I think it was an Eastern thing. Dave went to India originally to find out how they could motivate the Indians to build corporations; going for the Western model.

RM   Yes, he developed training programs to raise the level of need for achievement motivation, which his social psychology research had shown was related to economic development and growth, historically, in different cultures. I liked McClelland, and I admired his skill and insight as a researcher in his field. His work on the need for achievement, the Protestant ethic, and how that relates to cultural change and economic growth is very interesting. He also did fascinating studies on different kinds of power needs, and affiliation, and how drinking alcohol affects that. But he was not an easy guy to approach. You had a pretty close relationship with him, though, very close.

RD   Yes, at Wesleyan University, I had been his graduate student research assistant. Much later, he became fascinated by India, by what I had discovered there and he started to give himself little doses of Indian philosophy.

RM   So that was a big change of attitude for McClelland. Because originally, in the early days of the Harvard psilocybin project he had circulated this memo saying India, with all the cannabis use, was a kind of decadent society, not achieving much. At the time of your re-union, his attitude had clearly become much more positive.

GB   Ram Dass, we spoke of your being fired from Harvard. Leary and you were the first faculty members fired in how long? Ever?

RD   Ever.

RM   Well, Tim did some research and found out that Ralph Waldo Emerson had been fired from Harvard for his unconventional views about a hundred years earlier.

GB   What was your reaction emotionally, Ram Dass?

RD   I was in a state of existential shock. I felt I hadn't done anything wrong. It was just the play of energy. I didn't have any reaction. My mother had a reaction, but I didn't. It was all just: "Those straight people." I was infatuated with the drugs. They were going to teach me something I hadn't known before and I was on a holy quest.

RM   That's similar to what Tim said too: Being fired from Harvard upset him only because it upset his mother.

RD   I came over to Harvard President Nathan Pusey's office and there was Kennedy's Secretary of State, who was a professor at Harvard. Pusey only wanted to ask one question: "Did you give drugs to an undergraduate?" I said, "Yes" and he said: "You broke a promise to the Dean and we just can't have that." Maybe I was sort of blank, I don't know. It didn't strike me as serious at the time.

GB You do make the point in your writing that being a professor at Harvard and being the over-achiever was your reason for living.

RD Yes, until then. Then, I was in a state of mind that I had joined a holy quest. We were going to show Harvard what psychology was all about. We were dealing with states of consciousness that they hadn't considered.

RM That's exactly the way I felt too. We were exploring some areas that were incredibly relevant to psychology and the understanding of the human mind. Harvard didn't want to hear about it; so we were content to leave and get on with the research as we wanted to pursue it. No hard feelings.

GB Now, looking back on it from your vantage point of forty years later, was it really that small in your life or do you feel maybe you were carried along by the current and there was an ego-inflation there, a grandiosity?

RD You know, when I look back at my life, if I hadn't taken the drugs, I wouldn't have gotten to India, dot, dot, dot. So, from where I sit now, I see that incident was very positive because it connected me to the Spirit and I just didn't have any of that before. I was a psychologist, I talked to psychologists and the world was made up of psychology. The way I was before psychedelics, if I had been fired, I would have freaked. But psychedelics opened up new vistas and Harvard seemed very small. We were exploring a new thing and Harvard said, "No, you must not." As to my grandiosity – I was so bugged that Harvard didn't allow us to do this. Because Harvard was liberal and they treated their professors wisely; and here we were, their professors doing a brand new thing and they were scared. Who I was before those drugs, would have been scared, too.

GB Can you say more about the specific incident that led to your firing?

RD There was an undergraduate, Ronnie Winston, who was an English major at Harvard also involved with rocket fuel research at MIT; a really brilliant guy, from a very moneyed family. And he was hanging around our project. His friend was Andrew Weil, who was an editor of the student newspaper, the *Harvard Crimson*. I turned on Winston and didn't turn on Andy, and that cost me. Andy Weil wrote an article in the *Harvard Crimson*, condemning me because I was giving drugs to undergraduates.

RM   Because he didn't get the psilocybin session that he wanted?

RD   He didn't get it.

RM   You didn't give it to him?

RD   No.

RM   But he knew you'd given it to Ronnie Winston.

GB   In the book *Timothy Leary: Outside Looking In*, editor Bob Forte interviews Andrew Weil, who says:

Richard Alpert was fired and the investigative reporting that I did in the undergraduate newspaper certainly helped bring that about ... The university had wanted to get rid of Leary and Alpert, for a lot of reasons ... The newspaper saw a great opportunity for investigative reporting and made a deal with the administration that if they came up with the information that would help them get rid of them, then the University would act on it and then give The Crimson *exclusive news rights. ... The Crimson initiated this ... The University felt they couldn't act; they didn't have grounds on which to dismiss them.* (p. 307).

RM   I heard the rumor that it was that undergraduate's father, a wealthy and influential man, and also R. Gordon Wasson, the New York banker who re-discovered the Mexican mushroom cult, who were putting pressure on Harvard University to get rid of us. Wasson did not like Leary.

RD   Andy Weil was overweight in those days. He said, "I would like to be your student." I said, if you want to be my student, you need to lose some weight, which he did. He went and took psychedelic sessions on his own.

RM   It's interesting, isn't it, that Andrew Weil went on to be a major proponent of and model for a healthy diet and lifestyle, and a holistic and integrative approach to medicine.

RD   After the *Crimson* story about my giving the psychedelic to an undergraduate was published, it got to the *Boston Globe* and then to the *New York Times*, and so on.

RM   Andrew Weil writes, in that interview, that he felt "there was a lot of wild, questionable stuff going on in their (Leary and Alpert) circle, whether they were directly involved with it or not. And their presence at the university created a certain amount of tension." He thinks it was bound to happen "one way or another."

RD   Yes, years later, I guess, Andy had gone to Harvard Medical School, and he called me up from Washington. He was trying to do a drug study and they were not letting him do it. He called me up and said, "I'm in the same situation you were in at Harvard."

RM   Yes. He came to the same realization as Tim and you, that universities and governments are deeply threatened by consciousness-changing substances and are never comfortable with supporting much research with these unless it's negative. I've heard him say that when he was applying to do the research with psychoactives and being turned down, he was told that if he would just cast his research to the negative about psychedelics then he could get whatever funding he wanted. That's the way the government science game is played: We'll pay you if you provide the findings we want and need for our policies. In the case of mind-drugs, the policy is basically prohibition.

GB   Did this episode with Ronnie Winston happen after you had been prohibited from giving drugs to undergraduates?

RD   Oh yeah. And they knew about my homosexuality and drug use.

RM   They knew about your homosexuality? You were out to your colleagues?

RD   Yes, to some. Let me tell you a funny story from when I was a therapist at the Harvard Student Health Service (HSHS). I had a Mercedes Benz that a friend of my parents had brought over from Germany. I had put a big Jewish star on the bumper and it also had the seal of the HSHS. I lent it to one of my lovers, a guy from New Hampshire, a very young fellow. He tried to proposition one of the psychiatrists of the health service in my car. So, Dana Farnsworth, director of the HSHS, called me in and said, "Richard, one of your patients is driving your car." And I said, "It wasn't one of my patients, it was one of my lovers." That was all before the drug scandal. I could have said he was a patient, but I didn't.

GB   So you told Dana Farnsworth you were gay?

RD   Yeah, he knew.

RM   That is a funny story. I certainly was not aware of your homo-sexual side till much later.

RD   Before I got involved with Tim, I was leading a shady life. I was a professor and I was cruising parks and men's rooms. That was my wild side. And that wild side converted to drugs. I wasn't a totally upright college professor. The sexual orientation thing interwove this whole story. My claim to fame was that I was thrown out of Harvard. They always say it was because of the drugs but it wasn't only the drugs, it was also my homosexuality. Because I wouldn't have turned on those undergraduates if it wasn't for my sexual benefit, I'm sorry to say.

GB   Do you care if this all comes out?

RD   No, I don't care. But what do I say now, when I'm a big spiritual leader?

GB   Was faculty sleeping with undergraduates a big issue in the universities back then?

RD   It was a definite no-no.

RM   I gave drugs to my girlfriend, a lovely Radcliffe girl, from Puerto Rico, called Idalia. She participated in some of the early psilocybin experiments. You got fired giving undergraduates drugs; I gave an undergraduate drugs, too and I didn't get fired.

GB   You didn't get caught. Did you graduate in good standing? You completed your doctoral and post-doc year?

RM   Well, for one thing, I didn't really have a job I could be fired from. I was just a graduate student research assistant. Secondly, this was a rule Harvard made for Leary and Alpert, as faculty members. I was not a faculty member. All the people in our project conducting the studies were graduate students and the people participating were their friends or relatives. For example, my brother who was a graduate student in physics at MIT at the time, also participated. And of course, students at Harvard had access to their own sources of psychedelics, quite apart from our project, although no doubt inspired by it. For example, mescaline was legally available, for those who knew where to look. Undergraduates gave me drugs – Foster Dunlap turned me on to marijuana. Most importantly, we were being sanctioned not because the students had complained about bad trips or having been harmed. Quite the contrary; they were all having good trips and wanted to have more.

RD   Yes, I know it. Ronnie Winston was asked by President Pusey: "Did Dr. Alpert give you this drug?" And the kid said "Yes, and it was the most profound experience of any one of the courses I've had here."

GB   Harvard didn't want to hear about students having great experiences, because they wanted to block the whole thing.

RM   No one had told me I couldn't do that. I was turning on a fellow student. So I felt justified. It's not like we were coercing or tricking people into having drug experiences they had not requested. It was always consensual and mutual, as we say in regard to sexual relations.

RD   I felt justified too.

RM   Yeah, you just broke the rule, the agreement you'd made. I got lucky.

RD   I broke our contract. On the front page of the *New York Times*, the day after I got fired, it said: "Harvard professor lies." But I wasn't lying or denying. I broke a contract. To my family, all that was just politics about drugs. They conveyed to me they weren't happy. But their friends, my mother's friends, said, "What are you doing to your mother?" My father was so caught up in his power games that it barely registered.

RM   I remember my father had a great line: "I don't want to expand my consciousness, I have enough trouble with my consciousness the way it is. So expanding it would just cause me more problems." He was a businessman, like your father, in book publishing. So his way of keeping in touch with what I was doing was to read books, articles and everything he could find out about it.

RD   He'd go to his edge by that method.

RM   Yes, he learned all about psychoactive mushrooms. He already liked edible gourmet mushrooms. He collected the information. He'd send me newspaper articles, in German. So he appreciated it from his point of view. That was his way of exploring it.

RD   As far as my parents' reaction to my firing … I mean in Boston, Harvard is it. To get thrown out of Harvard is a big deal. On the other hand, for my father money was the big thing. One time Dad and Mother both came the day I was marching in a commencement procession, and Dad asked, "What do you suppose these full professors are making?" And I said, "Well, I don't know." And he said, "You don't want to stay in this business." (Laughs)

About the notoriety, my mother's friends came to me later and said, "You were a trial for your mother." But I never noticed it. She was so good at being supportive. She was like, "go, baby go," when you were doing what you wanted. I don't think she anticipated how far I was going to go. (Laughs)

GB   You said that there was an article in the *New York Times* which was very negative about you and that your father stuck it on the wall.

RD   Yes, that was years later when I was Ram Dass. It had a beautiful picture of me. I don't know if he read it. But he liked the fame and notoriety.

Ralph Metzner and Gary Fisher,
Zihuatanejo, Mexico, 1963

RM   Tim was not fired for breaking any rules. He just walked away from the University; decided that he'd completed his scheduled courses and the University dismissed him, or failed to renew his contract. They clearly wanted all of us away from the University, or even the area, following the IFIF experience. Tim didn't seem to have any hard feelings about it. He said universities can't be expected to support something that makes you question conventional and traditional worldviews. So he went to Zihuatanejo, to continue working on the *Tibetan Book of the Dead* adaptation, and to prepare for the training program we were planning for the summer.

GB   Jack Downing, a psychiatrist who was Director of the San Mateo County Mental Health Department at the time, came to Zihuatanejo as an observer-participant and wrote a favorable newspaper article about the program in Zihuatanejo. He talked about a psychotic woman who'd come uninvited and was accepted and taken care of and calmed down without any anti-psychotic medication.

RM   Yes, and she wasn't given any psychedelics either. She was already on her own self-induced psychotic trip. That was the kind of situation that R.D. Laing and John Perry had envisioned, where psychotics could go safely crazy. That was perhaps the ideal environment to do it. I remember we took turns keeping her company. When she wanted to go in the ocean, I went in the ocean with her. We listened to whatever she had to say; we didn't judge her.

RD   The second Zihuatanejo retreat we took very seriously. We were going to transfer our entire operation there.

RM   It had become clear it was not possible to offer that kind of program to the public in the United States whereas Mexico has a tradition of alternative health programs of all kinds. So, we rented the Hotel Catalina again and sent out brochures to our IFIF mailing list.

GB   I thought I read that you had rented the place for two years?

RD   Yes, we had the Hotel Catalina, just for the summer program.

RM   I remember the banner headline in the *San Francisco Chronicle*, $200 for a tropical paradise, three or four guided LSD sessions included, for a month. We had more sign-ups than we could handle. You (RD) were stuck handling all of the sign-ups, screening applicants, and getting the first issue of the *Psychedelic Review* printed, while we got to cavort on the beach.

RD   I cavorted too.

RM   In Zihuatanejo, we converted one of the cabins into a session room, decorated with India print drapes and equipped with pillows, candles and incense. Often, however, a good part of the session would be spent on the beach or in the water. We found that the surf in the protected bay proved to be an excellent way to bring someone through a difficult phase of a trip. Simply to lie at the water's edge, letting the waves wash over you, rolling the body across the sand, merging into the eternal currents of air, ocean, sun and earth, seemed to clear away much fear, suspicion, frustration and other emotional baggage. There were usually three or four persons in a session with one experienced guide. Much of the guiding was done by my wife Susan and me. We were on a very busy schedule: Sessions were started every morning and every evening. A minimum of three to four days had to elapse between sessions for all participants, to let the tolerance effect wear off. Thus, there were always groups either starting or ending a session or in the middle of one. Sometimes Susan and I went several days and nights without interruption, catching short naps "on the wing." Tim guided some of the sessions, but much of the time he was away in Mexico City, handling the political and diplomatic work necessary to allow the operation to continue.

Tim, Zihuatanejo, Mexico, 1963

One of Tim's creative inspirations was to build a ten-foot high tower platform on the beach, open to the sea. Here, one person would be on a trip at all times. We thought of him or her as a sort of inner-space lighthouse, a beacon representing the highest state of consciousness; one could tune in to this "high witness" in order to recover one's bearings when over-involved in the mundane or when lost in the hellish bardos. Each morning and evening, someone else took over and we would have a little ceremony, a changing of the celestial guard, the cosmic watcher of the day or night. I spent an unforgettable night on the tower, watching the moon rise and travel over the bay, its silvery radiance reflecting from the murmuring surf. As the sun rose behind the mountains, the pink-orange light of dawn suffused the sky. Swimming at night, one could move one's hands through the water and watch strings of pearly phosphorescent particles cascading from each finger-tip. Hour-long electrical storms soundlessly shattered the sky into shards of yellow, turquoise and violet.

The Tower on the beach was like an inner-space lighthouse

RD   Later, at Millbrook, that was the same idea for staying a week at a time in the tennis house.

GB   Ram Dass, you were back in Boston while they were in that second summer of Zihuatanejo?

RD   I was at Harvard. I had given Tim money for buying off government officials. He bought a speed boat instead. It was that same money.

RM   Tim left several times during the weeks we were there to go to Mexico City to talk with officials and psychiatrists. I think the expulsion was initiated by a psychiatrist, Dr. Nieto. Tim had delivered a paper on our work to a meeting of Mexican psychiatrists. The reaction was frostily hostile and Dr. Nieto started a campaign to have our work stopped. We had not consulted him sufficiently. We should have hired him as the resident psychiatrist. We should have had a Mexican resident psychiatrist in that position. He was very critical, hostile and very threatened by the whole thing.

RD   This Dr. Nieto had had a bad mescaline trip.

RM   So they notified the government health ministry. Journalistic distortions and fabrications contributed to the problem: For example, an axe-murder that had occurred in the area shortly before our arrival, was promptly laid at the feet of the *gringos* and their *hongos alucinantes*, by a local chief of police overzealous for promotion. Anonymous accusations in a newspaper, once made, are difficult to refute. Our project also inadvertently attracted a sizeable number of uninvited American marijuana smokers who camped out nearby, adding yet another layer of suspicion and notoriety. One of the uninvited visitors, according to Leary, was Carlos Castaneda, who later attained fame for his books on Latin American sorcery.

The Federales were polite and friendly; two men in suits and white shirts. They told us we were being expelled because of all the bad publicity. Personally, they said they did not believe the rumors and felt we were good people. One of them even expressed interest in taking LSD. But they said we had twenty-four hours to leave: The technical reason was that we were on tourist visas and were running a business. Tim managed to buy us a couple of more days while he shuttled back to Mexico City, met with his lawyer and tried to prevent the deportation. But apparently, calls from American authorities – the ambassador, the CIA and the Justice Department – had confirmed the decision to deport us. Tim maintained in *Flashbacks* (p. 129-130, 162) that repeated calls and messages from his secret (I never met her or heard about her at the time) friend Mary Pinchot Meyer, who was J.F. Kennedy's long-term mistress and confidante, had warned him repeatedly that individuals and groups high up in the American government were fine with him doing the drug experiments, but would destroy him if he became too public and drew attention. She herself was assassinated in Washington, DC, one year after JFK, under mysterious circumstances that have not been solved to this day.

Tim talking with the Mexican Federales about the impending expulsion

GB   What do you think would have happened if you had been allowed to stay in Mexico?

RM   Potentially, I think it could have been wonderful. We were learning how to run sessions to be optimally productive for people. The setting was gorgeous. We were getting fantastic feedback from our participants, many of whom wanted to stay longer and have more sessions. We had excellent reports from observers like Dr. Jack Downing, who later became a really good friend of mine, and was one of the pioneer psychiatrists involved in the therapeutic use of MDMA.

RD   But we weren't stable enough to run a stable institution.

GB   Why do you say the group wasn't stable enough to run the resort?

RM   The fact that we didn't get permission to do it. We were expelled. I believe that in Mexico we violated territorial instincts. Perhaps the Mexicans felt that we were there to do something that would be considered too crazy to do at home – and in a sense they were right. Medical and government authorities in the US were condemning what we were doing, and passing laws to make it illegal as fast as they could. You have to talk to people, plan it, and organize it. Tim was just waltzing around, in a way. He either underestimated the opposition that he was arousing, or he didn't care much about that. I tend to think he knew it was a long shot, but decided to chance it anyway. Life is a risk and he liked risks. Why not give it a chance, maybe it will fail, but we'll have fun anyway.

RD   As our stock went down at Harvard, then these fantasies seemed real.

RM   When word about our expulsion went out among the forty or so American guests who had signed up for our program, there was great disappointment, and several of them pleaded with us to run another LSD session for them, that they had already paid for, in the last three days before we had to leave. Tim and all of us were totally exhausted. If we'd had any sense we would have refused. The set and setting could not have been worse – we were under indictment and threat of expulsion. But I think we felt guilty, so we agreed to run the sessions. Two of them turned out to be major psychotic catastrophes, though no one died. Since the whole ambiance had been poisoned, most of these sessions were bad; some of them very bad. One man developed a religious mania and shouted the Lord's Prayer at the top of his voice across the Zihuatanejo bay. Later, he fell off some stone steps and fractured his jaw. He punched Tim, so that Tim fell down some stone steps and bruised his ribs. Four men held him down, while Jack Downing gave him anti-psychotic medication (which we normally never used).

Another man, for whom I was the reluctant guide, on the day after his session, decided to walk home to Boston, taking off on foot and in underwear, heading toward the village. While everyone else was packing, we'd have to from time to time send someone out to keep bringing him back from his long walk home. He was impervious to any rational persuasion. Once we got to the Mexico City airport, in the late evening hours, our restless traveler continued to pace up and down, tailed by tired staff members. He would go to the ticket counter and demand a ticket to "infinity." The clerks politely asked him to return in the morning. Finally, by trickery and luck, we managed to get him into a taxi and to our hotel. But our troubles were not over. Running on manic energy, while everyone else was dead tired, he paced the streets, demanding a taxi to take him to Boston. We finally took him to the American hospital, where, to my surprise, after one last maniacal lunge, he meekly followed the nurse's orders to undress and get into bed.

This was the first time I understood something I was to experience personally and observe several times: Under certain conditions when all the internal structures maintaining our view of reality have been undermined, a person might well accept any available external structure as better than none at all. We learned later that this man stayed in the hospital for two weeks. He wrote us, stating that the experience, though painful at the time, had taught him some valuable lessons. Part of the reason for his excessive paranoia, we found out, was that he had come to Zihuatanejo against his employer's wishes. He was involved in national security work and feared that the drug might make him reveal classified information. This fear was enormously heightened when the Federales arrived to evict us. We regrouped our scattered and battered forces at the house of a friend in Mexico City. Tim arrived, bandaged and limping from his encounter with the religious fanatic. Dick Alpert and Peggy Hitchcock flew in from Boston. We buried what remaining drug supplies we had in the ground near the hotel, because we were afraid of going through customs with them. We never saw them again.

RD   I came down to meet with them, in Mexico City, and I took a bottle of liquid LSD with me because I knew they were all being watched as suspects. I had my trip paid for by a business man who was in the waste handling business. He lived near Boston and he called me and said: "I think it's terrible what they're doing to Tim." I told him that I was going down there to help them out. And he said, "If I put up money for your plane ticket, can I go too?" So he and I travelled together, though I didn't know who he was. I had the bottle of LSD in my suitcase and we flew to one of the Southern cities on Eastern Airlines. He was right there with me the whole time. We were looking out of the plane as the bags were being unloaded. We could see the attendant kicking the bags. The next bag that came down was mine, but I said nothing. Later I found out the bottle of liquid LSD had broken, spilled and absorbed into my white silk suit. We cut up the white suit afterwards into little pieces, to salvage the doses.

RM   Did you ever find out who he was?

RD   No.

RM   At our meeting in Mexico City, we had a long discussion about what had happened and debated what to do next. Several hundred people had signed up for the training and sent in deposits. We wanted to salvage the operation somehow, in view of the positive results we had obtained with the forty or so we did take through the program before the final fiasco. So we decided to try to relocate somewhere else immediately.

Most of us returned to Massachusetts, to our house in Newton Center. A reconnaissance group consisting of Gunther Weil, David Levin and Frank Ferguson was sent to the Caribbean. We had received an invitation from an American living on the island of Dominica, in the British West Indies. Initial reports from the scouting group sounded positive so Tim took off with a larger group. Pretty soon the reports coming back, via telegram, to the rest of us sounded very positive, fairly bubbling with enthusiasm. This was the place, Tim wired. We prepared to leave. A few days later, another wire: Something had happened, the group was leaving Dominica. But they were going to the neighboring island of Antigua, which was much better anyway, so we should come down.

Tim and Richard, Psychedelic Training Program, Antigua, 1963

GB   In his book *Flashbacks* (pp 181-182), Tim says that he met with members of the opposition party on Dominica, who thought they were going to come into power in an election and they wanted to bring in tourist trade. They thought the training program was a good way to do it and they offered him everything. But then, the conservative party suddenly decided to bust him, instigated by reports and calls from American authorities, and to charge him with trafficking heroin. He had to leave quickly and that's when they all went to Antigua.

RD   Ralph, you went down to the Islands with me.

RM   Yes, you and I were the last to arrive, with the Land Rover and we shipped a hundred pound bag of Morning Glory seeds, which was to be our LSD-substitute for the seminar program we still wanted to salvage. (They never really worked very well for that purpose – tasted terrible).

A motley crew of fifteen had assembled. It included Gary Fisher, a psychologist from Los Angeles, who had done pioneering work using LSD in the treatment of autistic children; and also his wife and two young children. Barbara Dunlap and her son came; Gunther and Karen Weil and their daughter; as well as Tim's children. There was a family-like atmosphere, with excited speculations and stories about pirate adventures. Tim had rented an empty nightclub compound by the beach, ominously named "The Bucket of Blood." This was evidently someone's idea of a joke, associating it with pirate marauders, but the place had peculiar vibrations. The atmosphere between the two of you was pretty tense.

GB   Leary writes in *Flashbacks* (p. 183) that "when he (Richard) saw us frolicking on the sand, he flew into a rage. Poor Richard, the summer had been rough on his hopes for becoming respectable. He scolded me bitterly for blowing the $20,000 that Peggy (Hitchcock) had given us. Deported from two countries in two weeks. It didn't take long to raise the number to three."

RM   Yes, because we were also deported from Antigua eventually.

RD   That was where Tim and I fought, in Antigua, at the Bucket of Blood. I was bringing the Land Rover to Dominica and had stopped in Antigua on the way. I was swimming on the beach when I was surprised to see Tim and the group coming toward me across the sand.

RM   Yes, because they had already been thrown out of Dominica as well, and you didn't know that.

RD   I was pissed off. He can't go anywhere without getting us into political trouble. And here I had brought the Land Rover and the bag of morning glory seeds. Tim has just been thrown out from yet another country. We did a session and Tim and I got into a fight. The others watched us fighting.

GB   Verbally?

RD   No.

GB   Physically?

SUSAN HOMER

I was in the first wave, after the scouting group. In Dominica, there were three hundred and sixty five mountain streams, one for every day of the year, rushing down the volcanoes. Rain. Narrow, black sand beaches. Frogs were everywhere – all over the road at night so that you couldn't drive without running over them, squish, squish, squish. And on restaurant menus, crapeaux-this, crapeaux-that, three meals a day (Dominica had been a French colony earlier). The croaking din at night was unremitting.

Susan Homer Metzner, Hotel Catalina, Zihuatanejo, 1962

RD   Yeah. Tim was being irresponsible. Actually, each of us was irresponsible at one time or another. I used to think that Tim was the irresponsible one and I was the poor person to be in the middle of all the things. But I have re-evaluated it. I was just as irresponsible as he.

RM   Nevertheless, we strategized how to get the psychedelic training project going again. We re-wrote parts of the Tibetan Buddhist manual. We talked to all of the island's six medical doctors, trying to enlist their support for our venture, getting lukewarm responses at best. We did some LSD sessions, to try to get insight into our problems. But the set and setting were not good. Most of the sessions we had there were "bummers;" some were horrendous. Our approach to any kind of problem solving was to take LSD again. Kind of nutty when you think about it in retrospect, considering what we knew, even then, about the importance of set and setting. I remember you and Tim went on a trip and you both ended up bummed out with each other. I have this vague image of you and Tim sort of wrestling, almost in a sexual kind of way. You were, we all were, in that kind of freaked out state, when you feel uncomfortable just standing around, thinking, what do I do now? I was just barely holding it together too. Then Frank Ferguson freaked out and Frank had never freaked out before. He was super cool, like from another planet, this totally detached super intelligence. I thought he was immune.

RD   His state of consciousness seemed so pure.

RM   For several days we could not determine what was happening to him. He would sit morosely silent for hours, apparently trusting no one except his girlfriend Lora. Finally, we pieced together (or rather, I thought, and wrote in my chapter in the Bob Forte book) that Frank had decided, in his madness, that the main opponent of our operation in Antigua was a certain black psychiatrist, who was a lobotomy specialist, and very conservative. Frank wanted to sacrifice himself by offering to be lobotomized, in exchange for our getting permission to stay and work there. One day, he actually started toward the capital in order to carry out this demented martyrdom.

RD   My perception or recollection was a little different: Frank thought we were making a bargain with the devil and he felt that he had to stop us from doing this. That was his hallucination, his LSD trip. So he, in his bathing suit, got to that doctors' office and he volunteered himself for a lobotomy. He was going to sacrifice himself to save us which was a very beautiful drama.

RM   I thought originally his hallucination was that if he got himself lobotomized, then the physician would like us and give us permission to stay there. We (you and I) recently got to talk with him, forty years later (!) and check this story out. His account is more in line with what you're saying. He says it was that he was trying to save us from ourselves. By his having a lobotomy, we would stop the project and say, we've got to pack it in, this is it, we've got to go home. In a way, his agenda worked; we did go home after that, although fortunately without his being lobotomized. His girlfriend Lora stayed with him constantly, gradually nursing him back to health over the next several weeks. He reconverted back to the Catholic Church, from which he had come. It reminded me of the guy I took to the American hospital, after we were expelled from Zihuatanejo: he needed some structure. When all your reality structures collapse, you gravitate to some known certainties. Frank did not, however, communicate with any of the rest of us for years. And, as far as I know, he never came anywhere near psychedelics again.

LORA FERGUSON

The pace of life was quite slow and relaxed in Antigua, compared to what had been going on in Newton Center and even in Dominica. A lot of time for thinking where it all was going. Then, there was the LSD trip (to help decide what was going to happen next) that included Tim, Dick, Susan, Ralph, Gunther, Frank and me. The trip during which Tim and Dick did their "sexual wrestling," as Ralph called it. I think that was a clarifying event for Frank.

The next morning Frank told me he was seeing several flying saucers, which from the age of twelve he had suspected existed; now he could no longer repress or deny their reality. He said he now knew for certain that ETs existed. After another day or two of remoteness from the group, during which time I know he was mentally sorting out things, he set off on his walk – I think without any ulterior motive. By this time, he had not had any sleep for at least a couple of days and also nothing or almost nothing to eat. I think this was the cause of his freaky demeanor, which was frightening or unsettling to us who had never seen him like that. (Subsequently, I was to see it again at least a couple of times in the next year, always coming after days of not sleeping). He talked to island residents during his walk, and was directed or actually taken to the mental hospital because of his strange behavior. He did not seek out the hospital himself. There, according to Frank, he was immediately injected with a large dose of Thorazine.

Lora and Frank Ferguson on their wedding day, 1963

FRANK FERGUSON

I groggily came to consciousness in an outside hut, with bars. I knew that I could not leave the hut at will. I was immediately concerned about not being forced to have any more Thorazine. On the first day in the hut I saw only an orderly or attendant. As dusk came, I was given something simple to eat, which I did not eat for fear that it contained more tranquilizers. That first night, I hit upon the idea to counteract the Thorazine by drinking my own urine as the Vikings did to prolong their high (with fly agaric mushrooms – RM). I realized later that the urine pan contained a good amount of insecticide. One of the most meaningful experiences or epiphanies of my life followed that night. I went backward in time; saw that we were part of the Creator of the Universe and that the Giver of Light was in us. Some moments took the form of looking through the bars with total empathy at a large frog who was trying unsuccessfully to poop. At other times, it was difficult to watch Jesus on the cross. I traveled in time but not under my own direction. This now seems to me as a Near Death Experience (NDE) occasioned by the insecticide.

I visited Frank the next day, after Tim met with some authority (either government or hospital-connected) to arrange it. I thought that it was dangerous for Frank to stay in the hospital and that he should act convincingly straight so that he could be released. He agreed with me, but I didn't think his behavior changed much, if at all. I was very worried. But somehow he was released — maybe it was only a day later — with the proviso that he had to leave the island. There just happened (!) to be a visiting American psychiatrist who would be on the same plane with us returning to the U.S. I remember thinking that this doctor probably had a supply of Thorazine with him and was ready to use it. He sat next to us and asked Frank questions about LSD, IFIF, etc., until we landed in Boston.

For the next few weeks in Boston, Frank and I lived with the group in the Kenwood Avenue house. We got married a few days after returning from Antigua and when the others returned there was a big party at the house to celebrate. We moved with the others to the house in Millbrook, New York, but Frank was not participating in the planning discussions for the future. He told me that he now saw the "interdimensional nature of reality" as a result of the insights he had after the LSD trip and the night in the hospital in Antigua. He thought LSD would lead everyone else to come to this realization eventually but that it would be a long and difficult time. Their current vision of the future was not Frank's.

After about a week at Millbrook, there was a group meeting during which Dick Alpert told Frank that he could not continue living there. I think Frank would have made the decision to leave on his own eventually but it was hard to leave what we considered family. We continued to stay in frequent contact for the year that we lived in Cambridge and Boston and then for the sixteen months that we lived in New York City, while Frank was going to graduate school. Coincidentally he was sitting in class next to Anita, who married Abbie Hoffman and later was with Tim in Algeria and during some of the last days before his death. We visited Millbrook occasionally after we moved to Washington, and Ralph visited us there once. After everyone moved away from Millbrook, we had to wait until the advent of Google to reconnect.

RM   These events dealt the coup de grace to our stay in the ill-fated "Bucket of Blood," in Antigua, and indeed in the Caribbean. Gary Fisher and Susan and I briefly explored the option of moving the project to the French-controlled island of Guadeloupe, but our money ran out after a week. Everyone returned to the States. Indeed, it seemed that Fate had sealed our attempted psychedelic training center for ever. Escalating political sanctions and legal prohibitions had by now made open experimentation with psychedelics virtually impossible.

Leary, Alpert and I, together with a few others, moved to a huge estate in Millbrook, New York, owned by the Hitchcock brothers, where we established a research and training center for consciousness expansion, without drugs. The Millbrook Center, named the Castalia Foundation, became a sort of unofficial national headquarters for information and advocacy concerning psychedelics. It was also the center of an ever-changing scene of magic and creativity. Others members of our little band of adventurers dispersed to different parts of the country to build careers and normal family lives. Raising children and having a mortgage does wonders for making pragmatists of all of us.

Richard and Timothy in Antigua after being expelled from Mexico

The Big House, Millbrook

Part 3

First Year in Millbrook, New York Fall 1963 to The Castalia Foundation and Journeys to India Winter 1964

Fall 1963

Taking up residence in the "Big House" at Millbrook: Tim Leary and his two children, Jack and Susan; Dick Alpert; Ralph and Susan Metzner; Peggy Hitchcock (part-time); Gary Fisher, his wife and two daughters (who leave after a few months). Later, the group is joined by jazz trumpeter Maynard Ferguson, his wife Flo and their four small children. Frank and Lora Ferguson stayed for a short while, as did Foster and Barbara Dunlap and their two children.

Tim Leary and friends at Millbrook

The group begins a series of experiments in group living, designed to help apply the unitive insights of psychedelic experience into the mundane details of interpersonal and group relationships. Several restorative gardening and small building projects are begun on the estate and land. Leary and Alpert give frequent talks on psychedelics on the college circuit (sometimes joined by Metzner), at conferences and at congressional hearings. Leary and Metzner continue working on the adaptation of the *Tibetan Book of the Dead* for psychedelic sessions. Leary writes an important article on the production and interpretation of religious experience. Metzner continues editing and publishing the quarterly *Psychedelic Review*, returning occasionally to Cambridge for that purpose. Frequent visitors include graduates from the Harvard Project – Rolf von Eckartsberg, Gunther Weil, Michael Kahn, George Litwin, all of whom had moved on to academic positions at other universities. The Millbrook commune is also visited by jazz musicians Charles Mingus and Allen Eager; writer Robert Anton Wilson; visionary artist Allen Atwell; journalist and editor (of *The Realist*) Paul Krassner; Felix Morrow, publisher-president of University Books; as well as numerous other professional colleagues, including well-known Scottish psychiatrist R.D. Laing and Willem Nyland, a teacher in the lineage of G.I. Gurdjieff. Another visitor and later part-time resident is Art Kleps, who wrote a book about his Millbrook experiences. November 22, 1963 – On the same day that Aldous Huxley, revered sage

Ralph and Tim, Millbrook, 1963

of psychedelic exploration, dies of cancer, taking a small dose of LSD for his passing; President John F. Kennedy is assassinated in Dallas, Texas.

Spring 1964

Castalia Foundation, named after an esoteric spiritual community in Hermann Hesse's novel *The Glass Bead Game,* is founded, in part to provide a source of income for the group. Experiential weekend seminars, using non-drug methods of consciousness expansion such as meditation and yoga are offered, attracting widespread interest.

Summer 1964

July, 1964 – Ken Kesey and the Merry Pranksters visit the Millbrook community in their painted bus, a visit described in novelist Tom Wolfe's *The Electric Kool-Aid Acid Test. The Psychedelic Experience – A Manual Based on the Tibetan Book of the Dead,* by Leary, Metzner and Alpert is published by University Books (New Hyde Park, NY). The book becomes an underground best-seller, published in many languages and editions (some pirated), and is still in print.

Fall 1964

Susan Metzner meets and falls in love with a black photographer, spends time in New York City with him and moves there completely in late fall of 1964. Two fashion models, Nena and Katy, arrive at Millbrook. Timothy and Nena fall in love, as do Ralph and Katy. Working in collaboration with a number of visionary multi-media artists, including the USCO group with Gerd Stern, a series of Psychedelic Theatre performances are presented in theaters in New York. Ralph leaves for India, accompanying Gayatri Devi and her entourage from a Vedanta Ashram. Tim and Nena von Schlebrügge get married in Millbrook and also depart for India on their honeymoon. Filmmaker D.A. Pennebaker makes a short film of the Millbrook wedding called "You're Nobody Til Somebody Loves You."

Winter 1964

November and December 1964 – Letters from Leary, describing Millbrook scene, to Ralph in India.

Beginnings of the Millbrook Community

RD   So then we came back to Newton Center, and Peggy Hitchcock said, "My brothers, Billy and Tommy, have bought a large estate in upstate New York, near Millbrook, where they're breeding cattle. It's got a big house on it, which they're not using. Maybe we could set you up in that; it's a kind of castle." And I said, "Peggy, let's go see it." So she and I went up to see it and we toured it holding candles, it was too dark. We were going through sixty rooms or something like that. It was just wonderful. I had turned on her brothers to psychedelics, so they were amenable to the idea.

RM   Yes, Billy and Tommy became big supporters of our project. From a business point of view, it was a tax write-off for them. We paid them nominal rent, a dollar a year, so they could say this was a big tax loss, which they needed to shelter their cattle ranch. They had another more modern mansion on the estate that they called the "Cottage," where they would go and live sometimes. We had the old "Big House," which had some sixty rooms, four floors with towers, built of big stones. The three-thousand acre estate had all these stones lying around. The guy who had built it, Dietrich, was a German engineer who invented the gas lamps that lit America's streets at the end of the nineteenth century. He was a multimillionaire, as a result. So he had this estate that was filled with rocks. We heard that he had imported three hundred Italian stone masons to come and work there. There were huge lawns, neglected over time, and smaller stone buildings, including a two-story chalet, with stones on the roof, which was set up as a bowling alley.

RD   There were beautiful stone bridges over the creek, and various little towers and walkways.

RM   The gate was like a medieval German castle gate, with towers and a portcullis. The Big House, the lower part, was all these stones piled up and the upper part was regular wood construction with gables, tapestry on the wall, wooden floors. It was an amazing place.

RD   The brothers were socialites. They were in the "Cottage," built of Italian marble. Beautiful. They would bring models and other rich boys up

The Gatehouse at Millbrook

The Big House; face image painted by Allen Atwell, 1964

to their place. One of their visitors early on was looking in through our windows in his helicopter.

GB   You mean somebody was sort of spying from a helicopter on your scene?

RD   Yeah. We were the weirdos that the boys had living at the Big House.

RM   So we moved in there: Tim and his two children, Jack and Susan, who were 14 and 12, I believe. And you – Ram Dass; and Peggy Hitchcock was there with Tim, while keeping her apartment in New York; and Susan and I; and Gary Fisher and his family, from California, for the first few months, until it got too cold for him and he disagreed with the direction our work was taking. He was looking for more of a Vedantist ashram.

GB   What about Maynard Ferguson?

RM   Maynard and his wife Flo, and their four young children, moved in, I think, a little later in the fall. At first they lived in the Big House with the rest of us. Later, they moved with their family into the Gate House.

Susan, Tim and Jack Leary, 1963

One experience stands out in my mind: We used to go walking at night, in the moonlight, with the sounds of our boots crunching in the snow. One freezing cold November night, we heard of the assassination of JFK. All of a sudden, it was like uffff, a low body blow. Your life came to a stand still as it did for everybody. A few days later we heard that on the same day as JFK, Aldous Huxley had died of cancer, with a dose of LSD administered to him by his wife Laura – as he had described in his utopian novel *Island*. What a synchronicity that was.

RD   Was Gunther Weil there?

RM   He visited often, in the early days. Then he went to Boston University. All the other graduate students from the Harvard project, feeling the demands of young families went on to academic careers at other universities. Michael Kahn to Yale University, Paul Lee to UC Santa Cruz. All of them would visit often during the first year.

RM   George Litwin visited too. He'd started teaching at the Harvard Business School. Rolf von Eckartsberg went to Duquesne University, where he became a leading voice in the phenomenological psychology movement. He and his wife Elsa came to visit often. He had been in Zihuatanejo the first year.

GB   What about Gary Fisher?

RM   Gary Fisher and his wife didn't stay very long, maybe a month or so. He and Tim never really clicked very well. He still doesn't like Tim, to this day. He thought, on the basis of what Tim had told him, that this was going to be a kind of ashram along the Vedantist model, which it didn't turn out to be. He was very psychic and had learned to do this kind of healing, working with moving energy through the body with hand movements that he learned from Russell Schofield, about whom he told me. Schofield later (in the 1970s) became my teacher of Agni Yoga, or Actualism.

GB   What can you tell us about the experiments in group living?

RM   Well, we started this series of experiments in communal relations. The idea was, we had taken all these psychedelics, including LSD, that resulted in mystical states of oneness with all life and everyone, and

Susan Leary & Gary Fisher, 1963

The "Bowling Alley"

yet we still had these neurotic hang-ups, and sometimes didn't get along and got into conflicts. What can we do about it? Is there a way to minimize the gap between the high unitive experiences and the inevitable differences in everyday life and living together? We wanted to see if we could live in a way that would cut through the kind of oppositional thinking that comes up between people. The first experiment we tried involved the separate little house known as the Bowling Alley. We'd have a community meeting, draw lots, and two people at a time, chosen at random, would live in the Bowling Alley for a week, alone together. They wouldn't have to do any household chores, like cooking and cleaning; we would bring them food. They could take LSD or not, whatever they wanted to do to explore their relationship. I think my wife Susan and Flo Ferguson were the first couple. They came out after a week and seemed happy enough, though they didn't report any great breakthroughs. The next pair was me and my former girlfriend from Harvard, a lovely Irish Catholic girl from Boston, named Shelah O'Brien – who has since died, bless her soul. When the two of us lived in the Bowling Alley, there was not much of a connection between us. I had a camera and I would photograph her walking away from me, down a path. So, that was kind of symbolic of our relationship; her back turned to me, walking away down the path. We didn't become closer, we weren't particularly close anyway – we weren't lovers or anything. We didn't become lovers or stop being lovers.

GB   Did you take LSD during that week?

RM   I think so, or perhaps morning glory seeds. But nothing particularly stands out about it. Did you do a session in the Bowling Alley with one other person, Ram Dass?

RD   I did one in the Bowling Alley later on; with five people. Just staying in there and taking LSD.

RM   That was later, when Tim and I were both in India. I think we gave up on the Bowling Alley experiment after a couple of more turns. It didn't seem to lead to anything useful. Of course, we were doing group LSD sessions fairly regularly, taking turns being the "ground control," programming the sequence of music, and so forth. We next decided to implement what we called the "Third Floor Experiment." It had to do with transcending sexual possessiveness. We agreed that those people who wanted to transcend their couple relationships would live on the third floor, where each would have a room; those who wanted to stay in their conventional marital arrangement, like Maynard and Flo for example, would live on the second floor. And so would the children, of course. Those of us on the third floor would have to choose and negotiate who our sleeping partner was going to be every night. So that was the experiment.

RD   That was the heteros' experiment. I did not participate.

RM   But you also lived on the third floor.

GB   Why do you think you didn't participate?

RD   Because that was a heterosexual scene.

RM   That sounds right. I don't remember whom Tim was sleeping with at that point. Sometimes with Susan. But there was also a lovely young woman with blonde curly hair, called Carol, who had an eight year

Ralph Metzner and Susan Homer,
Millbrook, 1963

old boy named Eric. I slept with her a couple times and Tim did also. My wife Susan was there. I slept with her sometimes and not other times. We were slowly drifting apart, but still very good friends. My memory of the outcome of the "Third Floor Experiment" is that it involved an inordinate amount of time. You had to spend time during the day negotiating who you were going to sleep with that night. It seemed excessive. The usual arrangement is a little more convenient if you wanted to get anything else done. I guess if you had lots of time to spare it would be okay to play that game. It seemed like a game. I don't know how long it lasted, perhaps three or four weeks.

RD   You see, we were all psychologists and when psychologists live together, they have to do psychological experiments.

RM   It's true that we were researchers, interested in consciousness. You can't research consciousness unless you explore your own consciousness with intention, and try to learn from what's happening.

GB   Were there kinky scenes on the third floor or anywhere?

RM   No, there was nothing particularly kinky about it. Just the choice of sexual partner was elaborate and ritualized. Visiting for a while was a young woman who was bisexual-lesbian, who regaled us with stories of orgies she'd participated in. But I never saw or participated in any orgies myself, although I would sometimes hallucinate them during psychedelic sessions. We were still on this track of trying to resolve our sexual neuroses through these different experiments and then we would do LSD sessions. I remember I sometimes had paranoid sexual hallucinations in group sessions. It was so outrageous, it made me realize I was paranoid and delusional during the time of the session and then I would wake up to what was happening to me.

For example, there might be a session in which there were several close couples, but I was without a partner. The room was darkened but I perceived there was some smooching and cuddling going on between the couples. With my eyes closed, I would begin to hallucinate that they were actually having sex right there and I knew I was not. Pretty soon everybody else was having sex except me. It's a sexual orgy in which I am not participating. It seemed I could even hear the sounds of an orgy, sounds of lips smooching and bodies heaving. Then I would open my eyes and would see people were just sitting there quietly. My deluded mind would tell me – but see that guy over there, his hair is a little bit off, and he just tidied himself up for the exact moment when I would be looking. As soon as I close my eyes, they'll go to it again. At that point I realized, Ralph, you have gone too far. This is paranoid and delusional. It was sobering and fortunately, did not carry over into my post-session state of consciousness.

RD   I would take DMT and go to that little room, the gold tower room. I would have the robe that Geshe Wangyal wore on his way out of Tibet. I'd wrap myself in it and I would ask myself a question. And I remember Tim had started to use the word "ecstasy" and I was terribly opposed to our use of that word because it sounded too sexually provocative in my mind. I wanted to use words like "bliss." When I put this robe over me, during the session, I saw a grotto with beautiful sensual girls swimming around. I mean it was a *meshugeneh* thing, you know. So, I went back to Tim and said that we needed to stop using the word "ecstasy."

RM   So your DMT experience was a vision and it sounds like the vision was negative for you – it made you uncomfortable?

RD   Yes, I had sexual problems I had worked on for years. During psychedelic sessions, I would try to counteract my homosexuality by looking at slides of women and listening to poetry of women. I was trying to change my feelings about women.

GB   Sounds like you were trying to re-program yourself.

RD   Yes, but I was really trying to get away from myself, to a higher plane of consciousness.

RM   I did sessions like that too, trying to overcome my neurotic hang-ups. My sexual issue was of being excluded. Like those hallucinated orgies in which I didn't get to participate in. More generally, everybody else knows something I don't know and it has to do with sexuality. I have sometimes wondered if that may be a residual memory of a past life as a celibate monk. When you've committed yourself to celibacy for the sake of your spiritual practice and you live your entire life that way, you've got to be thinking "everybody else knows something that I don't."

Jack Leary with prize catch, 1964

And that something is a really important and intense experiential knowledge. We would sometimes have meetings and discuss all our paranoias.

GB   How did families and children fit in?

RD   We had family sessions by the fire. Tim's children, Jackie and Susan, were around and sometimes sat in with us but they never took any psychedelics.

RM   They weren't smoking any pot either. And pot wasn't a big deal for the rest of us in the early days. The New York musicians and demimonde brought it to Millbrook.

RD   Tim and I disagreed over my smoking pot. He was afraid pot would ruin us because it was associated with certain marginal aspects of the culture.

RM   I was nervous about it because it was illegal as hell. Remember the other psychedelics we were using were not illegal, at that time.

RD   And later on, it was Tim who got busted for pot, crossing the border in Laredo, Texas.

RM   So here we had this family, the Fergusons, with four young children, plus the two teenagers. In the spirit of community, we had a meeting and decided that all the adults should be responsible equally for all the children. Babysitting duties should be rotated, drawing lots. I remember you and I babysat the Ferguson kids one whole day, while their parents went to New York or something. The kids were beautiful and I loved babysitting the kids and I loved hanging out with you. But I wondered – is this what we're supposed to be doing? Isn't there a better use of our time? Somehow it didn't feel appropriate. Shortly after that they hired a black woman from the South to be a nanny, which made a lot more sense.

GB   Did any of the children go off to school?

RM   Jackie and Susan, and I think the older Ferguson daughter, went to school in Millbrook. The others were below the age of five. And one of them, Lisa, is now making a movie about her childhood in Millbrook.

GB   You consciously went into what you called experiments in living, and breaking up traditional social roles and *mores*. What would you say about that now?

RM   Yes, we tried living in community rather than lika a traditional family. A lot of people tried that in the 1960s and beyond.

RD   We were a motley crew. Maynard and Flo were New York musician types. Then there were poets and scientists who visited and we played touch football and other games. We'd take LSD as a group and we would look at one another on LSD, and we could see that we were all souls. And then we were functioning with our egos and making bread and things like that. We did have a higher vision of how we were trying to live life. We were interacting with people with whom we would not normally be compatible in certain ways. For example the gal, who Maynard and Flo brought to watch the kids, was a young black woman from the South and she became part of our scene. We were breaking the rules of caste.

GB   You mean caste as in race, class and so forth?

RD   Yes.

GB   You said you had a higher vision of yourselves. Did you still feel as if you were on the edge of a wave of utopia, of a new way of living, a transformation of society?

RD   Yes. Don't laugh. We learned from our community, and we learned a lot, about human relations and consciousness.

RM   I would agree with that. I remember feeling that way in the community, quite often. And I remember thinking it didn't seem possible that we, that I, could actually live like that; be that open to one another and be that flexible and that adaptable to outwardly distressing circumstances. There was so much closeness between us, it was amazing, and complete trust. We always trusted we could work things out by using psychedelics for problem solving.

GB   What did you all do for income? How did you support yourselves financially?

Richard carries Elsa on a horse ride with the kids

Jack, Susan & Tim Leary, 1963

Flo Ferguson with son, Bentley

J.F. Kennedy was shot just as our family of six, consisting of my father Maynard, my mother Flo, my two sisters, myself and our little brother – ages seven through two, were moving into Millbrook. I remember we all just stopped what we were doing and watched the newscasts over and over on television, sitting around on cardboard packing boxes. It seems like it was weeks before we found it within ourselves to get going again with our lives. After about six months living with the rest of the folks in the Big House, our family moved into the Gate House – all stone turrets and portcullis, like a medieval castle gate.

There was a waterfall on the property we swam in every summer, and lakes that froze over in winter for ice skating. There were apple orchards, which I remember pruning with Charlie Mingus during my first year there. Tim had given me a quick lesson on how the tree could renew itself. And there were fields of corn and sunflowers.

All of the structures looked like mythical castles. There were little towers and stone bridges and other fairytale cottages. There were woods full of gargantuan trees where my sister Corby and I would play, engaged in one heroic adventure after another– so enthralled in our wildly epic imaginings that we would be half frozen by the time we realized night had fallen and we should run home.

There was a fork in the road leading from the Gate House to the Big House, and dead center of the fork, there was a wishing tree. Every time we passed it, we would wrap our arms around its girth as best we could and press our hearts to its heart and feel its aliveness. Once, we decided to go home a new way and got lost in the middle of a huge cornfield, not knowing which way was out. Finally Corby had the idea that I should stand on her shoulders so we could see up over the tall corn and spot one of the main houses.

There was a magic that permeated every thing. I remember standing on the edge of a field of sunflowers when I was seven thinking that I was going to have to tell this story someday, because otherwise no one would ever believe it.

My early repeated flying dreams often involved my room turning into an Arabian Nights type of room before I flew out. These went on for well over a decade. It was so extreme I was convinced I could fly – that it was just a simple trick, a shift of belief that would bring my dream reality into my other reality. I was convinced

I could do it. I had constant bloody noses from falling out of trees, trying to fly, and I got all the other kids involved in these games where for hours we would hurl ourselves off of high up things, hoping to finally "nail it" and start flying. In my flying dreams I would fly at night and I could tell where the light ended and the darkness began and so I would fly just on one side of that line so people wouldn't see me.

Alan Watts came to our house once and created a ritual where one by one we all followed him around in a procession through the woods with torches and incense, chanting and worshipping like little wood nymphs.

RM   We had very little money. It's a good thing the rent was only a dollar. You, Ram Dass, and Tim were doing some lectures at colleges and conferences, and got paid for that. We even did one event where all three of us presented at a conference in Toronto. But mostly it was you two guys; I was too inhibited still, to give lectures. And the three of us took turns, each of us for a month, keeping the checkbook and paying the bills, keeping track of debits and credits. But I didn't have a clue as to where money was coming from. I remember that's when I learned from you how to live on credit cards. I remember saying to you, how do we do this? We've got all these bills and no money. You said, oh, you just use credit cards and you just pay a little bit every month. I said, wow, what a concept. It opened a whole world of possibilities that had never occurred to me. You and Tim were my money mentors.

RD   None of us had money knowledge.

RM   But I thought you knew – you were the wealthy playboy, at Harvard and Stanford and so on.

RD   I didn't know.

RM   So that was just part of your image? You had the money, but you're saying you still didn't know how to handle it? You didn't make that money.

RD   I didn't make that money.

RM   That makes the relationship to money different than if you earned it. Tim wrote about how proud he was of the fact, that the two of you figured out how to support yourselves and others independently, by your wits, without steady jobs. Of course, this glosses over the fact that he left debt in many situations he was in and incurred stupendous debts because of his legal problems. I remember after the Mexico fiasco, a woman came and said, "Look Tim, I think the best contribution I can make to you and your work is to give you $40,000 so you can pay off the debts you guys incurred here." She just felt moved to respond to that need. But I always thought you were more conservative and responsible about money than he was. At least that was my perception. But you're saying, at the time of Millbrook, none of us had any idea about money.

RD I didn't either. I wanted the role of the straight guy, compared to Tim, that was going to keep it all together.

RM Where Tim was the crazy creative Irishman, you would take care of the dishes and the household.

The Castalia Foundation

RD So then, we started these seminars at Millbrook, as the Castalia Foundation.

Tim at Millbrook

RM We had to generate income. We had been reading and were very inspired by, Hermann Hesse's books: *Steppenwolf; Journey to the East; The Glass Bead Game,* when we were living in Newton Center and at Millbrook. That's why we named the place Castalia Foundation, after this mystical community of seekers in his novel *Das Glasperlenspiel.*

GB Did that come from you or did it come from Tim?

RM I think it came from Tim, like most of our ideas. He and I were writing an article about Hermann Hesse as "Poet of the Interior Journey" (which was published in the *Psychedelic Review*), interpreting Hesse's books as disguised psychedelic myths, especially *Journey to the East.* That became a sort of a guiding myth for all of us. We all ended up going to the actual East, to India, one after the other. Although in the Hesse book it was a metaphor for the spiritual journey, on which we had already embarked. We were all kind of stumbling around on that spiritual journey. We weren't on any well-established traditional path. The Castalia seminars were like the human growth or human potential seminars, starting up independently around the same time at Esalen, in California, which we didn't know about until much later.

RD They were focused around psychedelics but without taking psychedelics.

RM Right, and anyway we didn't have any LSD; or not enough. Plus it was already much too sensationalized to give out to people at a public seminar. We were very aware, from the Mexico experience, of how easily

Castalia Foundation brochure cover design by Allen Atwell

Location: The setting for the weekend workshops is a large estate in the mid-Hudson valley, two hours by car or train from New York City. The house and grounds have been arranged to provide external support for consciousness expansion.

Schedule: Weekend workshops began at 7:30 Friday evening with dinner and an informal introductory session, and end on Sunday afternoon following lunch. The programs will vary from weekend to weekend depending upon the special skills of the staff members in attendance. However, the schedule for each weekend will provide for a balance between verbal and non-verbal, between the didactic seminar and the experimental laboratory.

Staff: In addition to Drs. Leary, Alpert, Metzner and their associates who live on the estate, there are a number of visiting staff members each weekend. Because these visiting staff members vary from one weekend to another, each weekend workshop has its own unique character. Therefore, participants may wish to sign up for a series of weekend sequentially programmed. Such an arrangement is best made following a first introductory weekend.

For each weekend there will be a sufficient number of staff guides so that considerable individual contact of the participants with the staff will be possible.

Recommended Dress: Informal.

Facilities: In addition to the seminar rooms and living rooms, the houses and grounds contain a variety of meditation facilities, forest paths, lake for swimming, vegetable gardens, art and photographic facilities, music and book libraries of relevent selections both Eastern and Western, and a library of tape lectures and experiental films.

Financial Arrangement: Each participant is invited to contribute a minimum of sixty (60) dollars to the Castalia Foundation (a non-profit educational foundation). Special rates can be arranged for more than one person, and a limited number of scholarships are also available.

Reservations: This invitation was extended to you by a friend who thought you might be interested in participating in an experiental weekend. If you wish to learn more about the program you should communicate with the Foundation through the person who gave you this announcement or directly by writing.

Castalia Foundation
BOX 175
MILLBROOK
NEW YORK 12545

someone's trip could go wrong and then we'd be stuck with a three-day madness. We said we'll show you how to run a session, a simulated session, using all the elements of set and setting and how to conduct a ritual. And then you can go home and do your session. It was still like the IFIF idea, but we were no longer trying to also be the suppliers. We'd use slides, music, candles, incense, pictures. I remember preparing tape recordings of suitable music that would play for hours.

RD　When people came to the seminars, we had them eat in the dining room, alone, in silence, while we'd be up on the third floor, with a microphone, telling them, from a distance, to eat slowly and meditatively.

RM　Yes, when you came you were not supposed to talk or engage in all the usual social rituals. That was Tim's thing, still using the game theory language, "drop your games." Don't talk, don't socialize, just go to your room and meditate and read instructions for tomorrow. We'd do things to break the perceptual set, the normal expectations – just as a psychedelic experience challenges your normal expectations. Maybe the butter would be colored green, the milk would be bluish. So, you would look at food and it wouldn't look the same as it usually does. We'd do hatha yoga. I taught them basic yoga asanas at some point during the weekend. I learned a lot from doing all those things, experimenting with ways to change consciousness without drugs. I thought it was worthwhile.

RD　That was show biz.

RM　Yes, I suppose so, though I didn't think of it that way because there was no audience and performers. We were all in it together. It's true that some people were guiding the show, but we were all participants. It was very egalitarian in that sense and educational; that's why I liked the seminars – they were educational seminars. They were billed as such. That gave us a structure and also gave us a source of income. One of the first seminar participants was Khigh Dhiegh, a television actor and expert in the *I Ching*, who initiated us into that ancient system of divination. Another reason for starting the Castalia seminars is that we all concluded, after being in Millbrook for a while, that we needed a structure to handle the huge numbers of visitors, both invited and uninvited. People seemed to just come up and help themselves to food and drink and hang out in the house. I think our reputation in New York was: Let's go up to

Millbrook for the weekend and have sex and take drugs. And some would bring their own drugs. We gradually felt we had to impose structure. Otherwise the crowds were impossible to deal with, and that got more and more so as time went on.

Millbrook Visitors – Musicians, Mothers, Merry Pranksters

GB   Who were some of the visitors that came to Millbrook during that first year?

RM   We had several visits from a group of innovative multi-media artists and explorers who called themselves USCO, which included Gerd Stern and Steve Durkee. They had an artists' commune in nearby Woodstock, New York. It was fun hanging out with these very creative men and women; we often discussed how the psychedelic experience could be translated into visual and auditory artistic media. Later on, in the fall of 1964, we co-created with the USCO group talk-plus-multimedia shows which we called "Psychedelic Theatre" and presented in New York City theatrical venues. I think these were forerunners of multimedia psychedelic presentations that later flourished, especially in the Haight-Ashbury urban tribal scene of San Francisco.

Maynard and Flo Ferguson,
mid 1960s

We also experimented, in that first year, with gardening, trying to grow some of our own food. Later, there was an extensive vegetable garden. I remember one sweltering summer day spending several hours in our new cornfield with Steve Durkee (who later converted to Islam and founded the Lama Foundation in New Mexico) and Stewart Brand (who later founded the *Whole Earth Catalog* and *Review*). The three of us made rows with a tractor, planted corn, then sprinkled dried blood around the perimeter to prevent the roaming deer from getting the corn. It didn't work – the deer got most of it anyway. But these experiments also foreshadowed the later extensive migrations of psychedelic "hippies" to organic farming communities out of the large cities, trying to become more self-sustaining.

GB   Any other musicians besides Maynard Ferguson?

RM   One person that impressed me a lot was Charlie Mingus, the jazz musician. I don't know how he came to be there or what his psychedelic experiences had been. You know he had this reputation of being very volatile, sullen and aggressive. I saw him once, in a club in New York, throw his cello at the audience and smash it, because he felt they were being inattentive and disrespectful, which they were. But at Millbrook. he was like a different man. There was this old beat-up piano there and he would play on it; it was very lyrical, very sweet and beautiful.

RD   He'd stay in the grape arbor, in a little cottage among the trees

RM   He spent time pruning the fruit trees. After you prune the trees in the orchard, you put black tar paint on them. He said, "I'm turning all these trees into blacks." He was a great guy. Once, he was going to eat a steak. He had this steak in front of him at the table, and addressed it quietly, "Well cow, this is it. You loused up your karma, and I'm going to eat you now." It was his way of doing his prayer, honoring the animal he was eating. He was a wonderful person, a big soul.

RD   He had a sports car. I took a drive with him and we had this very funny conversation. He was trying to arouse compassion in me toward him for his blackness. And I said, well you think you have a problem. I've got a problem – homosexuality. And it's not an easy one. And he said, "Ah, God, Man that's tough."

GB   Was there a lot of music at Millbrook with all these great musicians around?

RM   In the summer, when it was warm, we'd go out at sunset and meditate on the roof and Maynard would come out sometimes and play the trumpet. It was beautiful. But our immediate group didn't have musicians who could jam. And Maynard was on the road a lot.

RD   I think we talked. We talked and we had fun hanging out. But none of us were musicians.

RM   Very occasionally we conducted LSD or morning glory sessions for outsiders. I was a guide for Allen Atwell, who was a painter and taught art at Cornell University. He had made quite a deep study of the Indian Tantra tradition and the relationship of meditative states to painting, as in yantras and mandalas. In his session he laughed like I had never seen anyone laugh before, non-stop for six hours. It seems he'd discovered the psychic burden of effortful discipline that he had imposed on himself for years was unnecessary and could simply be dropped. Everything made him laugh. If I sat quietly and did nothing, he'd look at me and laugh and roll over. If I offered him an orange, he'd roar with laughter and pound the floor. When I left the room I could hear him laughing uproariously throughout the house. Allen later painted a huge tantric visage on the outside of the Big House; in New York City, he painted the entire inside of Van Wolff's apartment to look like the inside of one's body during a psychedelic session. He and Tim were rivals, for a while, for the affections of the beautiful blonde Nena von Schlebrügge.

GB   What kind of setting did you have for your own psychedelic sessions?

RM   In the summer months, we preferred to be outside for our own psychedelic sessions, especially as the stream of visitors in the Big House increased. We found a favorite hill with a sunny meadow, in the back wooded area of the estate. No houses or roads were visible; you had to walk a good way to get there. There were shady trees and places to sit, with beautiful views. It became known as "ecstasy hill." There was another hill, used more often for full-moon night-time sessions, sessions that often seemed to have a more romantic or passionate quality to them. This second magical spot became known as "lunacy hill." These two places soon became charged with immense and palpable power, with spirit of place.

Another practice that Tim introduced was a follow-up to our High Tower on the beach in Zihuatanejo, where one person stayed on "high" retreat for 24 hours. There was a little separate cottage on the Millbrook estate, not far from the Big House, down on the lawn, called the Tennis House. We would take turns staying there alone for a week; a kind of hermitage retreat, not having to do household work and having meals brought. Just meditate, take LSD, do whatever spiritual practice you had. I also spent time weeding and gardening during my week there. So, that was more focused on spiritual growth for the individual, less on interpersonal dynamics like the earlier community experiments.

PEGGY HITCHCOCK

I sometimes brought friends of mine to visit. Musician and composer Charlie Mingus, who was a friend, visited first in Newton Center and later in Millbrook. I remember one weekend in Millbrook, Charlie had a surge of energy and severely pruned many of the ancient apple trees in the orchard, painting the pruned branch ends with black tar. I don't think those trees ever bore fruit again. I knew Charlie through my past relationship with Allen Eager, who was a jazz saxophone player and cyclical heroin addict. Allen was never happy with his addiction and had unsuccessfully tried various forms of therapy. I thought perhaps psychedelics might help him. I gave him some mescaline and he totally freaked out. I could not understand why he had such a terrible trip. In retrospect, I think it was because he used alcohol to sedate himself and quiet his demons. At that time, I certainly did not know how to help him through his bad experience. He was a very intelligent and fascinating guy when he was not using, but definitely had an addictive personality. Over time, unfortunately, the addictive personality won out. Later on, Allen lived for a while in the Bowling Alley at Millbrook as part of the Bowling Alley experiment with Richard Alpert and some other people.

Charles Mingus playing at Tim and Nena's wedding

GB   How did the Gurdjieff connection come about?

RM   We first got very interested in Gurdjieff's teaching through reading Ouspensky's *In Search of the Miraculous*, which was also about a journey to the East, and a spiritual teacher, a very unusual one, from the East. In the early days at Millbrook we experimented with a variant of Gurdjieff's "stop" exercise, which we also then used in the Castalia seminars. At unpredictable intervals during the day, a bell would ring, and then you were supposed to stop whatever you were doing for one minute, and just observe what you were doing, just become conscious of your physical, emotional and mental state. It was exquisitely difficult to do, very frustrating as well as enlightening. Then we heard of a Gurdjieff teacher in New York City, Willem Nyland. It was probably through Felix Morrow, who was the publisher of *The Psychedelic Experience*, and a student of Gurdjieff, that we made contact with Mr. Nyland. We invited him to come up for a discussion about Gurdjieff's teachings and consciousness expansion. He wouldn't come to the Big House, but agreed to meet with some of us at the "Cottage," where the Hitchcock brothers lived. The meeting did not go very well. Nyland refused to consider the possibility that Gurdjieff might have known about and used some unknown psychedelic. I asked him, about this passage in Ouspensky where Gurdjieff says there's a Fourth Way, the way of the sly man, who takes a pill that allows him to go beyond personality and become aware of essence. Nyland protested, "No no, Ouspensky didn't know anything."

Tim asked him, "Don't you think Gurdjieff would have improvised? His entire life looks like a series of improvisations to changing conditions and experimentations with various methods of teaching." Nyland said, "I have been teaching 'the work' exactly the way Gurdjieff taught it, for the past twenty years." He seemed to take, as a point of pride, that his words expounding the Master's teachings, hadn't changed and were exactly the same years later. We thought it was kind of rigid and judgmental. But he then proceeded to give a comprehensive, very lucid, condensed outline of the Gurdjieffian system and that was very beautiful. So then, some of us started going down to New York City to attend Nyland's weekly meetings. On our trips down to New York, on the Tacoma Parkway, a two hour car ride, someone would read aloud from *All and Everything* for the others. In a stuffy New York apartment, with Nyland droning on about being conscious and remembering yourself, it was often hard to stay awake. About a year later, Tim, Dick and I had a private meeting with Nyland. He had been scolding me on the phone about Tim's behavior. Was he conscientious, was he responsible, or wasn't he just a publicity seeker? During the meeting he lectured us sternly, like a Dutch uncle. He said whatever the drugs did, they could not give you an "I" or help you develop one, and that this was the real task. Tim and I both lost interest in Nyland after that, though we did not lose our high regard for Gurdjieff. My wife Susan became a dedicated disciple of Nyland for many years after.

GB   Ralph, you said your mother also came to visit the Millbrook community. Can you tell about that?

RM   Yes, and she took LSD. Did you meet her when she came to Millbrook, Ram Dass?

RD   Yes.

RM   She came to Millbrook in the summer of 1964, and she stayed for two or maybe three weeks, I think. She talked to people and hung out. After about a week of getting to know people and the place, she said she really enjoyed being there and I talked to her about maybe joining the community. She was fifty-eight at the time, divorced from my father. She was Scottish by birth and was living in Paris – she had an executive secretary position with UNESCO. She said she would have to think about it and that if she came to Millbrook, she thought she could take on managing the laundry. So she found a role for herself. She saw a need, a niche she could fill. I think it showed an instinctive understanding of how a community functions, how everyone has to have a function.

After being there for a week or so she also said, "You know, I think I should like to try this LSD of yours." She'd read the *Tibetan Book of the Dead* manual. So we arranged a session. Tim sat for her the first time, he introduced her to it. It was beautiful and she had a fantastic time. The following week, she had a second session that I guided for her. Shortly after she got back she wrote me a letter and described the experience that she'd had in very glowing terms – how she understood so much, the incredible beauty. It was very, very positive.

Letter to Ralph from Jill Metzner, 1964:

My first impression of your group was that you were a religious community, essentially, and that there was a very close interpersonal relationship amongst you all and that communications could be made with a glance. At the same time, different temperaments stood out quite clearly ... Maybe if you go away from each other, there will be periods of longing to be back. The pattern of the whole community was fluid and flexible. There was, I thought, a marked laissez-aller as concerns this world and one's daily life but at the same time a certain desire for it to be "put in order." Right?

I think I now comprehend that those visions are indeed one's own thought patterns that one sees. I think I now also understand that that is where the teaching about oneself begins. If one can figure out during the sessions that those are one's thoughts, then it gets clearer what it is ...

If ever I did reach any stage of transcendence then it was for a very short time. I do remember recognizing a true and incontrovertible reality. That's sure, and knowing myself to be part of the process. In my first experience there were many representations of energy transformations, while in my second I was aware more of visions of changing colours and forms. I was once, with Tim, a meteor rushing through space, all sorts of other beings rushing or rocketing about ... I was part of an atomic explosion, which I could hear clearly, like fireworks (it didn't frighten me) and its downward fall became transformed into glittering rain of diamonds. Then, I seemed to be a cell within a whale. I was part of a primeval forest. Also, with Ralph, I saw many microscopic processes inside my own body, inside my own head even. I was microscopic and then macroscopic. They were visions of extraordinary beauty, in both cases ...

I experienced some incredible lovely music; the notes were simply living, vibrating clusters of energy, and then later, just dancing gaiety. My wrathful visions included one where I was encased in a white metal container which was hurtling downwards. My legs and arms could be seen trying to get out. Fire and blood were coming out of it. But it melted away ...

I had visions symbolizing my erroneous attempt to install order: I was seeing riveted metal domes around me... the clear blue skies became metal domes. Then I saw a whole boxful of metal robot figures. I was myself a clay figure, crumbling to dust.

I had a compelling vision where I seemed to be at the feet of archangels, where St. Michael seemed to be exhorting his forces. It was a heaven of majesty and awe. I got quite attached to that one, alas. I should not.

Among very positive visions, first and foremost the certainty, the reality, the forms, shapes and vistas full of radiant color and variety and sparkle, the sense of being a part of it, of belonging to all living, dancing energy.

RM   I said to her, when she was leaving, you know it's going to be tricky for you, going back. There'll be nobody to talk to who would understand what your experience was about. About ten years later, she wrote in a letter "I took that LSD one summer and it was terrible, it was so frightening." She had completely reversed it in her memory. Fortunately, I had kept the original letter, so I sent her a copy. It was as if she had been brainwashed by the media propaganda machine. In the absence of a supportive community, all the stuff about the "terrible drugs" had gotten to her.

GB   Do you find that sometimes, people have very positive experiences but then the memory fades?

RM   It can happen, clearly.

RD   And it can happen the other way, too. Negative experiences can be remembered as a positive session; but they don't remember the negative aspects.

RM   And then they want to do it again. Which is probably a good sign, because it indicates they want to learn from their mistakes and overcome the fear. As if they're saying, bad or good doesn't really matter that much, I learned something from the experience and I want to learn more.

GB   Can you tell about your memories of the visit of Ken Kesey and the Merry Pranksters to Millbrook? It's described by Tom Wolfe in his book *The Electric Kool-Aid Acid Test* and the impression is that they received a cool reception. According to Wolfe's book, they felt that "there is a general vibration of – we have something rather deep and meditative going on here, and you California crazies are a sour note ... this was Millbrook, one big piece of uptight constipation, after all this."

RD   Everybody had gone to bed before they arrived. We had an acid scene the night before. We were in that soft feeling, chilling out. We saw the bus; there was a speed component to it. Neal Cassady had a wonderful thing going. He called Tim "Dick" and he called me "Tim." He had a wonderful mind. (He died in 1968).

RM   I had very little memory of that whole interaction. I was surprised to read about it in Tom Wolfe's book. It didn't seem such a big scene to me. In *Flashbacks*, Tim says he was sick with the flu, and that's why he was unavailable – not because he was feeling superior and meditating. He says Ken Kesey and he did talk briefly, and they've "been allies ever since." I know Kesey said very glowing things about Tim at his funeral.

RD   It wasn't such a big scene for us.

RM   For one thing, we didn't know they were coming. If we had had advance notice, I'm sure we would have loved to have given them a big welcome party. It was nighttime, we were going to bed or already retired. Tim was too sick to even come down. But I remember I came down, and you (Ram Dass) did, and Susan and I went around with them. We showed them around and we took them to the "Cottage." I remember they were constantly throwing conversational riffs around at each other. They were probably high on speed, or speed-acid combinations, like a permanent trip kind of thing. And then they would look at the paintings and say "oh look there's this guy," and they would identify themselves in the painting. Play games. It seemed okay. They were nice people but I remember we were sort of not prepared. To put that in a book, it's unfair of Tom Wolfe. Made it seem we were these chilly, arrogant guys who thought they were superior.

RD   From the bus we must have looked that way. Instead of going towards them, we did pull back. We went to bed because we'd had enough.

RM   Yes, but we showed them around and I spent some time with them. Susan actually spent more time with the Pranksters than I did. I found out only much later (or else I'd forgotten) she actually gave Neal Cassady an injection of DMT. There's a picture of her doing that in the photographic memoir *On the Bus*, by Ken Babbs and Paul Perry.

RD   I spent a couple of hours with them.

DOROTHY FADIMAN

Dorothy Fadiman, c. 1965

My visit to Millbrook, in the spring of 1964 was the culmination of an identity crisis that had been percolating since I'd left Pittsburgh, three years earlier. After becoming a graduate student at Stanford in 1961, I'd lived in a state of perpetual confusion, anxiously and eagerly sorting through all the old rules and values I'd carted across the country from my hometown in Pennsylvania. With every new "adventure," I went through figuring out what to discard and what to keep. As I broke away from old messages telling me to beware of strangers and to be guarded both emotionally and physically, I took in new messages: an expansion of consciousness came to life through psychedelic drugs and sexual freedom that I could never have imagined in Pittsburgh.

During my second year in California, a handsome, virile visionary named Ken Kesey tapped me on the shoulder and invited me to be one of his girlfriends. His energy was magnetic and effulgent all at once. I accepted. He had an "open marriage" and assured me we wouldn't be cheating. So, for the next year, living two lives became a way of life. Every weekday I wore a girdle and nylons, put on lipstick and worked a nine–to–five job as a speech therapist at the Palo Alto Veterans hospital. Every weekend, I joined Ken and his friends, the colorful band soon to become "the Pranksters." I immersed myself in a heady freedom that shattered my defenses, and opened me to feelings of both exhilaration and excited fear that I had never felt before. On the weekends, I wiped off my lipstick, took off my bra, and cast my fate to the winds.

Words like "ecstatic" and "universal" and "dissolving boundaries" entered my vocabulary. I didn't know what to do with these new feelings, and had no guides, but that didn't hold me back. I was drawn deeper and deeper into this awakening. Even while opening up light years beyond where I'd ever been, I still held back. I had neither the courage nor the abandon to dive in completely. Being Ken's girlfriend had given me a relatively secure place in "the scene" but not membership in "the club." I was still too fearful of losing whatever control remained. I did not join the pack on their journey into uncharted waters when the bus finally took off. Yet I knew, now that I'd tasted a certain "inner freedom," that I wanted to continue looking further and discover more of whatever this experience was.

I had heard about a place called Millbrook, described as an experimental community, where psychedelics were used as a sacrament. Intuitively, I knew that

Millbrook was my next destination, if only for a day. So, I set out on a cross-country journey. Uninvited and unannounced, I got on a Greyhound bus and headed for the mythical retreat called Millbrook.

From the moment I arrived, I stepped into yet another dimension, a land of enchantment. I found a mysterious, elegant world of lithe women and magical men, gliding through the corridors of a once grand, now aging mansion. The members of this community (and the regular guests who came and went) were working together to build a full life there, with day to day routines, in addition to their open-ended spiritual work and hedonistic gatherings. I remember being deeply touched by how welcoming and genuinely hospitable they were to a stranger. They offered me a bed and food while I was there, and asked for nothing.

Soon after I arrived, I learned that the Pranksters, now traveling in their bus "Further," were on their way to Millbrook, and would arrive that day. I hadn't known they were coming. It was an eerie convergence for me. The moment when the bus appeared on the horizon, was completely surreal. The people on the bus – Ken Kesey and the Pranksters – lived in a reality that had never really been mine, but I hadn't yet let go of the fantasy that I might someday be brave enough to join them. The Prankster path, as well as I could tell, was to get high (not asking how much of what you were taking) and see what happened! That mindset was about to collide with this other delicately arranged, carefully crafted, but still elusive vision: the promise of a safe place to be guided, guiding each other through the terrains of consciousness with psychedelics.

As the Prankster bus traveled closer to Millbrook, the boldly painted rainbow vehicle felt like a brawny force from my recent past blustering into this other, new world of Millbrook. I had broken out of the emotional straightjacket I'd worn in Pittsburgh, into the intense, circus-like world of the Pranksters. Now, I was moving on, drawn toward the possibility that Millbrook symbolized.

But for the moment, I didn't really belong to either "scene." No longer Ken's number one girlfriend, I didn't have that protection any more. Because of my own fear of "losing it," I didn't really belong on the bus. Just having arrived at Millbrook, where everything seemed to be choreographed like a ballet where I didn't know the steps, I certainly didn't feel like I belonged there either.

Like so many of us in those years, I had to decide with each breakthrough, how then shall I live? I have come to realize since then how we were all searching, passionately, honestly, some of us desperately searching. Sometimes we found what we thought we were looking for, in a person, in a psychedelic, but more often than not, we'd find the key to a door which led down a path to yet another door. To allow myself to be at Millbrook, I had to close the door, at least for now, to the world of freedoms the Pranksters were offering to the wild and willing.

Because of the extraordinary dedication of a core intentional family, Millbrook was more than another door for many people. It was the gateway to another universe. My first night at Millbrook started out strangely, and went on to become deliciously memorable. The hosts and guests for that night were gathered informally around a kitchen table, exchanging pithy wisdoms and clever jokes with familiar ease. I was in awe at their quick-witted comments and piercing reflections, and felt awkward as I watched.

Silent with shyness, I listened, overwhelmed by the flow of candid insights being shared by what seemed like everyone except me. Through the stardust of my being enchanted by these exchanges, it seemed that I was in a room of enlightened beings. As the evening wore on, I remained painfully unsuccessful in finding anything to add to that glittering circle of psychedelic intelligentsia.

I didn't know how to contribute, and I didn't know how to leave. At one point, deeply uncomfortable, I looked up and, in a split second, was drawn away from the tension of trying to find the right words. Across the room, my eyes met the eyes of a man, a radiant being! A slender, handsome man was gazing at me. He didn't speak, just watched me intently. My heart quivered, because with that steady gaze, he was talking a language I understood, a language I could speak: the language of pure energy. We didn't say a word to each other. There was nothing to add to what hung in the air between us.

That "knowing that we know," that recognition met my real hunger, to be seen. We seemed to say to each other, silently, "I see you, in all your glory." In that gaze I felt accepted for who I was and I was able to receive him in return. That complete communication didn't need anything more to make it real.

The man turned, went on to do whatever he'd been doing, and now, feeling connected to Millbrook through that exchange, I was able to slip away and go to bed. There were lots of rooms, places for travelers to stay for a night. I settled into a small room that had been assigned to me earlier. It was a warm evening. I lay naked under the sheet, drifting off to sleep, fantasying about what it might be like to be with this exquisite man.

What happened next unfolded like a dream. A crack of light appeared as the door to my room gently opened. The man from the kitchen knew, without asking, that he could come to me this way. Not a word was spoken, nor was it needed. He slowly, quietly approached my bed. I welcomed him. His touch was electric. We made love throughout the night, a deeply sensuous physical merging, riding the waves of passion, a language of its own, our mutual desires urgently whispering to each other's senses for hours. When he left before dawn, we still had not spoken.

The next day, I learned his name ... it was Ralph. I asked others where I could find him and was led to his office to say "Goodbye." I hoped he'd speak to me now and wanted him to say something memorable. He was working on the *Psychedelic Review*. I walked in and he looked up, smiled quizzically and said, "I have a question." I held my breath, now having a huge crush on him, hoping he would say something romantic about our night together. He spoke matter of factly and simply posed a question: "You have the body, and the passions of a woman." He paused and said, "Why is your hair so short?" That was it. That was all. Nothing more! He said "Goodbye" in a friendly way and returned to his work.

As I stood there and listened to his question, asking why my hair was short, it seemed to be a shaggy dog ending to a lyric tale. But, as I look back, I realize that, in between the words of his question about my hair, he managed to embed a compliment about my body and about our time together ... obliquely.

My actual psychedelic breakthrough came a year later, neither with Ken Kesey nor at Millbrook. I went back to California, and during the following year was guided by a wise entheogenic guru on a trip that aligned my intention to be of service. I had the psychedelic experience I had been yearning for at a place with a very unromantic name: the International Foundation for Advanced Study. It was also in that setting that I "connected" with Jim Fadiman, to whom I've been married for more than forty years.

When we got married, Ralph sent us a note, handwritten into a copy of the *Psychedelic Review*: "May your days be luminous and your nights be ecstatic." More than four decades later, Ralph and I are still friends.

RM   That seemed appropriate under the circumstances. Tim writes, in *Flashbacks* (p. 205), that you said, "I feel like we're a pastoral Indian village invaded by a whooping cowboy band of Wild West saloon carousers." I think it's just a good story. Tim called it different tribes with different styles. Tom Wolfe exaggerated the weirdness of the situation.

Romance and Journeys to India

GB   How did Tim Leary meet the blonde Swedish model Nena he called "Nanette" in *Flashbacks*?

RD   Nena came with Van Wolff and that New York crowd.

RM   Van Wolff was a kind of PR-agent-impresario, whose New York apartment was a hub for the glamor set from fashion, photography, film, and the arts. It seemed to be always buzzing with vibrations of seduction, intrigue and gossip. Nena's picture was on all the New York City buses advertising Winston cigarettes at that time. Tim called her, "A thoughtful and romantic woman, an icon of beauty, surrounded by, instructed by, manipulated by the technicians and producers of the fashion industry." When they took their first LSD session together, he wrote: "... Nanette allowed her jet-set facade to fall away, just so much childhood scar tissue. From within, emerged an archetypal nobility, the radiant essence of a Valkyrie. ..I fell under her spell." (*Flashbacks*, pp 203-204). She moved into the Big House with Tim and set up a routine of being there and working in New York a few days a week. His relationship with Peggy Hitchcock had for some time before evolved into more of a friendship – which continued long afterward. In one of those strange synchronicities, Nena had a close friend, Katy, also a model, whom she brought up to Millbrook. She had auburn hair and green eyes, she was gorgeous. I fell under her spell.

GB   Where was Susan?

RM   Our relationship too had been evolving into a more open pattern. She had met and fallen in love with a photographer from New York, and moved to the city part time to be with him. We've remained friends; and she got very deeply into the Gurdjieff work with Mr. Nyland. It

Ralph, Nena and Tim at the Taj Mahal, 1964

seems like the repeated group psychedelic sessions had a tendency to dissolve traditional structures of interpersonal relationships as well as intrapsychic defenses. But then, new patterns of relationship were being created as well. I went with Katy on one of her modeling assignments in New York and I too noticed the mechanical, manipulative behavior by the fashion professionals setting her up to project the desired abstract images of glamor. We took LSD together in her apartment in New York. Here's what I wrote in my journal about that experience:

We took LSD in Katy's apartment. She wandered around, reciting to herself "my apartment, my dog, my cat, my lover…," as if trying to keep the pieces of her world together. It was not frightening to her, she trusted the process. She got into a bubble bath and I turned into a monkey, sitting on a branch, curiously observing the plant and animal life around me, chattering merrily at the goddess lying languorously in the foam. We lay on soft blankets on the floor and traced the lines of light in the space between us, gossamer golden threads from finger tip to finger tip; iridescent beams from eye to eye. With my hand resting on her side as she was lying on the rug, I watched her body transform into different bodies, some darker-skinned, some lighter, in rapid succession. One of them was a gleaming white skeletal form that flashed for a second as if I had

X-ray vision. I remembered reading Buddhist meditation manuals that recommended visualizing a woman's body as skeleton to overcome the distractions of sexual desire. As she lay back, her face broadened and rounded, all-knowing magnetic receptivity emanated from her eyes and face. The fragrance emanating from her set off fountains of ecstasy in deep recesses of my brain. The curves of her breasts, her abdomen and thighs were the rounded hills and valleys of Earth. The downy hairs on her pubic mound were golden sheaves of wheat. She was the bountiful Grain Goddess; she was Eve, the Mother of All the Living. I spoke the name "Eve" and she gave a little start, turned back into her form as Katy and said "I'm not ready for that yet."

When we drove back up to Millbrook in the car, she turned to me with brimming eyes and said, "Now that you've got me, what are you going to do with me?" I replied that I didn't think I had her, that if anything it was the other way around. It amazed me that though she was very beautiful and had had many lovers, including some famous ones, she seemed to need almost constant verbal reassurance that I loved her."

Nena was a very young, very beautiful, very successful fashion model. Today we would call her a super model. She was born in Sweden in 1941 and had lived in China with her family as a refugee during World War II, before returning to Europe. Her father, who was a German baron, was much older than her mother and had died when she was a child. When I first knew her, she was in her early twenties and had been the sole support for her mother, the baroness, and her younger brother, since she was fifteen. I don't believe she had much of a happy childhood. I remember feeling protective towards her. As I remember, she and Tim first connected at my brother Billy's birthday party on her first visit to Millbrook.

Nena on her wedding day, 1964

When Tim phoned me to let me know about his impending marriage, I was devastated. We had each had our little flirtations but I remember thinking that Tim and I would eventually get married and that we were moving in that direction. I felt very motherly towards his two teenage children, Jackie and Susan. I went to Tim and Nena's wedding at Millbrook in November of 1964. Shortly thereafter, I became engaged to a doctor, a relationship which was certainly very much on the rebound. Later that winter, I remember meeting Nena's mother at a party and being shocked when she said to me in a very matter of fact way, "Peggy, don't worry, if you really love Tim, I'm sure it will work out. Stick around because their marriage is falling apart." By that time I was engaged to be married. I did get married the following June. All my Millbrook friends attended my big Long Island wedding, including Richard, Tim and Nena. By that time Tim and Nena were leading separate lives. My husband and I were separated in less than two years.

After my brief marriage fell apart, I remember thinking my relationship with Tim was still unresolved. I went up to visit again in Millbrook and Tim and I briefly resumed our romance. I also remember an incident which was the turning point in the relationship, although at the time I tried to forget it. We were up in his bedroom one evening and his daughter Susan came in to talk with him about something of importance to her. He dismissed her in what I thought was a very brusque and cold way, which deeply shocked me. I thought very sadly to myself, "I could not be married to a man who would treat his child this way." For me, at that time, having children was the only reason to get married.

Something that touched me deeply in the letters from Millbrook that Tim wrote to Ralph, who was in India, was that they revealed a wonderfully intimate side of Tim, which he seemed to have difficulty in showing in person. I think Tim had problems with intimacy. After reading some of Robert Greenfield's biography I did have some insights into the possible reasons for this issue. Greenfield discusses how, after Tim's grandfather died and his father abandoned the family, Tim was raised solely by his mother and maiden aunt. Growing up, he did not have any positive male role model to let him know it was okay for a man to show his feelings.

Richard helping Tim to prepare for wedding to Nena

GB How did your trip to India come about?

RM I had been wanting to go on a trip for a long time, following the mythic quest described by Hermann Hesse and many others. We all talked about it a lot. The Castalia Foundation was to put up money for the journey: It was to be a research tour, to study Indian yoga methods, and consult with Hindu and Buddhist teachers about the possible use of mind-expanding drugs as aids to meditation. It turned out that Gayatri Devi, an Indian lady guru in the Vedanta lineage of Ramakrishna, the 19th century Bengali saint, was planning a trip to India with her entourage and invited me to join her. She ran one Vedanta ashram near Boston and another in La Crescenta, California. She and several of her American devotees, including Fred Swain, had had a psilocybin session guided by Tim, when we were still at Harvard. Fred Swain, a former Air Force major, who had taken a mushroom session with the legendary Mazatec curandera Maria Sabina in Oaxaca, Mexico, had become a follower of Gayatri Devi. He had also been with us in Zihuatanejo, the first summer.

RD Rabbi Zalman Schachter had a psychedelic session also around the same time, in that ashram.

RM Yes. His account of that session is included *The Ecstatic Adventure,* an anthology of psychedelic experiences that I edited (published in 1968). So, Gayatri Devi was going to Bengal, India, to set up an ashram there for her Indian devotees, who numbered in the thousands. Going with her would be good way to go because I would get an insider's view of Indian religious culture, not the usual tourist's view. The opportunity was perfect. Gayatri Devi's party was going to leave in the fall of 1964. I wanted to go and tried to talk Katy into going with me. She was in conflict about it. She didn't have the same connection to India and Hinduism that I did. We talked endlessly, but she couldn't decide. Tim and Nena encouraged her also, and they were going to come to India after their wedding. Finally, I left, accompanying Gayatri Devi's party, and urged Katy to come afterwards. After a week's stopover in Kyoto, Japan, where we conversed with Zen teachers and visited shrines and temples, we landed in Calcutta, where Mataji, as they called her, had thousands of devotees. Enormously interesting visits to temple sites in Bhubaneswar, Puri, Konarak and Benares followed. Then to Delhi and northwards up into the hill country of Uttar Pradesh to Rishikesh, where the Beatles later visited the ashram of Maharishi Mahesh Yogi.

There I separated from Gayatri Devi's group and continued further northwards into the Himalayan foothills to the village of Almora, where Lama Anagarika Govinda, the Austrian-born Buddhist scholar, lived with his Parsee wife, Li Gotami, in a cottage on a ridge with an unbelievably spectacular view of the snow and ice peaks of the Himalayas. Every day I would walk a couple of hours to their house and they shared very generously and kindly from their immense store of knowledge and experience of the profound Tibetan Buddhist culture. Lama Govinda was impressed with the appreciative dedication we had written to him in our adaptation of the *Tibetan Book of the Dead*. He agreed to try a dose of LSD that I offered to provide and guide for him. After an initially turbulent period of confusion and anxiety at the intense somatic changes induced, he centered himself with the aid of mantra and mudra and had an illuminating experience according to the model of the *Bardo Thödol*. He expressed his pleased anticipation of a visit from Timothy Leary.

During my travels, I had been writing Katy and the Millbrook group my impressions of India. Tim wrote back letters in which he described the fantastic and joyous spiritual and social carnival that Millbrook had become, his deepening relationship with Nena, their wedding plans and travel plans for India, and his evolving ideas about the processes of psychedelic consciousness expansion. He was using, at that time, the ethology language of imprinting and de-imprinting. These ideas and understandings formed the conceptual framework for his work in translating the Chinese Taoist classic, the *Tao Te Ching*, into a session manual for psychedelic experiences. Tim's psychedelic poetic adaptation of that text was later published as *Psychedelic Prayers*. He was working on that while staying in Almora with Nena on their honeymoon, and meeting with Lama Govinda every day. It's my favorite of all his writings – wise, funny and elegant.

Letters from Millbrook to Ralph in India

Tim's first letter, dated Nov 16, 1964, describes the growing enthusiastic audiences that Tim and Dick were encountering on their lecture tours, and Tim and Nena's relationship moving toward marriage.

Dearest Friend and Great Spirit Ralph –

Your messages have been unforgettable – poetic, vivid ... they get us right there with you ... and you are so much there. Katy let me read some of your notes to her and they are lyric flute songs beyond compare. Beautiful. So much has happened dear brother ... so many millions of years have spun by ... I've tried to keep some sort of diary ... hopelessly inadequate and out of date ... Sometime we'll go over it...or probably not ... things show no sign of slowing down ... SAN FRANCISCO ... press conference ... bungling PR people ... but wonderful, far-out stories by amused and impressed reporters. BIG SUR ... incredible place ... gorges tumbling down to rocky sea, cliffs, redwoods, river canyons where only needle rays of sun penetrate...enormous turnout for weekend ... wonderful people ... seminars funny, relaxed, rapt interest ... Nena arrived on Sat., at Monterey ... the five days of separation were ... well, you know ... unbearable ... we lived in a glass front house overlooking the Pacific ... had incredible sessions ... one mainly inside each other and the second on a grassy hillside a mile above the Pacific ... involved part of the time in an Adam-Eve expulsion from Paradise scene which was the most moving and educational experience of my-our lives ... The week after the seminar was wonderful – we ran it like a Castalia weekend ... PALO ALTO ... two standing room crowds ... enthusiastic ... series of threat-carrot talks with Menlo Park people ... if I inform to the FDA they will certify us to give LSD ... if I don't I'll be in jail in a month etc ... we never gave it another thought ...

NEW YORK ... Cooper Union ... all 1300 seats filled and 300 standing ... crowds so receptive it was like whispering things in your lover's ear ... Richard was a smash at U of Minnesota and faculty cocktail party was held etc. The political-educational battle over psychedelics has been won and from now it's just a matter of time ... next generation ... my only concern now is to learn to use my own head and to pursue the incredible complexities that develop when two people begin to explore their potentialities together and in small tribal groups. Withdrawing energy and commitment from externals and materials, etc. You know.

Nena and I have been together almost every minute for the last three weeks and she is an unending series of beauty and wise lessons. We moved directly into the bowling alley which is now the most relaxed, warm, glowing room in the world. We are visiting the Episcopalian minister in town to arrange the most romantic, mythic wedding in history ... very soon. You have to give everything to it without reserve and then it all flows from one moment of happiness to the next ... well you know. The tribal scene is wonderful. Richard came back glowing with strength and new plans ... Susan has been spending most of her time here ... working on lectures and other PR business ...Katy is the divine woman goddess, beautiful lotus-lily, always and incredibly feminine. The trees are now leafless and etched black, like sumi-painting strokes and the dusk comes quickly late afternoons and fires are glowing in most of the rooms and the house breathes softly waiting for the next period of change and movement ...Nena and I will probably be joining you after the first of the year. Love. Love. Love. Love. And to Mataji our loving thoughts, and to Fred. We were delighted to read your descriptions of Mataji's joyful reception in India.

Tim.

I also got some letters from my wife, Susan, who was still at Millbrook, which spoke of a meeting she had in New York with my father, who was visiting from Germany (though he didn't come to Millbrook). Susan addressed me, tongue-in-cheek no doubt, as "Conqueror of Passions." I had written her and the others that this was the transliteration of the Hindu name Ripujit, that Gayatri Devi had given me when we were travelling in Bengal; which I accepted with some reluctance, since, in my Western psychological way, I preferred to think of my passions as something to make friends with rather than to conquer.

Nov 1, 1964

Millbrook Dearest Conqueror of Passions,

We have your two great letters & lots of postcards. You sound great ... so does Japan. It's very quiet here, slightly anarchical since Tim & Richard are away, but the weather is beautiful and bright. I left T & R at the airport Monday, then went to see Felix (Morrow), and then met your father at the airport. He was very surprised to have someone meet him & pleased of course. He had a bad cold & slight fever but was tanned and in good spirits. I had a long talk with him at his hotel, told him the story up to the minute. He was great – it really is great to be able to talk to a parent, he didn't even get too dogmatic – only mainly on a point which I think I agree with him, namely that a Third Floor plan (community, he thinks) is crazy as far as maintaining a marriage is concerned and having babies. He thinks we're crazy with this community thing. Then, it was funny because he insisted that I was far more upset than I was or have been, & he tried to tell me that was natural, etc. He wanted me to get on the plane with him, come stay with him, be his house-keeper, cook his meals! Who knows, maybe I will ... Funny to write you letters – I never wrote you any before. What more is there to say? I love you – I think of you all often.

Dearest Love, Susan

From Tim's second letter, dated Nov 20

Dearest Ralph,

Friday night. Seminar. Silent period. Busy day moving Katy's furniture into the house. Rearranging rooms. Sue Met and Sheila and Nena transforming library into seminar room. Incredible sunset from roof. Warm, moist fall weather — like spring with snow melting. Big month of fiestas, dear brother, saddened only by your absence. Enormous crowd coming Thanksgiving. Then Town Hall lecture, much publicity with party afterwards at Peggy's. Then wedding, Saturday December 12th in Episcopalian church here (tribal village center). About 100 people – Nena having fairy tale dress made, etc. Wedding causes some tension – everyone has to re-adjust their imprinted chess-boards – but all is sticking together. Beautiful Katy is "maid of honor" – incredible phrase! and Richard "best man," ditto. The meaning of imprinting is "GETTING INVOLUNTARILY HOOKED TO EXTERNALS and accidentally presented externals at that!!!" The process of DE-IMPRINTING is getting conscious-ness back to the flow and back to the body. RE-IMPRINTING is planned temporary hooking back to externals. Habits get built up around an old imprint. Which stresses the need for changing the environment to be in tune with your new imprint and to avoid automatically falling back. It seems to be clearer and clearer – how to use the head. An imprint lasts seven days unless you avoid the old environment and keep close to the new imprint, based on tolerance period plus clinical data.

We think of you constantly and send you messages – usually looking into the fire. Or at sunset.

Love. love. love. I'll try to write daily – now that we are into a routine flow of everyday new and wonderful.

SUSAN HOMER

I remember that Ralph was basically absent a close relationship with me by the time I met Mario. In any event, I didn't move into the City until winter 1965, after Ralph had departed for India. And after Tim had declared that we were just flotsam and jetsam floating down the river of life, bumping into other flotsam and jetsam along the way, caught up in the same eddies temporarily.

I don't remember much about the visit of the Merry Pranksters; I don't remember perceiving them as being out of synch with us. I do remember connecting with Sandy Lehmann-Haupt. I just had a sense that we somehow were old friends. So maybe that tempered my perceptions of the rest of the crew. And of course, I had a good time on that lovely sunny afternoon in the tower room with Allen Ginsberg and Neal Cassady. Only Neal wanted to try DMT. Allen sat with us. I think he had come up from the City when he learned the Pranksters were to be at Millbrook.

I don't remember anything called the "Third floor experiment." I did not participate. I slept with Tim maybe once at most in Millbrook and I don't remember it being part of any formal experiment.

The trust and closeness seemed pretty fantastic to me, not truly possible to achieve as promoted. Certainly, the intense clarity and feelings for others I experienced in LSD sessions was inspiring (as it is to this day) but it was soon obvious that there were no dramatic lasting personal or interpersonal transformations. And the idea of societal transformation to me was even more implausible.

I couldn't agree more with Ralph's father's comments about the impossibility of "marriage" in any usual sense of the word developing and being maintained under the circumstances in which we lived. We never really lived as a couple on our own; having spent maybe two nights together during four years (on our dismal October Maine honeymoon) without assorted others around. I don't really count it as a marriage – perhaps a legalized affair? And I have the sense that the possibilities of our relationship were cut off rather frivolously and irresponsibly, without the nurturance they deserved. Of couples, only Maynard and Flo survived; and they, of course, had a number of years' foundation and children to hold them together. But then again, life is filled with endless possibilities. I, for one, am still trying to figure out just what karma is: meeting it now, and creating it for later acquaintance.

Tim's Third letter:

Dear Ralph,

Wednesday, day before Thanksgiving. Enormous crowd coming – Gunther-Karin, George-Corky, Max-Dick, Mike Holl-Brita, Felix-Gloria Morrow, David Padwa et fam., Allen Atwell and kids, Peg, Paul Krassner, Billy Olney, Foster, etc etc. Mario too. Bitten [Nena's mother, Swedish Baroness] is cooking turkey and three geese. Bjorn [Nena's brother] & Sheila are romancing. Katy comes by train tonite. Sue Leary is glowing. Nine kids were thrown out of her school. She is popular with faculty – too Millbrookish to make it with the teenagers. Marriage plans ... we had a ring designed which is Nena caught in a blonde gold and diamond band ... license, announcements, blood tests, gown all taken care of ... we are inseparable these days, keeping humor and loving detachment while the turmoil swirls by. We think now we'll leave for the Orient right after the wedding. The bowling alley is a sanctuary where we preserve the psychedelic level. I have learned so much in the last six weeks. ... its amazing. Your letters are incomparable ... I've never read travel experiences which live and pulse like yours, dear brother. We go with you. We think of you constantly and look forward to seeing you soon. Richard is in high humor ... has good things going with Peggy and Annette (who is here now). Public relations going well ... The Big House will continue of course. I wish there was another person of maturity and professional status to join.

Allen Atwell has changed; the flickers you caught have flamed up into an amazing turbine fire of energy-power ... phoning Sec of Defense about LSD for paratroopers, Pres. of Air India to sponsor tour of India of models, Pres. of Pan Am and Bucky Fuller to put helicopter net over Pan Am building, etc. Maybe Dick can work something out with him ... My understanding of the "trap of externalization" becomes clearer. Imprinting freezes us to the outside – the trick is to withdraw once a week and then, each time, make a carefully planned re-addiction to the outside – systematically reducing the number of externals – and thus allowing for new complexity and subtlety. You know.

Nena has changed. More quiet, tranquil, amazing patience, she moves through the turmoil areas with calm. She has Chinese, Viking, south Sweden farm girl things at her center. The power of imprinting continually astounds me. Frightening, unless you continually and vigilantly recognize. Sue Met is happy these days – she and Mario seem to be working out a solid thing – they are closer to taking a place in NYC. I miss you so much. We delight in the prospect of seeing you soon. We travel with you. Your eyes are ours. Our hearts are yours.

Love love and love to Mataji and Fred. Tim

Fourth Letter from Tim, dated Dec 8, 1964

Dear Ralph,

Snow, deer tracks, Siva and Kali (two dogs) racing into the white fields. Sheila and Bjorn kissing on the stairs. Annette smiles at midnite in front of third floor fire and says – You have a house full of beautiful people. Richard has mutated. He has taken over "Tim's role," whatever that means and is genial, hospitable, radiating plans and welcomes. He is filling the house with creative men and beautiful women. Allen Atwell moves in after Xmas. Eduardo, an Argentine painter, wise, funny, masculine. Mario has moved in. Joan, an Elizabeth Taylor, is now Dick's secretary. Allen Eager is a genial house buddha. It's the most beautiful place in the world. Glowing. Wedding in four days. Incredibly long list of details all clicking into place. Nena is a pure, white fire of honesty and love. We have been together about 23 hours a day for the last four weeks. Six sessions in seven weeks. We leave December 15th ... leave word at American Express, Calcutta.

Katy ... every hour a new crisis. Nena and I have bought her a ticket around the world which she now has in her possession. I have made reservations for her to leave when we leave. We are putting no pressure on her – simply given her another card in her hands – a freedom card which she may or may not use. She is miserable. Your letters have been magnificent. I guess that is all you can do ... let her know you are waiting, without putting on a lot of pressure or emotion. Perhaps, by the time you receive this she will be on her way. In any case, and in all cases the only thing to do is to free oneself from internal distortions and external addictions.

We think of you always and with great joy that we'll be with you soon.

Love. Love. Love. Love.

RM   I took the three day journey by bus and train down from the Hill Country to meet Tim and Nena in Delhi. When I told them enthusiastically about Almora and my meetings with Lama Govinda, they decided they wanted to go there too. But before we headed back up into the mountains, we wanted to see the Taj Mahal. We had heard that once a month, around the time of the full moon, the grounds are kept open to visitors at night. We thought this would be an extraordinary setting for a psychedelic experience. During the day we took a tour of the mausoleum, our senses heightened by legally available ganja. Our guide enthusiastically explained the history behind this amazing structure. "Shah Jehan, who built this monument, was not only in love with his wife, Mumtaz Mahal ("Jewel of the Palace") but he also had a mania for construction." He built it in response to his wife's dying request to create something by which she would be remembered.

Tim Leary was very impressed by the fact that Shah Jehan built the Taj as an expression of personal-human love. He felt that the quest for enlightenment still always had an element of selfishness ("my enlightenment"), whereas the Shah's love for his wife was purely other-oriented. The question of how personal passionate human love could be integrated with the spiritual quest for liberation was clearly a central concern for Tim during this period – and perhaps a core theme of his entire post-psychedelic life.

As the sun was setting and the full moon rising, we set up our session blanket on the grass in front of the Taj. The sight of the Taj Mahal in the moonlight is incredible even to normal perception. With heightened senses, the effect is indescribable. After our eyes got adapted to the darkness, the light of the moon was brilliant as daylight, the white marble dome glistening pale blue and silver, while precious stones inlaid high on the dome flashed and sparkled. Like a mirage it hung in space, separated from the earth by a thin band of haze, glowing and humming with radiance in perfectly harmonious wave-field patterns.

For about a week I lived with Tim and Nena in a rented house on the ridge above Almora. There were visits with Lama Govinda, and also with Sri Krishna Prem, an Englishman who had retired to India and founded a very small spiritual community dedicated to the cult of Krishna and Radha. I think Krishna Prem was the closest Tim ever came to accepting someone as a spiritual teacher or guru. I also was very impressed by his teaching; he inspired me to examine my motives and intentions. What was I doing there? I felt I was avoiding dealing with my fractured relationship with Katy. It was also increasingly obvious to me that Tim and Nena were not exactly harmonizing. I left a few days later, on the long journey back to the U.S.; with a stopover in Frankfurt, Germany, to visit with my father and his family.

Cover of Psychedelic Prayers, *published in 1965*

Tim wrote, in *Flashbacks* (p. 223), about the break-up of his marriage with Nena, the end of their "Himalayan Honeymoon:"

"So we're moving on. We had connected as fairy-tale lovers in the enchanted woods of Millbrook, had lived out a season of courtly romance. She had taught me tender lessons of girl-love and female splendor. We had time-traveled through a few mythic incarnations, played out magical dramas in panoramic realms. Now we would have to rise to that most complex human art, gentle separation."

This was the big day at Millbrook, when the faithful converge on the scene and gather in the sleepy, small church of this placid town to witness a most unlikely occurrence – so everyone perhaps thought – only to be impressed by the sincerity of the intention and the dramatic demonstration of the resolve to engage in binding union and to publicly vow in the presence of this company, which was a most motley crowd representing a rather unusually wide spectrum of human possibilities.

How at odds this all seemed with the structure and institution of the church, which made even the minister tremble and feel insecure and hurry through his ceremony perhaps in the fear that something unlikely was to going to happen – which of course it didn't – or was it just that I felt an incongruity between "Christian purity" and "reckless but deliberate explorations of drug consciousness," perhaps as clouds of guilt momentarily arising on the horizon of my awareness?

I did not feel much moved in the church – it was not quite as festive for me, not as dramatic, not as shattering, not as experientially meaningful as I thought it would be, and the demonstration or implication of the significance of the event came to my awareness mostly after the fact as it showed itself in others' comments, such as Charlie Mingus, who said something like: "Many were saved today – Tim swore to love as the eternal binding power." Mingus is very wise, down to earth and basic, grounded, and we had a most meaningful encounter with him and his art, his bass, his "woman," whom he asks questions in the solitude and darkness of his attic, to whom he plays and is played and answered. What a sonorous strength it is that emanates from his bow and his strings that set up a column of vibration, rising like a twirling storm, transporting and elevating everything in its path. It penetrates right through the bones and opens the wide luminous landscapes of the internal, this fantastic otherworld of playful color and geometry, radiant energy and ecstatic resonance. Isn't there some primordial power which sits with love and plays with bow and strings at the flow of life?

Then there was the huge reception in the wide halls and expansive rooms with flowing waves of communicating people, so many levels, so many cells, so many dances, so many invitations, so many traces in the highly viscous and heavy medium of filled space. Who can follow it all up, who wants to? What else to do but to stay firmly rooted at one spot and flow with movement like a precious

Tim and Bjorn preparing for the wedding ceremony

water-lily at the end of a long snake-like, pliable stem weaving to and fro on the churning waters of a huge lake in beauty and harmony. The world readily flows by, in and around and through you. No need to move. The only need is to answer the call which you can hear loud and clear as you begin to drift away from yourself and your own projects. Just to let things happen and to affirm, to say yes, yes, yes to what is – how simple and yet how difficult.

And there I stand in the teeming, swirling sea of humanity, their songs and laments and the myriad dances of courtship and blandishment fill my space – yet I do not get dizzy. In the rhapsody of sound and movement there rises the pure melody of surrender, harmony and beauty, the poem of acceptance. And it is there, it is, it is beautiful whatever it is. The whole house has become a beckoning, enveloping, nurturing tropical ocean of forms, colors and sounds, as millions of fractured, incongruous elements are transformed into beautiful flowers and ornaments of a gigantic organism, radiating joy and peace. And as the bewildering eddy swirls around me there also enters, at the same time, a liberating and soothing quietness and harmony, a kind of embedded-ness beyond description, which allows me to affirm, to accept, to meet and respond to the staggering invitations to merge with this orgiastic organism in its innocent beauty and purity.

Everything fits: there is Monte, the queer Puerto Rican hairdresser turned rock-and-roll singer, all decked out, mannered and bejeweled like Louis XIV, holding court in fantastic and hilarious style, sending me sky-high in hysterical peals of earth-shaking laughter and benevolent affirmation; how incredibly funny, daring and beautiful in its grotesqueness. There are the stiff New Englanders who corner me with a word about existential philosophy, a seemingly out-of-context concern, which strikes me as unbelievably funny. Yeah, sure, there is that world too, how bony it is, without flesh and blood. There are the task-seekers, the legions looking for something to do, having selected a costume to better identify with their chosen job – to keep the fire burning or some such mundane thing, done with incredible vigor and enthusiasm, which to me spells fear of drowning in a sea of incongruity, a way to cope with the anxiety of unstructuredness, a response to the flood and onslaught of undisguised craziness. (How often I do exactly this.) There is the tribe of the rich and powerful, beautiful creatures in expensive fur and silk, who feel perhaps out of place, yet tied firmly to each other, an intrepid band of curiosity seekers, radiating sincere benevolence. There are the "down-to-earth" people who cherish and promote the food and sing a hymn to the value, significance and cost of the caviar, which is stacked bountiful on the table, together with roasted pig, salmon, salads, ham, punch and the champagne. There are the hardened non-conformists, who appeared in the church in big sweaters or fur coats; men who never change costume because they feel they might lose some of their precious ego-territory, or they plainly just don't give a damn. There are the far-out photographers, Susan in her twenty-first century costume, lovely, natural and deep as ever, and her teacher, the lanky, dreamy Jamaican who takes pictures without end to record this scene for posterity. Dick, whose show this is, the master-arranger and indefatigable worker, is half out of his mind soaring through rooms in ecstatic oblivion and yet taking everything in. And Tim himself in his formal suit, beautiful, serious, luminous, floating; his Nordic queen, regal in bearing, like an exquisite, mysterious flower, sophisticated and natural at the same time. There is the mercurial Peggy, darting here and there in her inimitable social dance, elusive and wonderful – could she ever slow down and stay firmly rooted? And there are all the mystery guests, explorers and experimenters, adventure-seekers and con-men, the serene and the passionately religious, the painters, the musicians, the would-be philosophers, the sensualists, the mystics, the robots, the schizoid, the lovers, the doers, the thinkers, the gamesters and the Buddhas.

They are all there – and of course the goddesses of all appearances: the lush and sexy dames who carry their wares in ostensible directness; the shy and gauzy who flutter around confusedly and softly; the languid, slouchy show-girls who model themselves and who carry their veils and banners; and the mysterious beauties, dark with bottomless open eyes, like Egyptian goddesses; the Cleas of our region, intense, passionate, wild and untamed behind frail disguises, intellectual and sensuous in curious combinations; the daughters of Zion with the halo of the occult and ancient knowledge. There are the masculine spoofs who seem lost and out of things, who circle about without roots, searching for the bottom or for the sky or both, who are always ahead of themselves. And there is always Charlie Mingus, who takes his bow and his bass outside into the night to play the wind, and to wrestle with God for love and his life.

*Darlene in the background sewing
Nena's wedding veil*

I was brought up to Millbrook with Monte Rock (a well known to the New York scene hairdresser) to make the wedding veil for Nena. I was twenty-three years old and worked as a fashion editor at *Mademoiselle* magazine. Monty called me one Friday afternoon and said, "I want you to do me a favor and go to the millinery district and buy three yards of white tulle and three yards of pink tulle and come to my house Saturday morning at 10 a.m. I am doing Nena's hair, she is marrying some ex-Harvard professor and I want you to sew a veil putting the pink and white tulle together somehow. I have a car and driver and we are going to this estate in Millbrook to the wedding.

When we arrived at Millbrook, we went to the Tennis House where the bride and bridesmaids were getting dressed. The bridesmaids in their spring gowns were scattered here and there around the room like flowers, light blue, yellow, pale pink. I found a comfortable place to sit, shook out the pink and white tulle and began to sew, all the while being filmed by Ricky Leacock. Monty was flying around Nena, placing flowers in her hair. She was glowing blonde and gorgeous, and beautiful light was pouring into the room through the leaded windows. Monty handed me a glass of punch, spiked with LSD and told me to drink it. It was my first time.

When Nena was ready, we all somehow got in limousines and then we were in the church and I do not remember much. The next thing I know I'm in a hallway of the Big House and these ladies are floating by me in mink hats … probably the Hitchcock contingency. Then I met Nena's fabulous mother, so tall and regal and warm. I wanted to go home by then, to some quiet place, because I was feeling drugged and needed to lie down.

That was my first trip to the Millbrook estate; the following year I went back many times with Van Wolff's crowd. Tommy Hitchcock was there a lot with his girlfriend. I went to Millbrook for about three years until it totally blew the mind of whoever I thought I was, and I morphed into a beautiful, very turned on young lady — or at least I thought I was pretty hot stuff.

I could write a great deal more about all the weekends I spent at Millbrook. It was all amazing and interesting, sometimes shocking and sad. One time Timothy interrupted some wonderful tears I was having — it was a great cleanse, and he asked me to come outside and look at the stars. Then I was out there with him looking at the stars and all of my deep feelings had vanished. So I was annoyed by his interruption. I didn't play Tim's games with him. I don't really know why he didn't appeal to me, but I didn't want to dance. I loved meeting Ralph; one time, I was walking in the Big House and he had been standing on his head for what seemed to be a long time. As I walked by I said, "Hi" to his upside down self. And he talked to me upside down and I loved it, though I don't remember what he said.

Susan Leary (left), bridesmaid, with Nena getting ready

Ginsberg, Leary and Metzner with mylar Buddha, Psychedelic Celebration, NYC, 1966

Part 4

Millbrook After the India Journeys
Spring 1965 to Summer and Fall 1966

Spring 1965

Ralph returns to Millbrook, finds the scene in the Big House divisive, depressing and chaotic. There appear to be two camps, one in favor of minimal orderly housekeeping, the other devoted to staying as high as possible all the time. In an uneasy arrangement, the latter group, which includes Richard as well as Michael Hollingshead and several others, decide to move to the Bowling Alley.

Ralph's relationship with Katy is over. At a lecture given jointly with Richard in New York, he meets Barbara, a young woman who comes up to Millbrook to be his devotee and girlfriend.

June 1965

Tim and Nena return from India. In an attempt to save the marriage and the friendship, Richard, Tim and Nena take LSD together. The attempt fails and the trio disperses. Nena moves back to New York City, Richard goes for a long vacation in the south of France. Bob Thurman, ex-Harvard undergraduate, visits in his form as Tibetan monk Tenzing. He and Nena eventually leave together and get married.

Summer and Fall 1965

Tim and Ralph team up with a group of visual media artists, who call themselves USCO, to present theatrical "Psychedelic Explorations" in New York City, to enthusiastic audiences. Tim meets Rosemary Woodruff, who moves to Millbrook and becomes Tim's partner, lover and later wife. The Millbrook community flowers again with creativity, spirituality and romance.

Fall 1965

When Richard returns to New York, at a meeting with Tim and Ralph in a coffee shop in Poughkeepsie, he is asked not to return to Millbrook. Michael Hollingshead is given the assignment to take doses of LSD and copies of *The Psychedelic Experience* to his native England to facilitate the burgeoning psychedelic movement there.

Ralph's girlfriend Barbara, having become pregnant, undergoes a personality change, falls in love with a New York light-show artist and leaves Millbrook to live with him. Ralph decides to move to an apartment in New York, to work with a film crew on further psychedelic theatrical shows.

December 1965

Tim, Rosemary and Tim's two children, drive to Mexico, via Texas, for a vacation. The Big House is closed down and boarded up. Tim plans to relax and write a book in Mexico. In Laredo, at the border crossing, through a confusion of circumstances (possibly set up) he and his daughter are arrested and charged with possession of pot. Released on bail, they return to Millbrook, the house is re-opened and the Leary Legal Defense Fund is launched – the first of Leary's many legal battles throughout much of the rest of his life.

Winter 1965 and 1966

Ram Dass goes to England, has mysterious session with radical psychiatrist R.D. Laing; then to France, where he has session with a wealthy French art-dealer playboy.

Winter 1965 and Spring 1966

Leary's public media activities (on behalf of his own legal defense and the position of marijuana and psychedelics in society in general) increase dramatically. New summer school programs are planned and organized for Millbrook. Ralph visits Millbrook often on weekends, including the one in May 1966, when the Dutchess County Sheriff's department, under G. Gordon Liddy (of later Watergate burglary fame) busts Leary and others at the Big House, in a night-time raid with thirty Sheriff's deputies. Leary organizes a new church: League for Spiritual Discovery, as religious umbrella for his increasing public activities. Leary, Ralph and light artist Don Snyder tour eight Eastern cities, with day-long simulated psychedelic sessions.

Summer and Fall 1966

Psychedelic celebrations and pageants in Millbrook, with hundreds of people, evolve into theatrical presentations in New York, attracting several thousands. They consist of talks by Leary, musicians, slide-shows, dramatized journey stories. The first one, "The Death of the Mind," based on the Magic Theatre scene from Hermann Hesse's *Steppenwolf*, is a smash success, getting rave reviews. The second one "The Resurrection of Jesus Christ," more controversial, ends in fiasco when it turns out the person chosen to play the lead is a police informant, who breaks down and confesses. The third one, "The Illumination of the Buddha," is produced and directed by Ralph, together with Gray Henry and a group of New York filmmakers and photographers lead by Bob Lowe. A combination of the first and third celebration on Steppenwolf and the Buddha, is taken to Hollywood, and turned into a movie called *Turn On – Tune In – Drop Out*.

Tim Leary, Millbrook, 1964

Ralph Returns to Millbrook – Community Divisions

RM   When I arrived back in Millbrook after my journey to the East, I found a scene of depressing chaos. I was freaked because the scene had completely changed from how I had remembered it. A seedy, drugged-out guy met me at the front door – wearing my clothes. This turned out to be Arnie, a punkish artist from New York, whom Richard was now admiring as his teacher. Gone were the serenity and glowing warmth of Castalia weekends, the joyous enthusiasm for consciousness exploration in a family of seekers. Instead, it seemed as if the Millbrook mansion had become a scene of decadence and depravity, of vicious arguments and conflicts. Millbrook had become our *Morbio Inferiore*. This was the name of the place in Hermann Hesse's *Journey to the East*, where the pilgrims mysteriously start to argue and mistrust each other and eventually disperse, having forgotten what they were doing. I was very distressed.

Ralph Metzner, c. 1966

Tim Leary writes, in *Flashbacks* (pp 221-225):

Six months of changes … had converted Millbrook from a community of scholars and scientists to a playground for rowdy omnisexuals. In my absence Dick had fallen in love with Arnie, a flamboyant photographer from Brooklyn who liked to project color slides on walls during acid sessions, leading the vulnerable brains of his audience through a Coney Island funhouse of hallucinatory pranks. Always the en-thusiastic lieutenant, Dick had promoted Arnie to the position of Adored Guru. It was Arnie who now set the tone and directed the scenarios … Michael Hollingshead had reincarnated in Scottish kilts and scarlet capes, zanily lecturing on the relativity of the brain. It was a James Dean juvenile delinquency script. Tough street New Yorkers using LSD for mischievous fun.

Arnie and crew specialized in playing pranks on each other during acid sessions – a neurological demolition derby, pushing insanity pedals to the floor, deliberately trying to confuse, frighten, spook each other. For two weeks they camped out at the Meditation House, intoxicating themselves with hundreds (hundreds!) of doses of acid, undeniably breaking all records for conspicuous over-consumption.

Needless to say the antics of Dick's Band of Rascals had scandalized the Hitchcocks and everyone else who viewed Millbrook as a dependable spiritual base. Everyone waited to see what would happen when I returned. "To clean up the mess," as Ralph put it. He had returned before us from India, loaded with serious Oriental wisdom, and was ostracized as hopelessly humorless.

Tim mows lawn, Millbrook, 1965

RM   I remember you (RD) and I met and talked over the situation. There were two camps: One, consisting of Nena's mother and her brother Bjorn, my old friend Shelah O'Brien, a young couple from New York and myself, that wanted to maintain some semblance of normal order in the house, with cooked shared meals, and cleaning and so forth; and the other, consisting of Arnie, several other friends of his, his ex-wife, girlfriend and Michael Hollingshead, who just wanted to stay high all the time. They spooned LSD in the form of a paste several times daily from a mayonnaise jar. Because of the build-up of tolerance, doses repeated at such short intervals are likely to have less and less of an effect. There was quite a bit of tension between the two factions. I was very turned off by what I thought was Arnie's "mind-fucking:" Sitting in a meeting and saying to his girlfriend, "I know you're lying, because I'm telepathic and I can read your mind." I think you and I agreed that the best solution was to separate the two factions and have the "stay high all the time" crew, which included you, move to the Bowling Alley, while the ordinary housekeeping team stayed in the Big House. It did make a sort of sense, in that you guys were focused on maintaining a high state of consciousness, whereas I was more interested in living in such a way that changing states of consciousness could be integrated into normal life, while doing other things as well.

GB   Ram Dass, what was your take on the changes at Millbrook that Ralph was referring to? You say you were okay with the way things were going, you were enjoying the experiment of staying high?

RD   We had a wonderful time. I was among them for twenty days.

RM   Didn't you get sick? You were really sick. I was totally alarmed. I thought you were going to die.

RD   I was determined to go, go, go.

RM   You just wanted to take more LSD and get rid of the sickness that way? I tried that once. It makes you more aware of the sickness. Do you remember what it was?

RD   It was the flu. I did find at the end that we weren't getting along. That big bottle of LSD – every time you thought you needed it, you took some. We weren't high. All the personalities in that room, oh boy. I wasn't enjoying that, I was enjoying the idea of it. But the reality was … I had picked the wrong associates.

RM   Yes, it made me wonder about your judgment.

RD   I didn't have good judgment.

RM   And that freaked me out because I was always looking up to you and Tim as being my guides in the world, older male mentors who showed me the ways of the world. I thought what's going to happen to me next? That was the fear. It was very uncomfortable for me.

GB   There's a story – you were apparently sick and cold, Ram Dass. You had taken some sleeping pills and were passed out. Arnie injected you with DMT and LSD and put on a sound and light show and you woke up out of a deep sleep. Do you remember that?

RD   No. No.

RM   Who tells that story?

GB   Michael Hollingshead, in his book *The Man Who Turned on the World*, published in 1972.

RM   With Michael you never know if it's made up or not. Tim's stories definitely have more credibility. With Michael, there often didn't seem to be any purpose to his madness; just a game, often a verbal game, for its own sake. Tim was also into game theory but he was a visionary.

RD   The concept of game playing describes both Michael and Tim but with two different uses of the word "game."

RM   Yes right, both game players and having appreciation of the game aspect of human behavior. I think that's one of the things Tim liked in Michael. Whatever you get involved in, take it lightly, like a game (even things that perhaps shouldn't be taken so lightly).

RD   Michael had come to the Harvard project originally from New York where he collaborated with Doctor John Beresford.

GB   Apparently, he and Beresford and Jean Houston had started a center, the Agora Institute, in New York. They did a lot of LSD sessions. That's how Jean Houston got started with psychedelics.

RM   She and her husband Robert Masters wrote up their results in their book *The Varieties of Psychedelic Experience*, published in 1966. I liked Michael a lot, but I was wary of him.

RD   Michael had a sweetness and compassion too. He was clever, very clever.

GB   Ram Dass, maybe you can comment on the veracity of a story about Arnie, told by Hollingshead. He says you had brought three psychologists to Millbrook; you were sitting around and told everyone to keep cool. You wanted to make a good impression. And Arnie came in a suit, reading the *New York Times* and he sat down. He had put in his mouth green dye which started flowing out of his mouth and onto his clothes. Do you remember that?

RD   I don't remember it, but it's possible. See, that shows my dualism: I'm on the side of the psychologists; I'm playing the game. But the whole thing was a sham,

RM   You were the core of that group of rebels for that particular time period – which was a relatively short time period.

RD   I learned something in that time: We got so inward turned, that I neglected to pick up some youngsters from the school for retarded kids, that Tim had hired to do some work for us. They were waiting at the cold bus stop for me. And I was doing my experiments. I was full of guilt for falling down on my responsibility on that one.

RM   I remember also that during that time when I had come back from India, but before Tim and Nena came back, you and I did some lectures and presentations in New York, in part to raise money for the Millbrook community.

RD   Yes, the Village Gate was one of the clubs in New York we visited; on Monday nights, they wouldn't have their regular program and let others have use of the club. So, one Monday night, several of us from Millbrook came down and ran a scene at the Village Gate. We had all our slides and multi media paraphernalia and I was the master of ceremonies. The owner came up and said, "You're sensational, you're a natural-born comedian. I'd like you to open next Monday by yourself. So I had to get a soft hat and I was making it big in the City. I came back the next week, doing my solo; Charlie Mingus was supposed to be the main attraction. It was "Mingus and Alpert." But Mingus didn't show and another musician came instead. The whole audience was bugged and when I got up, they said, "Come on, get off the stage. Let's have the music." They just weren't my audience.

RM   Yes, I remember that event. I squirmed with embarrassment for you.

RD   I was in charge at Millbrook and trying to raise money to keep it going. Tim had not yet come back from India. Paul Desmond, from Dave Brubeck's group, was coming every night and he was giving me some support. We were at a table and in comes Timothy. And he stays for one set and he's a great friend of the musicians. I said, "Well, Tim, what do you think?" And he said, "It's absurd." (Laughs) I didn't perform again after that. I needed somebody to tell me to forget it.

GB   You had to wait a few years to find your audience.

RD   That's right.

GB   One thing we haven't discussed, Ram Dass: What was your relationship to Ralph in those days, the Harvard days and the Millbrook days. Were you close?

RD   We were close, but he was a graduate student and hung out with the graduate students, and I hung out with Tim and the rest of the faculty.

GB   So he was a junior member of your team, so to speak.

RD   Yes. He was a junior member but he was the intellectual backbone of the project. I was more like the heart of the project.

GB   And Tim?

RD   Tim was just Tim. He didn't have the intellect that Ralph had and he didn't have the heart that I have, but he did have a sense of history. He was very much a scientist. And he was very expansive, bringing in

Richard Alpert giving lecture at Town Hall, New York, 1965

everybody. For example, when I was cooking at Millbrook, I knew for how many people we had cooked. Then somebody would come to the door, it could be anybody. Tim would invite them in to sit down, and I'd say, "Well Tim, we don't have enough food." And he'd say, "Well, here's my plate."

GB   So Tim was expansive, inclusive, visionary, you're saying?

RD   Yes. He was expansive – socially. But he didn't like social games; he liked football and such, but he didn't like gamey social relations. He liked the people of the town of Millbrook. However, he was not intimate with people. I think most of the women he was with would back me up in this. He wasn't intimate with his children or with me. I don't mean intimate sexually, I mean intimate as being close to a human being. He didn't know how to do that. Ralph is an intellectual but he knows how to get close to people.

RM   My perspective on our three-way relationships is a little different. I agree in the Harvard days, I was the junior member of the team, the graduate student, while you were the professors.

I felt connected more with Tim on the level of shared vision and intellectual, historical interests. We wrote and published several essays together – one on Hermann Hesse and another one on "Programming Psychedelic Sessions." With you, Ram Dass, I felt more friendship, as with an older brother. You were always very kind to me which I really appreciated and still do. My memory of our interaction in the first year at Millbrook, is that you and Tim would think up some scheme or idea for us to do (to bring in money) and you would bring the idea to me to check it out. I think you even told me that I would at first be skeptical and raise questions; and then finally agree. It seems you were using me as a kind of pragmatic sounding board.

Tim and Nena Return from India

Tim describes what ensued in *Flashbacks*, (pp 225-226):

Dick listened to my worries about parting with Nanette. He suggested that we three take LSD together. In hindsight this was the height of folly – we were three willful wary souls, already alienated from each other.

Dick appointed himself shaman. His heavy-dose experiences with the Pranksters had taught him impressive psychedelic barnstorming flourishes. He used a long glass tube to titrate the clear liquid LSD. And he blasted us!

He panicked first, thinking, my god these two have been tripping together so much they have an unbreakable bond. I'm cut off. He lay motionless, watching like a wary cat. Nanette was thinking, why am I here? I was trapped in my battered time-ship, power-failing, drifting off, rudderless.

Here was a classic example of negative re-programming. Each of us was as vulnerable as a newborn babe. In this kind of situation the first one to take a decisive position will initiate a new reality for the others.

Dick made the first move, and it was a blind-side tackle. He accused me of being a disapproving moralist, a prude who condemned his homosexuality.

How I reacted to this first move would be crucial. Response A: I laugh and genially point out that the love and humor among us three will conquer all. Outcome: fusion. We unite as a triumphant merry trio of divinities. I don't spend four years alone in jail, while Dick doesn't paint himself into the lonely Holy Man corner, and Nanette maintains two wise friends for her blossoming career.

But I could do no better than Response B: guilty silence. Outcome: fission. Dick and Nanette exchanged a conspiratorial glance of superiority, which with X-ray sensitivity I caught. I drifted off leaking spinal fluid, leaving Nanette and Dick bonded together in a surprised uneasy alliance.

If Dick or I had been more secure, either one of us could have strobed the other out of low spirits with a blast of loving humor. But no. This acid session was about severing connections. The lines went down, and we never got the same current going again. It was the last time we took acid together.

GB   I was asking you, Ram Dass, about a session where you tried to save Tim and Nena's relationship, and somehow that made it worse. And that lead to separation between you two.

RD   Yes. They had fights all the time. And there were sides: I felt Tim was right and she was also right. Then Tim's fury, "What's a friend for?" I was welching on his friendship. They were both wrong.

RM   I remember thinking at the time, the very idea of that three-way session was sort of mind-boggling. I think you told me she came onto you, in a way. Do you think she came onto you to make Tim jealous?

RD   Not to make Tim jealous. She wanted to change my opinion of her; and they were both upset about Arnie.

RM   About the whole scene, probably. I basically agreed with Tim that this whole split in the community, with some of you out there taking acid all the time, was a disaster. The way Tim articulated it, and I agreed with his perception, you were unable to prevent that split from happening. Whether or not you were interested in preventing it, I couldn't tell but that's what it looked like. I was totally freaked. It was something I had never come even close to encountering before. You two were my closest friends and mentors and we had done all this fantastic pioneering work together and now everything was exploding in the ruins of interpersonal conflicts.

RD   I was going further and further out on my edge.

GB   So the scene was getting too anarchic, hedonistic, chaotic?

RD   They were keeping the game together, the scientist game, the professor game, teaching and all that. And I, without them, was just partying with the group at the Bowling Alley. I was there with Arnie and his girlfriend for many weeks. We all grew to hate one another and then this horrible thing happened: I forgot to pick up those people from the school for the retarded and then felt guilty for letting my fun get in the way of responsibility. Boy, that freaked me.

GB   When you were in the Bowling Alley, who did the laundry and such?

RD   I think the group over in the other house. This was a closed experiment.

RM   Yes, but my memory is that the people in the Big House were doing their laundry. I didn't think they were doing your group's laundry. There didn't seem to be much interaction between the two camps.

RD   Well, I don't think you're right. It was like with the Tennis House hermitage: bringing food and doing laundry for the separate group was part of the experiment.

RM   It didn't seem viable to me.

RD   I was going on a track that Tim didn't like.

GB   Could you say more about that? Millbrook was supposed to be an experiment in communal living.

RD   Tim always assured me that the sky was the limit and I tried my sky and it wasn't – his limits were different. I'm following his advice and when it runs through my personality, he doesn't like it. After the session with Nena, Tim came up to the room where Jackie, Susan and I were sitting, and he said to the kids, "I want you to know that Uncle Richard is evil." It was because I had sided with Nena.

RM   He saw you as having broken up their relationship. But he didn't think that later.

RD   Later we were close again. But that freed me, because he was a good Catholic, and to call someone "evil" is serious. Jack said, "Oh dad, he may be a jerk but you don't mean evil." But Tim was very serious.

RM   Did you ever talk it out with him, that particular difference?

RD   It digressed into "you're evil," "no you're evil."

RM   Ram Dass, you and I had a conversation at the Omega Institute, in the café in 2004. You asked me if I thought your homosexuality and Tim's problem with it, was at the root of the split between you. I said it wasn't a problem for me, I didn't know about Tim.

RD   I think that I was defensive about my homosexuality, and that's the way I dealt with it with Tim. I know nothing of his sexuality.

RM   Sounds like maybe it was an element, but not the core element. In my perception of you, I thought your sexuality was mysterious, because I did see you also having relationships with women. I remember once or twice, you said to me something like, "When I get through this, I hope you and Tim will teach me about sexuality." I was so surprised. What did I know about sexuality? The other thing that impressed me: You seemed to know a lot about people's sex lives, when you told stories from your various travels. I thought, how does he know all this stuff, who tells him all of this stuff? I've wondered whether that's a gay thing. I picked that up too when I read Gore Vidal, whose writings I really love. He's talking about the sex life of the Kennedys and people in politics and the arts. How does he know all this?

RD   I feel that it might be.

RM   Maybe women tell gay men stuff that they don't tell straight men. And they tell each other stuff that straight men don't talk about.

RD   Yes, that's true.

RM   That must be it. They're receptive to hearing about sexual behavior that's unconventional. It's one of the benefits of having an unconventional attitude, you learn about unconventional behavior.

GB   Ram Dass, you're talking about your homosexuality more freely now than I've ever heard before. Have you talked publicly about your sexuality before?

RD   There's this book out, *Gay Soul*. I have an interview there and I figured the only people that would read it would be gay people. Tim reacted badly to my homosexuality and I think, in that period of my life, his attitudes ruled the day. The gayness would offend people that I wanted to socialize with. Drug-taking was an area of my life I thought of as positive but I think I treated gayness as a sickness: That it was my fault and it was my cross to bear and I never laid it on people.

GB   You came of age in a time when it was seen as a sickness.

RM   Yes, and the drugs we were taking were not illegal, so that was positive socially – at least at first.

GB   Homosexuality was considered a psychiatric syndrome until the 1970s.

RD   Yes. In therapist meetings, the psychiatrists at Harvard Student Health Service would assign any students that were gay to me. Not because they thought I was gay, but because I could handle them. And then there was that episode of one of my lovers, driving my car, propositioning the psychiatrists. Throughout prep school and college, and at Harvard, I was leading a double life. I mean, I had very wonderful girlfriends, but then I'd go out in the park. I had been leading this double life for so long that I couldn't openly bring the homosexual part out. And now that gayness seems to be all right, that isn't me at all.

GB   Did gay liberation affect you at all?

RD   No, because I was scarred from way back. I'd always felt that I was bad.

GB   In that fateful session with Tim and Nena, Tim quotes you in *Flashbacks* (p. 226) as saying, "Tim, I've always thought you were being judgmental about my homosexuality."

RD   I remember that.

GB   Did you talk with Tim about your homosexuality? Did you exchange views?

RD   Always in a kidding way. You never talked intimately with Tim, because it was just hard to do. That's why I never talked to him about my sexuality.

RM   I never talked with Tim about sexuality either – his, mine or yours. It wasn't something men, at least straight men, talked about, period.

GB   Ralph, what happened in your relationship with Katy?

RD   When I came back, Katy wouldn't have anything to do with me. She had fallen out of love and into hate. I just met her once, at a party in New York City. She had moved out of Millbrook when the punkers moved in and seemed to be blaming me and Tim for the negative changes that had happened there. When I saw her, at the party, we barely talked. When I looked at her, it seemed to me as if her eyes were blazing with intense hate, same as they had shone with intense love before; the same quality and intensity, but reversed polarity.

I was reminded of something Gurdjieff wrote about three different kinds of love. I had been reading his *All and Everything* while traveling in India. There's a passage where he says feeling love tends to turn into its opposite, whereas conscious love evokes the same in the other. So when I looked at Katy's eyes, I saw that reversal. It helped me not to take it so personally, though in a sense, it was totally personal.

RD   What's the third kind of love?

RM   The third kind, physical body love, he says is a matter of type and polarity.

It's interesting, isn't it: both Tim and I had these intense romantic idealized involvements with two incredibly gorgeous, glamorous women. Millbrook reached a kind of high point of creative and spiritual celebration, then we went to India and both relationships crashed. Then, the hard work of community building had to start all over again.

GB   When and how did Barbara, the mother of your son Ari, come into your life?

RM   Some time after I returned from India, and before Tim and Nena returned in June, 1965. Richard and I were giving a talk in New York, raising funds. I talked about India. There was a young woman in the audience with whom I connected, who then pleaded with me to come up to Millbrook. I resisted at first, because we had just made an agreement to close the community off to further immigrants, setting some limits to growth, trying to keep it simple, simpler than it was. But she was persistent and I was permitted an exemption. We went back to having sunset meditations on the roof, doing regular yogic meditations and things like that. I was still totally in my Indian yogi persona and she decided to become my devotee. She'd set up Hindu shrines in the house

Barbara Taliafero, 1965

with candles and devotional pictures of Krishna and Radha, and do chanting of Kirtans. She looked like an Indian woman, with huge, limpid brown eyes, and she'd look at me and say "is it all right if I adore you?" What was I to do? Still nursing my narcissistic wound from the rejection by the imperious Katy, I was captivated. All was well, for a few months, until she became pregnant.

GB   How did Bob Thurman connect into the scene?

RM   He was a Harvard undergraduate very interested in psychedelics and Eastern religion. He used to visit a lot when we were living in Newton Center. He had a fascinating mind and ability to articulate complex spiritual topics. He had lost one eye in an accident while changing his automobile tire. He then had a glass eye, which he would sometimes remove manually, a rather unnerving habit.

RD   He was a good friend of Foster Dunlap.

RM   I didn't know that. After Harvard, Thurman and another friend of his, Jeffrey Hopkins, went to a monastery in New Jersey, founded by the Mongolian Buddhist lama, Geshe Wangyal. They immersed themselves in the study of Tibetan language and Buddhist scriptures and meditation. Before I left for India, I visited him and the lama at the monastery, to ask for advice about my upcoming trip. The old lama was delightful, very kind and with gentle humor. Thurman and his friend were wearing monk's robes, had shaved their heads, and were talking English in odd sentences, like their teacher. He had adopted the name Tenzing.

GB   So then he showed up at Millbrook, after you guys had come back from India?

RM   Yes. He showed up as Tenzing, the "mad monk," wearing his dark red Tibetan monk's robe. I don't know whether he took LSD in Millbrook or elsewhere, and had a bad trip, but he had turned against psychedelics, and against Tim's ideas and projects. He was coming around and issuing warnings about this LSD stuff is not good, and you guys are going crazy. Or you're already crazy, you shouldn't be doing this. He was now an authority on Buddhist meditation and spiritual practices. Do you remember that?

RD   Yea, something like that. Then he and Nena went off together. That's when they got married.

RM   He left the monastery and went back to graduate school, I think Harvard, to get a PhD in Eastern religions. Then he became a professor of Eastern Religions at Dartmouth, and later Columbia University. He's regarded as one of the foremost Western authorities and teachers on Tibetan Buddhism. And I believe he's still quite critical of psychedelics and their use. Their oldest daughter is the famous actress.

Psychedelic Theatre Explorations and Celebrations

GB   So how did the teaching and creative activities of Millbrook get going again?

RM   In the summer of 1965, after the debacle of the three-way acid session, Richard left for the south of France and Arnie and his cohorts left the community. Tim and I and Michael Hollingshead got together with the USCO community of visual media artists again, including Gerd Stern, Judy Cassen and later Don Snyder, a very gifted photographer, and started to offer what we called Psychedelic Explorations in theatrical venues in New York City. In part, these were continuations of the Castalia Foundation weekends, designed to carry the message of consciousness expansion to larger audiences and to bring much-needed financial income to the ever-changing Millbrook community. Tim and I would give talks on our discoveries in the realm of consciousness-expansion, and the light wizards would do their presentations.

Tim wrote, in *Flashbacks* (p. 230):

As prelude to the light presentations Ralph gave a charmingly pedantic lecture on the anatomical and physiological capacities of the various sense organs. I followed with a poetic-scientific sales-rap about the various circuits of the brain, describing what happened when they were turned on. Education, entertainment, and advertising were nicely blended.

The flyer for the presentations stated:

The Psychedelic Theatre is a new venture in direct, non-verbal communication of states of altered consciousness ... Through the use of multi-channel, mixed media presentations, involving slides, films, tapes, stroboscopes, kinetic sculptures etc.; a complete re-structuring of the sensory input is possible, permitting the systematic alteration of the usual modes of perceiving.

Audiences seemed to respond positively, enthusiastically to these presentations, in part, no doubt, because their senses were already heightened before they arrived at the theatre.

During this time, too, Tim met Rosemary Woodruff, who was to become his wife and partner in the next, much more social-political and public phase of his life. When she moved into the Millbrook Big House with him, Allen Atwell painted the tantric diagram of two intersecting triangles, symbol of erotic union, onto the brick chimney of the house.

Rosemary Woodruff, Millbrook, 1966

Later, in the fall and winter of 1965/66, Tim and I went on a road tour in eight eastern cities, together with light wizard Don Snyder. We offered "Psychedelic Sessions" – a ten hour experience of "programmed stimuli" to expand the mind and heighten the senses without drugs, but designed to duplicate or simulate programmed psychedelic sessions. The sessions were limited to twelve people, cost $40 per person, and were conducted in private homes in New York, Boston, Philadelphia, Pittsburgh, Cleveland, Cincinnati, Detroit and Chicago.

GB   What were your thoughts and feelings about this phase of your work, Ralph?

RM   I had mixed feelings. On the one hand, I was relieved that we were able to get creative projects going again that were in line with the basic vision of communicating the insights of psychedelic states, and which also served to bring in some income to the community. On the other hand, I was becoming increasingly uneasy about the direction we were going, which seemed to be geared more and more toward entertainment and publicity, rather than scientific and spiritual exploration.

GB   You mentioned a dream you had around this time that reflected this unease.

CASTALIA FOUNDATION and USCO
present
PSYCHEDELIC EXPLORATIONS

The program consists of psychedelic improvisations, lectures and discussion, the Psychedelic Theatre, and an informal question and answer period on the practical aspects of psychedelic research.

The **lectures and discussions** deal with the technology of consciousness-expansion, the practical and theoretical problems of psychedelic research. Methods of expanding consciousness, ancient and modern, Eastern, will be discussed, and where feasible, demonstrated.

The **Psychedelic Theatre** is a new venture in direct, non-verbal communication of states of altered consciousness. A group of artist-engineers, USCO, in Woodstock, New York, have created this theatre; they have presented their work in various universities and cultural centers throughout the country. Through the use of multi-channel, mixed media presentations, involving slides, films, tapes, stroboscopes, kinetic sculpture, etc., a complete re-structuring of the sensory input is possible, permitting the systematic alteration of usual modes of perceiving.

The Psychedelic Theatre illustrates and amplifies the themes discussed in the lectures, just as the latter provide the theoretical background necessary for an understanding of the new techniques of audio-olfactory-visual alteration of consciousness (AOVAC).

PLACE: NEW THEATRE, 154 East 54th Street, New York City

DATES: Every Monday evening, beginning June 14th

TIME:
Doors open: 7:00 p.m.
Psychedelic Improvisations: 7:15- 8:00 p.m.
Lecture — Discussion: 8:15- 9:45 p.m.
Psychedelic Theatre: 9:45-10:30 p.m.
Informal Question and Answer Period: 10:30-11:00 p.m.

TICKETS: $1.50, $2.50, $3.50 at the door

RM   In the dream I saw the three of us, Tim, Richard and me, as vaudeville song and dance men, doing our routines for a laughing audience. And I remember one time I connected with Maynard Ferguson, the bandleader, who was returning to Millbrook from New York, where he had been on a gig. I was also returning to Millbrook from New York, from a speaking gig. I liked Maynard personally. We were both traveling performers and we lived among other performers and models. Somehow, it all seemed far away from our origins in science and research and I did wonder and worry about that.

The Meeting in Poughkeepsie and its Aftermath

RM   So, after the summer, when we'd all had a chance to cool off and think about the future of the community, you returned in the fall of 1965, and the three of us had this fateful meeting in a coffee shop in Poughkeepsie. My memory of it is that it was the three of us. Tim writes in *Flashbacks* (p. 234) that it involved Michael Hollingshead too.

RD   You and Tim invited me to leave Millbrook. Not to come back. I had some LSD sessions to run in Europe. I thought, "I'll raise more money than them." And I thought it was a good way to get out of Millbrook.

RM   It was very hard to get a sense of harmony back into the community. It wasn't as if we were blaming you, although it must have felt like that. But you were the *de facto* leader of the rebel "stay high" group and seemingly weren't able to hold things together, while we were in India. There also was your attracting and idealizing of people like Arnie. When Tim suggested it, I couldn't see it going any other way, although I do remember feeling bad and wishing there was another way.

RD   Look at who I was left with, when you guys went to India: Tim's Swedish mother-in-law and brother-in-law, the woman who was minding the kids, Michael Hollingshead. These were all Tim's people, not mine.

PSYCHEDELIC SESSIONS

TIMOTHY LEARY & RALPH METZNER

FALL AND WINTER 1965/66

IN

NEW YORK, BOSTON, PHILADELPHIA, PITTSBURGH,

CLEVELAND, CINCINNATI, DETROIT, CHICAGO

PSYCHEDELIC SESSIONS

Conducted by
Timothy Leary, Ph.D. and Ralph Metzner, Ph.D.

During the fall-winter of 1965-66 a series of psychedelic group sessions will be conducted in these eastern-midwestern cities.

The aim is to produce a psychedelic or ecstatic experience without using drugs. The methods involve an intense ten hour inundation of programmed stimuli — sensory, emotional, intellectual, artistic, philosophic — which reproduce and induce the LSD experience.

In addition to the experience, the session provides a living demonstration of methods for running sessions, of systematic techniques for recording and describing the psychedelic effect, as well as a survey and illustration of ancient and current theories of consciousness-expansion.

BACKGROUND

Throughout 4000 years of recorded history men have known that there exists a range of energies and awarenesses beyond the imprinted symbols of the rational mind. Many models, myths, metaphors and methods have been developed to explain and produce the transcendental experience.

For the past five years a group of more than fifty psychologists, philosophers, and scientists has been developing models and methods for expanding consciousness using psychedelic foods and drugs (LSD, mescaline, psilocybin, etc.). This group, located successively at Harvard, Zihuatanejo (Mexico), and Castalia Foundation, Millbrook, N. Y., has concentrated on designing language systems for receiving and communicating non-symbolic levels of energy and techniques for programming psychedelic sessions.

Four books and over fifty scientific-scholarly articles have described these activities.

Since 1963, experimentation with these sacred biochemicals has been restricted by federal law to mental hospitals. The Castalia group has adapted to this government repression (not unfamiliar in the history of visionary research) by working out non-drug methods of producing the "going-out-of-your-mind" phenomenon.

During 1964-65 these methods have been demonstrated at weekend workshops held in Millbrook, N. Y., and in presentations of the "Psychedelic Theatre" in New York City. In order to provide these experiences for a larger number of persons in a more economical manner, one-day sessions will be run in several metropolitan centers listed on the back-sheet of this brochure.

RM I agree with you there. Michael was definitely a loose cannon. He could do good things too, but you never knew if what he was going to do was good or bad.

RD With all these people as raw material, how could I?

RM It felt uncomfortable for me to have that conversation with you, extremely uncomfortable. And I felt it put tension in the relationship between you and me for years afterwards. But, at the time, I went along with Tim, because I agreed with his perception of the situation and couldn't see any other solution.

GB At that point, what were your differences with Tim as far as your vision and Millbrook and the psychedelic movement were concerned?

RD There were a lot of differences. I'm more of a heart person. I didn't know where we were going to go. I wanted it to go where it must go.

RM What was your perception of the scene after Tim and I came back from India? Did it seem harmonious? Did you feel that it had changed from before? Did you feel it was a good change or not a good change?

RD I felt the change; it was that hard edge that Arnie and Michael represented. We all tempered each other. When I didn't have you guys around, I was getting high. (Laughs) What am I going to do here – make a silk purse out of a sow's ear? I was irresponsible.

© Don Snyder

"Like Knights saddling up ..."

RM So my recollection, and yours, is that Tim and I asked you to leave Millbrook, or rather, not come back. The way Tim tells the story of this meeting; it's four of us, including Michael, deciding to all go off in different directions:

Dick arrived back from Europe in the fall. Michael, Ralph and I met him at the Poughkeepsie station, and we convened a cheerless conference in a restaurant. We agreed that we had gone about as far as we could go at Millbrook. The fun had stopped. The money, energy, able bodies, and utopian idealism needed to maintain a sixty-four-room castle had been dissipated.

Like knights saddling up we four resolved to pursue our separate quests and illuminate our respective realms. Dick struck off to start a new reality in California. Although he had seemed too neurotic, too sexually avant-garde for our scholarly-scientific scene, from the minute we separated, his moral pendulum began to swing in the opposite direction. Five years later, when I was being called the "most danger-ous man in the world" Dick had become America's most respected Hindu swami. Baba Ram Dass. A veritable saint.

Ralph Metzner went to New York to write a book on consciousness. Michael Hollingshead, always ready for an adventurous assignment, was elected to bring the message of brain-change to England. A new spirit of experimentation was emerging in London ... I announced that I would close Millbrook and retire to Mexico to write the story of our adventures. A literary agent had phoned to tell me that New Amer-ican Library would advance me $10,000 on an autobiography I later published it in 1968 as High Priest. *We used some of the money to buy a passage on the Queen Elizabeth II for Michael, who sailed with 1000 doses of M.G.'s [morning glory seeds] and two hundred copies of* The Psychedelic Experience.

From *Flashbacks* (p. 234)

RM   Then you went off to England and did your sessions, with Ronnie Laing and others, is that right? You had other travels too, to California, yes?

RD   Yes, I still had the math project at Stanford.

RM   I didn't realize you were still running that while you were living at Millbrook.

RD   Yes. It was the School Mathematics Study Group research on teaching the new math that I had started at Yale. At Stanford I came up with the finding that attitudes of women teachers in elementary school affected the child's future attitude towards numbers. Jim Fadiman was one of my assistants. That's how he got out to California. He was a stu-dent at Harvard and I brought him to Stanford.

RM   So, after the Poughkeepsie coffee shop meeting, you never came back to Millbrook except to visit.

RD   That's right.

RM   Which is basically similar to my story: I left for New York in the winter of 1965, when Millbrook was boarded up, temporarily, and only returned for visits and participated in Psychedelic Theatre presentations in New York.

GB   Ralph, what led to your departure from Millbrook?

RM   Well, after that meeting in the coffee shop, Ram Dass left and Michael Hollingshead also left for England. We had been putting on Psychedelic Theatre presentations in New York City during the summer, collaborating with the visual light media artists.

I moved to New York in the fall, taking over Rosemary Woodruff's rented apartment on West Ninth Street. I needed to continue working on putting out further issues of the *Psychedelic Review*, which was getting harder and harder to do with our vanishing financial resources. I was also trying to land a contract with a publisher to edit a collection of psychedelic accounts, which did eventually appear as *The Ecstatic Adventure* (Macmillan, 1968). But my departure had a lot to do with Barbara, my girlfriend, getting pregnant. Shortly afterwards, she underwent a 180 degree personality change: She lost her infatuation with me and lost all interest in the Millbrook Hindu-tinged meditative practices the community was trying to maintain. She used to accompany us on the trips to New York to work on the psychedelic light-shows. She wanted to shop and buy clothes and hang out and listen to music. One of the light-show artists was an advertising designer named Richard Aldcroft. He had a machine consisting of a rotating transparent cylinder filled with liquid, in which colored pieces of plastic floated; a light beam radiating through it projected these ever-changing colored shapes on the wall. It put you into a kind of soporific visual trance. He also had a high-paying job on Madison Avenue. Barbara became entranced with him and, on one of our trips to the city, moved in with him: "I'm not coming back with you." She was six months pregnant with my child. So, part of the reason for my moving from Millbrook to New York City was also to try to generate some income so I could assume responsibility for the child. Millbrook was broke.

GB   You said you learned something about that story only recently. Can you say what that was?

RM   Well, for thirty years, I've told the story of that episode as a victim. I felt distraught and humiliated. This woman left me, when pregnant with my child. She did that to me.

RD   Yes, yes – you did it to her.

RM   That's what I realized much later. I was in a workshop with Hunter Beaumont. He was saying we each have a story that we tell ourselves about who we are and what we are. And I realized that I had never empathically looked at that situation from her point of view. When I did, I saw she did what any woman would do. She was pregnant, she needed a nest. In fact, when I saw her once later in Aldcroft's apartment, sitting in the loft, she was like a mother hen brooding in her nest. I couldn't provide a nest and he could. I had nothing to offer except participation in a spiritual community, which was not what she needed or wanted. She did what she felt she needed to do, not because she wanted to do something to me. So that enabled me to drop the victim story – which was a big relief. I was thankful I wasn't married to her; I didn't want to marry her. I'm glad I didn't, it would have only complicated matters even more. And I'll always be grateful to Barbara for bringing Ari into my life.

Barbara Taliafero, 1966

GB   How did that work out?

RM   Ari was born in May 1966. Barbara took a small dose of LSD while giving birth to him. I wrote it up in my book, *The Ecstatic Adventure*, along with that of another woman who gave birth that way. I interviewed her. She said it actually facilitated the birthing and helped her deal with the contractions. She could become detached and be aware that her body was contracting but not be identified with it. The pain was still there but she wouldn't react to it so much, just let it be there. Which is similar to what Dr. Eric Kast had found, giving LSD to terminal cancer patients. Barbara and Aldcroft split up shortly after the birth. She gave the child up to her parents, who lived in the Bronx, to take care of and went to London, England to live with a rock group. She was kind of a rock groupie. Six months later, the rock group threw her out. So, she went to try to get the child back, but her parents wouldn't let her. They considered her an unfit mother, called her an alley cat because she abandoned her baby. She asked me to help her get the child back, because I had more credibility, vis-à-vis her parents. There were all kinds of dramatic hysterical confrontations. Eventually, we did persuade her parents to release the child back to her and my shared custody and caretaking. That worked out more or less for another year or so in New York, and then we both moved, separately, to California, with the child. She had the habit of going off and changing her mind: "You take him now, it's too much for me; no, I want him back now." A lot of painful and difficult back and forth, for years until he died in a bicycle accident at the age of eight, in Southern California. But that's another story.

PEGGY HITCHCOCK

By the time Tim and Nena and Ralph were in India, I was no longer directly involved with the Millbrook scene. I was in the process of getting married. To the extent I was aware, I was upset by the situation at the Bowling Alley. I blamed my ex-boyfriend Allen Eager for the use of addictive drugs which I believed was taking place. I was shocked and disappointed in Richard's behavior and felt sad about the degeneration of the whole community. When I heard about the meeting you all had on Tim's return, I thought it seemed like the only sensible solution to the problem. In retrospect, I think it was the best thing which could have possibly happened for Richard. He had bottomed out and burned his bridges, so to speak. It was a turning point in his life. He went on to India, where he found his life's purpose and came back as Ram Dass.

One afternoon, a friend of mine, Allen Atwell, an extremely talented psychedelic muralist, came to see me at my New York apartment with his partner, Susan Firestone. They were very concerned about their friend, Rosemary Woodruff, who was involved in a destructive relationship with my old boyfriend, Allen Eager. She needed to get away from him and they asked if I thought she could come to stay for a while at Millbrook. I had met Rosemary; she was a lovely person, and I was most sympathetic to her situation. I quickly made arrangements for her to visit, which she did. In time, she became Tim's devoted partner and wife.

The whole slogan, "Turn on, tune in, drop out," felt to me like a disaster in the making. Our original emphasis in taking psychedelics was on the primary importance of set and setting, in order to ensure that one's exploration of consciousness would be, in so far as possible, a positive and nurturing experience. Now, with Tim's very public pronouncements, the emphasis suddenly was on taking psychedelics with little regard for where or with whom the experience happened. Psychedelic substances have traditionally been used to explore consciousness within a safe and even sacred setting. I felt strongly that Tim's pronouncements diminished the value of what we had been trying to accomplish with our experiments. It seemed to me he was completely ignoring the dimension of the sacred and the intention for spiritual awakening implicit in the psychedelic experience. Tim seemed not to want to hear how his message was being construed and misconstrued. The focus of his public activity shifted more and more from the educational to entertaining, with the psychedelic celebrations. These celebrations were created to financially support the community in Millbrook and later to raise money for Tim's legal expenses. I watched him go through a gradual transformation from educator to media personality as he took center stage. After his marijuana bust, Tim was not deterred in the slightest from speaking his mind. He continued to publicly denounce the government's prohibition against psychedelic substances and, in my opinion, did everything possible to ensure that he would eventually be silenced by going to jail. He could not resist spitting in the eye of the establishment, as though he had something of a martyr complex. I didn't see very much of Tim during the next few years, as I was raising a family and he was in and out of jail. We reconnected when he was living in Los Angeles years later, and we remained friends until his death.

Peggy Hitchcock, 1965

Richard Goes to England – Meets R.D. Laing – Goes to India

RD   So I then went to Europe where I ran sessions.

RM   You went to England, right? You ran a session with Ronnie Laing, where you both took it together.

RD   He (Laing) convinced me that he was less knowledgeable about psychedelics than I was. He took on the role of the follower and he was not looking out for me; I was supposed to look out for him. Then he took off his clothes and stood on his head. An interesting session which I chronicled in *The Only Dance There Is*. (Anchor Books, New York, 1974, p. 22-24):

Ronnie and I decided to take LSD together and he said to me, "How much shall we take?" I said, "Well, why don't we take about 300 micrograms?" And he said, "Well, that's a little much for me. But as long as you're along, I guess it's all right." Now by his saying that he put me in the role of sort of being his protector, that is, he cast me into the role of being the guide, which bugged me a little bit. But O.K. I don't know this guy. If that's the trip I'm supposed to play, I will be John Responsible. And he can flip around the room, right? And my usual model of what's going to happen is I'm going to take it and I'm going to create a pleasant environment. I'm going to put on Miles Davis records (in those days) and we're going to lie around and, you know, do it. So we take it and the first thing that happens after we've taken these chemicals is he takes off all his clothes but his shorts and he starts to stand on his head. This doesn't fit into my model of what you do when you have psychedelics. I don't know anything about yoga, and it all seems absurd to me … So I watch with a certain, you know, disbelief. Then he walks over to me and he looks into my eyes and his face looks like the most defenseless child, just like my model had been that I'm going to have to take care of him … I'm going to be the guide. He looks like a totally defenseless child. He arouses in me every nurturant impulse I have. I felt tremendously protective of him. And I just feel like saying, "Oh, Ronnie." I'm not saying anything, but I'm like, "Ronnie, it's all right, I'm here." You know, "Count on me." He's just like a little child, wide open. And we were no sooner in that role than his face takes on the subtlest change, just muscle patterns like, it's as if a thought in his head manifests in a change in his face – he now looks like the most protective, fatherly, warm, nurturant being – and he arouses in me all those uncooked seeds of being a little, dependent child, see. And I become, "Oh, Ronnie, of, wow, you will take ... you are going to be my ... Oh, Ronnie, I can do it this time. Oh, Wow." The minute I'm in that his face changes again, and he is now the student and he's asking me questions. This is all silent. It's all mime and all just facial things. It's all thought forms ... Well, Ronnie and I in the course of the next six hours went through, I don't know, perhaps eighty or so different social roles. What we did was we'd go into a role, a symbiosis, like therapist and patient, and then we'd flip it around and be patient and therapist. We'd be prisoner and executioner and then executioner and prisoner. Some of them really scared us, believe me. It really is scary. In each one, you had to say, "Right, O.K., that one," and then flip over and do the reverse of it. And I began to see that Ronnie and I were establishing a contact in the place where we were behind all of that. You could say behind the people that were playing the game.

RM   You were trying on different roles, during the trip.

RD   Yes, we were trying on different roles.

RM   Were you doing this by talking or was it more non-verbal gesturing?

RD   Gesturing.

RM   He was big on non-verbal communication.

RD   That's all I remember.

RM   It sounds like you enjoyed it. It's interesting that you say he regarded you as being more knowledgeable. He didn't describe that particular session in the memoir book I have of his. He describes meeting you and says that when you take psychedelics like LSD with somebody, you know where people are at, basically. Meaning, he felt you were equals, that you were sharing knowledge on the basis of equality. At least that's the way I would read that. That's consistent with the story you tell about that session.

GB   What else did you do in Europe during that time?

RD   I went over to do a psychedelic trip, for a wealthy artist in France. He picked me up at the airport. He's got a big American convertible and we're to go down to his house near Paris, which has all these paintings of sailboats and gambling scenes. He said we were going to his castle in the country but in Paris we stopped at his mother's. His mother's place was a block long and a block wide. It was a nice session. But it turned out he had a problem, a sexual problem. He had a wife and kids and was a very reputable art dealer but into a leather scene. His mother paid for his upkeep, giving him these houses. He wasn't earning any living. We get into the session, and he's really far out. In that session he wanted me to pee in his rubber suit that he was wearing. I said you can use your own pee. Here he was sloshing around in this heavy suit. Then he said I'll go into my studio and paint. He came down after a while and said "I'm ruined as a painter. The LSD did it." He found he couldn't paint the same way as before. I left him and went to Deauville, the nearby seaside resort. I went to the gambling clubs and I was high. I wore my white shirt and dark glasses. Roulette was the only thing I used to play. I would look at the roulette wheel and the black ones were pulsing. I put money on black and won and won and won. I was so jazzed. But I thought I need to get away from this guy, the painter. So I took just enough money from the winnings, the exact amount for the trip to England, where I wanted to meet up with Tommy Hitchcock, who had a house there. Interestingly, eight months later, I got a letter from the painter saying one of his paintings had won first prize in a contest. So, he wasn't ruined after all.

RM   I also had some interesting encounters with R.D. Laing. On my way to India the year before, I stopped in London to visit him. He was just divorcing his first wife; he and I had several lengthy, intriguing conversations, over the course of a couple of days. A fascinating mind. On my way back from India, I was in Frankfurt staying with my father; and this gorgeous German woman Jutta, was there. She was a friend of my father's third wife. We had a brief but intense fling. But I was on my way back to the US, via England, where my brother Robin, a barrister, also lived. Jutta said, 'I'm going to England myself, I'm looking for a job." She was a clothes designer. So I gave her my brother's number, and Ronnie Laing's phone number, to look up in London. I didn't think anything of it. But months later, I heard they fell in love and got married. She was his second wife and they eventually had three children.

We stayed in touch by mail. Jutta, Ronnie and their children used to go on skiing vacations in the Alps with my father, his wife and their children. They would send me photographs. Ronnie wouldn't ski; he would just play the piano. He was a very gifted pianist actually. He was going to be a concert pianist before he went into psychiatry. So there was this funny kind of family connection between us and also a strange kind of parallelism between Ronnie and my mother. My mother is from Scotland, Ayrshire, which includes Glasgow, where Laing was from. He was a Scottish man who married a German woman and my mother was a Scottish woman who married a German man. A curious kind of synchronicity. They also died within days of each other.

RD   What happened to Laing in India?

RM   He went through a whole meditation program; he was into yoga and meditation. I think he was there for a year. He and Jutta published a journal which they called *FIRE*. Twenty years later, in the mid-eighties, I met Ronnie and Jutta again in London, and then that marriage was dissolving. At that time, I was working with the empathogenic substance MDMA in psychotherapy. The three of us took MDMA together. Ronnie liked MDMA; he said it made him feel "normal," implying that he usually felt more or less insane, involved in the madness of society. Jutta would sing songs by Schubert and Hugo Wolff, accompanied by Ronnie on the piano. It was very beautiful. He was such a gifted, insightful man. But he did have this strange quirk of sometimes unexpectedly turning on people, attacking them verbally, in group conversations; people who thought they were his friends, like Fritjof Capra, or Carl Rogers, or John Perry. He never did that to me though, luckily.

RD   He was originally a surgeon?

RM   Yes. In the British navy or army, the military.

RD   He was so insightful. I've been fashioning my house, which is a community, after Ronnie's place, Kingsley Hall. It was originally the house that Gandhi used (in England). That was Ronnie's place, where he and his family lived for ten years or more with a group of psychotics, other doctors and staff. But the doctors and the patients couldn't tell one from the other. It all went into madness. I love that. I just love that.

GB   Ram Dass, what happened between your trips to England in 1966 and when you went to India?

RD   I went to California and hung out with Owsley, the underground LSD maker, who made a form of LSD that was called "White Lightning." Owsley and I went to England because he knew this girl over in London. She ended up living with me in New York City. I said to her, "Ralph and Tim and Nena went to India. I have a real desire to go to India too." So along came David Padwa. David had sold his computer company to Xerox; he was the Hitchcocks' friend and he was a young, suave businessman, very smart. So, David was a person I had turned on to LSD. He called me up and said, "Would you like to go with me on a trip from Teheran to India in my Land Rover?" Well, there it was, my opportunity. We drove from Iran across Afghanistan to India. The Land Rover was stocked with tuna fish and Vivaldi tapes. We were not ready for India.

GB   Other than that Tim and Ralph had already gone, was there any other reason that you wanted to go to India? In *Be Here Now*, you said that you also had this longing to find someone who knew about these states of consciousness.

RD   I had been disillusioned by the psychedelic scene. They were all nutty or neurotic. Their lives were in turmoil and I was thinking that these are not my people. I got interested in Eastern spirituality years before, when Aldous Huxley had encouraged us to read *The Tibetan Book of the Dead*. It was about the things we saw on trips that we were not capable of putting into words. Aldous had said psychedelics provided "gratuitous grace." I thought if we are getting so much grace and we have so little knowledge as to how to use it well, that Eastern book was spelling out for my consciousness something that was not in the psychology of the West.

GB   So they were accurately describing states of consciousness that you were experiencing under the psychedelics?

RD   Yes.

GB   Earlier that year, before you went to India, your mother died.

RD   It seems to me that it was six months prior to my leaving and that was 1967.

Ram Dass, late 1960s

GB   What did your mother die from?

RD Well, that's a funny story. She died from a blood condition. Her enlarged spleen made her look pregnant. The day after I arrived at his place, Maharaji said to me through the translator, "Your mother died this past year." And then out of Maharaji's mouth came the only English word I ever heard him pronounce – "spleen." That was kind of a "Yeah!" The organ that killed my mother was awakening me. Beautifully poetic.

GB How did your mother's death affect you and your state of mind at that time?

RD I have four images that come to mind. I was going with Caroline, that was Owsley's girl friend. And she was wearing a miniskirt when I brought her to visit my mother. My mother was in a wing chair and dressed in her bathrobe. Mother didn't like Caroline, because of the miniskirt. That's the first image. Then, when I left her room and said goodbye, the plumber was coming in because her toilet needed fixing. She turned her attention to the plumber and it was ruining the goodbye scene. That's the second image. But a different goodbye scene had occurred a few weeks before. I came to visit her from the Newport Jazz Festival, with Maynard and Flo and Tim, and we were very stoned, I think on mushrooms. So, visiting my mother; they had given her morphine or something, and we were two old souls. And, in our old soul manner, we considered death and it was like that. That's the third image. I said, "Mother, the way I look at it, you're like a friend that is going to be in a burning building. Get out of the building. Get out of the building." I was talking to her as a soul. We had this wonderful talk, and that was the end of our relationship, not the scene with the plumber.

GB Didn't she say something like, "You're the only one I can talk to about death?"

RD Yes. That was because of drugs.

GB Because she was on drugs? Or both of you?

RD No. I could understand her because I'd had (psychedelic) drugs. See, the state of consciousness she was in at the time of her dying was exceptional for a Jewish middle-class person.

GB   Are you saying that her consciousness got raised through the dying process?

RD   Yes.

GB   You've written about your mother's funeral:

I took LSD to go to the funeral and it was quite interesting, because I experienced Mother and me hanging out watching the whole scene. She didn't seem particularly upset, nor was I. The family was seated on one side, and the rest of the people on the other, so that they could watch the family mourn. I was at the end of the row. It was a sunny day, and there was golden light coming out of the casket. Mother and I were hanging out watching all the people who were thinking beautiful thoughts about her. I wanted to smile, but I realized that would be the final straw: "Of course, he takes drugs, he smiles at this own mother's funeral!" A smile is not currently an acceptable social response at the time of somebody's death.

(From: Dass, Ram and Stephen Levine. *Grist for the Mill.* Berkeley. Celestial Arts, Revised Edition, 1987, p.117.)

RD   Yes. That's the fourth image. At the funeral, she was at my shoulder and we were talking. There were about three hundred people – on one side was the family and on the other side were the mourners. And she and I were laughing and we were happy because there were so many hearts – hearts so loving to her. You could see it.

GB   What was sitting on your shoulder – her Spirit, or was it a physical form?

RD   Well, it was her consciousness. (Chuckle) So then, in India, after Maharaji had made his remark about her spleen, he said, "She is a high soul." I said to the translator, "Didn't he say she *was* a high soul, because she's dead now." And Maharaji said "Ne! Ne!" He was seeing her as a soul and I was remembering her as an ego. Since that moment, with his "Ne!," I have never related to my incarnation mother. Because I now see her as a soul that took birth this time as my mother. And since that moment, I think of her as my rooting club in the beyond. She's just rooting for me.

The Bust in Laredo and Gordon Liddy's Raid on Millbrook

GB Ralph, you actually helped board up the Big House, when everyone left?

RM Yes, on December 31, 1965, after Tim, Rosemary and his two kids had left for Mexico, I had already moved into the apartment in New York. Everyone else had left; Allen Eager and I returned to Millbrook to board up the windows and lock up the Big House. I had many mixed emotions as we closed up the huge house that had pulsated with so much exotic and creative life-energy. As it turned out, the closure was not to last for very long. After Tim and his family were busted for a small amount of pot crossing the border in Laredo and they were released on bail, they moved back into the Big House in January. I was asked to come to Laredo to testify as a witness for the defense; to the effect that Leary's use of marijuana and other psychedelics was both scientific and religious, drawing on evidence for religious use of cannabis in India. The Texas judge and jury didn't buy any of it, of course, and he was given thirty years for smuggling a very small amount of pot. Four years, and thousands of hours and dollars later, the case was thrown out by the United States Supreme Court, as "cruel and unusual punishment." By that time, Leary was embroiled in several other cases. The authorities were definitely out to get him. While living in New York City, I worked for an *ad hoc* organization called the Leary Defense Fund, preparing for the trial as a test case.

GB Ram Dass, what was your take on that whole story?

RD The pot was found in his daughter Susan's underwear. And Tim wanted to make this the case of cases. But you don't make the case of cases when your pot is found in your girl's underwear. So he was fraudulent. But I went down to Brownsville, Texas, where the court was. He was in trouble and I offered my services, even though we were very distant at that time. I helped raise money for Tim.

RM   So the Big House was opened up again in the spring of 1966 and Tim and his family moved back in, along with a new cast of characters. Tim was planning legal strategies with various lawyers and consultants, and also a Millbrook Summer School to help raise funds. I was involved with preparing further Psychedelic Theatre productions in New York. I would go often to Millbrook on weekends. The weekend in May 1966 when Gordon Liddy and his deputies busted the Big House, I was there and disposed of a large chunk of hashish on my night table, when I heard them coming, by eating it. I was high for a quite some time that day. But that was also my last visit to Millbrook for a long time. It just became too dangerous for me, with the increasing exposure to law enforcement personnel.

Susan and Tim Leary with Ralph Metzner strategize their defense in Laredo, Texas, 1965

Ralph Metzner and Tim Leary at the time of the trial for marijuana bust, Laredo, Texas, spring of 1966

LISA FERGUSON

Lisa Ferguson, 1970s

Flo Ferguson, late 1960s

We were staying in the Big House when Dutchess County Sheriffs' deputies, under Gordon Liddy, did their raid. My father had gone ahead to the Tropicana in Las Vegas, where he had booked a long-term engagement, and the rest of my family had our bags packed, ready to head across country the next morning. I was sleeping in a room at the top of the second floor stairs, when suddenly the door burst open and police in riot gear thundered in grabbing the twelve year old black girl (our beloved baby-sitter) who was sleeping in the bed across from me. They grabbed her by the collar of her pajamas like she was a rag doll and yanked her out of bed in a very brutal way. I sat up, terrified.

"Don't move!" A man in full black riot gear lunged to within inches of my face and screamed. I froze and listened through the walls as everyone was taken away to be questioned. After a while, I heard footsteps on the stairs outside my room as one by one, people began returning back to their rooms.

The next day the headlines in the local newspaper screamed, "Young boy and girl caught sleeping naked in same bed!" What the papers failed to mention was that the boy and girl were Bentley and Wilder, my younger brother and sister, who were practically toddlers.

A few years ago, when I was filming "Children of the Revolution: Tune Back In," I felt like tracking down Mr. Liddy and asking if he wanted to pay my therapist bill for the traumatic anxiety. I made the film in response to what Tim Leary said to me, five days before he died, when he told me I would cure my alienation by "tuning back in." Over the course of six years, I tracked down and interviewed children who grew up like I did, and our radical parents. This film documents my experiences at Millbrook and reclaims the dream.

Millbrook After the Liddy Raid – More Psychedelic Theatre

GB   So Ram Dass was in England, you, Ralph were in New York, and Leary returned to the Millbrook house, with Rosemary and his two kids, now teenagers, is that right?

RM   Yes. And an ever-changing cast of characters and visitors: Many lawyers and advisors working with him on his case; publicists and journalists writing articles and helping him promote a positive vision for psychedelics in society. He wrote about several inspiring meetings with the Canadian media philosopher Marshall McLuhan, who encouraged him to be relentlessly positive. It was a message he took to heart and practiced the rest of his life.

In *Flashbacks* (pp 252-253) he wrote of this phase:

And that's how it happened, step by step from the Harvard firing to the deportations, from Laredo to the Liddy raid, I was pushed from scientific detachment and scholarly retirement into public opposition to the policies of the ruling regime.

By this time I no longer regretted being an outcast. I was beginning to enjoy the fray. And I was not alone in the rebellion. Millions of Americans, exactly at this time, were also pushed to open resistance to the group that had taken over Washington after the assassination. A cultural revolution was brewing.

My understanding of the situation was this: America was experiencing a quantum jump in intelligence. For the first time in our history a large and influential sector of the populace was coming to disrespect institutional authority, not as members of organized dissident groups but as intelligent individuals, highly selective political consumers who demanded responsive and effective leadership, which no existing party, no religion, no labor union seemed able to provide. Thus a conflict between the old industrial society and the new information society was to be played out in the new arena of power – the media. Those who understood this would create the future.

JEAN McCREEDY

I had experienced spontaneous mystical states while in Jungian oriented therapy in the early sixties, before I had heard of psychedelics and the work of Leary, Alpert and Metzner. When I became aware of the results they were getting, I became determined to find a way to pursue psychedelic exploration. In 1966, after attending weekend seminars at Millbrook, Tim invited me to move to Millbrook and participate in a new experimental community project he was starting. I moved most of my belongings to Millbrook and watched as they were dispersed throughout the Millbrook mansion. I was divorced, a very naïve middle class housewife and secretary to a vice president at the Riggs National Bank in Washington, D.C. A huge change for me! I was open and ready to explore my internal landscapes with a deep and innocent faith. I had absolutely no idea what was in store for me!

In the evenings I typed Tim's books. He wrote profusely and drank a lot of wine. He never edited his writing and would turn out endless pages to be typed and delivered to his editor the next day. He seemed to be an endless fountain of truth as he experienced it.

Everyday was an intense journey, both inner and outer! Tim always amazed me with his ability to accept people from backgrounds and lifestyles without stereotypical judgment. We were a mix of everything: artists, a probation officer, musicians, school teachers, ex-junkies, a Hindu nun, etc. etc! We were all in psychedelic training – committed to conscious set and setting.

Tim allowed for unstructured flow as he watched to see what would unfold! Very often chaos! With a minimum of structure, we were allowed to explore creative self expression and drop out of robot games so as not to be as affected by conventional programs. "Going with the flow" was a big watch word during those times. Somehow we were organized enough to have a semblance of ground floor order, most of the time.

Tim was very alive and "on stage" all of the time playing his part in the cosmic theater we called Millbrook. He had an electric quality that was magnetic and challenging – often exploding with new perspectives and ideas – always mutating, open and far seeing. At times, he was prone to project his own dogma and became frustrated and genuinely mystified when he couldn't understand why people behaved contrary to his belief system. He was vitally interested in everyone involved in the community we later called "The League for Spiritual Discovery."

We were experimenting on a regular basis with group psychedelic sessions and the meditation house was available for individual sessions. This was a great gift as we were totally protected from any intrusions from the outside world during psychedelic meditations and could stay for several days if we needed to. I experienced my most significant spiritual breakthroughs during those sessions. Every morning and evening the huge bell would ring to announce meditation and the community would gather.

In late 1966 there was a very big change when Tim invited a group of ashramites under the tutelage of Bill Haines, a self-proclaimed guru, to move into Millbrook because they were being ousted from a traditional Hindu ashram for their use of psychedelics. Overnight, we were suddenly confronted with integrating approximately thirty new personalities into our living situation. The energy and delicate focus that we were tentatively grounding was essentially obliterated. How typical of Tim to up-end the status quo! Now we came to the shadow side of the group process. Bill and Tim never could see eye to eye and when they took LSD together. Their sessions became a battle of personalities and ego clashing. The League and ashram factions never resolved their differences and we had a major personality dysfunction at the top. Bill's group moved into a different building and we became two very separate entities. I didn't buy it and maintained my relationship with both groups. At times, Tim would comment that I wasn't being loyal to him.

Meanwhile, my personal journey was blossoming as a result of my sessions in the meditation house. I experienced the property as a sacred place where I had been given the gift and golden opportunity to travel inward and rediscover that I have an immortal soul which is the very essence of who I really am. It was a joyous revelation for me when I experienced myself fully conscious, out of my physical body, moving through space, traveling as a subtle body through many dimensions, as a conscious point of light. In retrospect, I am amazed that I had no fear and no remembrance of my planet earth identification. I had a sense of comfortable familiarity. Whenever I was confronted with confusion and/or very intense electrical energy fields, my guidance would appear in the form of small bright lights. During one journey, I found myself in a capsule with extraterrestrial energies that communicated with me telepathically and brought me to where I could continue on my own. I was always protected and cared for.

During 1967, Tim announced that he would not be focusing as much at Millbrook because he felt called to go public with his advocacy of psychedelics. This took the form of lectures at universities throughout the U.S. and long sojourns in California with the Brotherhood of Eternal Love. My heart sank, as I knew that by drawing public attention to our experiments at Millbrook, it would be the beginning of the end. It was. In December 1967, we were busted (for the second time.)

It was a usual, somewhat early, Saturday morning. I was in a tower room on the third floor with friends hanging out, talking about tantric yoga. Something caught my attention outside. I stood up and looked down to the driveway below filled with police cars. Immediately we heard thundering footsteps throughout the house. I heard someone yelling to get up as we were being raided. I ran to the stairs to find my children and bumped into an officer who instructed me to go to the dining room where I joined my kids and the rest of our tribe. Tim and Rosemary were in California with the Brotherhood. Bill Haines, true to form, was taking a bellowing leading role. We were busted and it was really the end of our community! I felt strong and deeply sad.

We were subpoenaed to appear before the Grand Jury in Poughkeepsie. Most of the community members left when it turned out that the subpoenas were invalid. I chose to stay because I wanted to remain dedicated to my belief that our conscious use of LSD as a sacrament was our spiritual god given right. Naïve? Probably. I have never regretted that I made that choice to stand up for my convictions. I refused to answer any of the Grand Jury questions and, as a result, I spent two months in jail on a contempt of court charge. After I was released, I returned to Millbrook. My children and I were allowed to stay on the property until they completed the school year. When we left the property the police escorted us to the highway. I thought that was a little over the top!

Tim and Rosemary stayed on the West Coast and I never had any further contact with him. I have always felt grateful to Tim for making my two years at Millbrook possible. Being able to have those two years was the beginning of my new life with profound spiritual understanding – a wonderful gift!

RM   During the summer of 1966 an expanded group of artists and musicians gathered around Tim and Rosemary at Millbrook, experimenting with greatly expanded forms of the psychedelic talk, music and light-show celebrations that had been presented in New York the previous year. Now, a narrative element was added: The first production was called "Death of the Mind," based on the Magic Theatre sequence from Hermann Hesse's novel *Steppenwolf*. I played the role of Harry Haller, the neurotic intellectual trapped in his mind; Rosemary played Hermione, the enigmatic beauty who leads HH into the Magic Theatre, and Tim played Pablo, the magician, who gives HH the drug which initiates him into other realities. In this way, the sequence demonstrated the role of the guide in a programmed psychedelic session: Tim would intone passages from the *Tibetan Book of the Dead* manual to help HH, the voyager, get over his fears and confusion. Live musicians accompanied Tim, sitting on stage; while light artists with slide projectors and special effects devices projected an ever-changing panorama of psychedelic imagery.

Tim and Rosemary, late 1960s

GB   What was your involvement with these productions, Ralph?

RM   I was living in New York City by then, visiting Millbrook on weekends, collaborating with the visual artists, but not directly involved in the production. Rosemary's and my spoken parts were pre-recorded and heard by the audience while multi-colored imagery was swirling on-screen. My character, who was on a bad trip, would scream in fear, "Help! I'm drowning," giving Tim-Pablo, as the Guide, the cue to offer reassurance and philosophic counsel. Rosemary's sensuous voice whispered some of the psychedelic prayers that Tim had adapted from the *Tao Te Ching*. The first show attracted crowds and sold out for six weeks, generating considerable press coverage. The idea was to produce other multi media re-enactments of great religious myths, using the new light-technologies.

GB   Were any other myths given a psychedelic re-enactment?

RM   Well, the second show produced was called "The Resurrection of Jesus Christ," a theme with which I was never comfortable. It led to Tim Leary's name on the marquee, with the title "Resurrection of Jesus Christ" beneath it. It seemed almost blasphemous. Jesus was a character wandering around New York on a bad guilt tip, and Tim the guide joked and kidded him out of his martyrdom. It ended in a fiasco, after the first and only performance, when the young man chosen to play the role of JC, confessed that he had been set up as a police informant and fled.

GB   What about the Buddha show that you produced?

RM   Yes, after that, in a meeting with the theatre producer and Billy Hitchcock, who was financing these shows, Tim vigorously and generously supported my proposal to put on a production based on the "Illumination of the Buddha." I had been studying the Buddha's life-story and enlightenment experience and discussing various techniques of visual presentation with a film-makers cooperative on the Lower East Side, called The Third World. Their main leader was Bob Lowe, an experienced cinematographer who taught in Columbia University's film department. Another member of the group was Gray Henry, a blonde Southern belle from Kentucky, a very gifted artist, who had studied religion and philosophy with Joseph Campbell at Sarah Lawrence. She and I had worked together on the Leary Defense Fund and were now collaborating on this Buddha production. We became romantically involved as well, though I eventually lost her to a Venezuelan man, whom she married, with whom she converted to Islam and moved to Egypt and Saudi Arabia, raising two children and studying Sufism.

The film cooperative and I spent at least a month in intensive preparation for this show based on the enlightenment experience of the Buddha. We had collected hundreds, if not thousands of slides: Indian and Tibetan art, many of them from Allen Atwell; plants, flowers and trees; faces of live human beings as well as sculpted heads and masks; cosmic, stellar, galactic imagery, and others. Steve Ashton and I each had a pair of projectors with a dissolve unit and four sequences of images were all projected on the same screen dissolving in and out of each other in constantly changing combinations, accompanied by music and spoken word text. Compared with many psychedelic "light-shows" that I've seen both before and afterwards, these sequences had much more mythic and archetypal content – rather than just abstract color patterns, which are after all, only a minor part of a classic psychedelic journey. The scene of the Buddha's sexual temptation was filmed as a scantily clad female dancer moved in front of a silhouette screen. The attacks of Mara, the Lord of Death, involved demonic faces and masks of horror. At the climax, when the visionary imagery merged into cosmic-galactic realms, and to suggest the story of how weapons hurled at Buddha were turned harmlessly into flowers, Gray Henry and her assistants rushed down the aisles in the balcony and threw arms full of flower blossoms on to the audience below.

The show was such a theatrical success that a group of us, including Tim and Rosemary and several of the light-artists from the Third World Film cooperative, decided to take it across the country, during the winter of 1966/67. We did one performance in Chicago; then one in San Francisco where it garnered a scathing review from noted jazz critic Ralph Gleason; and finally one in the Santa Monica Civic Auditorium, where the entire audience seemed to be high on LSD, due no doubt to Owsley liberally passing out his "white lightning" tabs. A film crew from UPI studios, with Hank Saperstein as producer, filmed the Santa Monica show, mostly the talk by Leary and his musicians. But the slide sequences needed to be transferred to film in the studio; so Bob Lowe, Steve Ashton and I spent a month in a Hollywood studio, cloistered with our imagery machines. We also integrated the *Steppenwolf* story into the film, so it was like Harry Haller takes LSD, and then relives the enlightenment of the Buddha. We filmed a scene in a café on Sunset Boulevard, in which Harry Haller (played by me) meets Hermione (played by Rosemary) and falls in love with her. Then he goes on a bad trip and strangles her, which was filmed in silhouette, and Leary, as the trip guide, shows and tells the Illumination story of the Buddha. The resulting film – *Turn On, Tune In, Drop Out* – was released in 1967, but only shown publicly for about one week. Just around that time, possession and use of LSD and other psychedelics was being criminalized, and the studio withdrew the film from distribution – no doubt thinking, or being persuaded, that a film whose main character was advocating what had just become an illegal act, was not in their best interests to distribute.

I came from a family in Louisville, Kentucky, with a history of deep involvement in religion and spirituality. This ultimately led to my studying these subjects at Sarah Lawrence (class of 1965), where I took Joseph Campbell's classes in mythology and talked with him while doing my paper on the Hindu subject of Shakti-Shakta. Courses in primitive religion interested me in the Huichol Indians and their peyote religion. Since I was young, I have been interested in mysticism and later also in metaphysics, which complemented my studies in art history. I was also taking extra classes in New York City at the New School for Social Research. There I signed up for a course taught by Jean Houston entitled "The Varieties of Psychedelic Experience." I attended Jean's wedding to Bob Masters and subsequently was invited to take LSD under their supervision, with the provision that I write it up for inclusion in the book they were writing. This I did the day after I graduated from college.

In late 1965, I went to a party across the street from where I lived behind the Frick Museum in New York City. My friend Carol led me into a basement apartment inhabited by a man called Van Wolff. The walls and ceilings of his place were painted entirely with what looked like one's inner organs, by a famous psychedelic painter of the day, Allen Atwell. It was here that I met Ralph Metzner, while I was sitting on the floor next to Miriam Makeba and Peter Fonda. This encounter with Ralph led to our studio, The Third World, helping to produce the Castalia Foundation's psychedelic theatre presentation – "The Illumination of the Buddha."

Let me tell you what the experience was for people who came to this show at the Village Theatre on Second Avenue. As everyone entered the theatre lobby, there before them was a giant Buddha figure painted gold, which we had laboriously made from mylar at the Third World studio on East Second Street. As the show began, Timothy Leary and Allen Ginsberg were sitting on the left side of the stage, dressed in loose white pants and Indian shirts with strings of beads. Allen was playing a small harmonium and, as the lights dimmed, Tim said in a hushed voice, "Tonight we will travel together into the consciousness of Gautama and experience the process of enlightenment" (or something like that).

We had stretched across the entire stage a very thin silk cloth screen, which would serve symbolically as Buddha's mind. First, in silhouette, we were treated to the Buddha's life-changing encounters with an old man, a sick man, and a dead man. With his decision to sit beneath the bodhi tree until he reached enlightenment, Bali

Gray Henry in Third World Studio preparing masks for the film, 1966

Ram, the young Indian dancer who played the part of Gautama, was seated at the center of the stage behind the filmy screen. We projected a moving colored protective aura from behind. At first, he is tempted to give up his quest by an alluring, sensual, naked woman. At the studio we had a dancer wearing only jewels filmed in three ways and in three colors. These were then mixed together, her large, inviting eyes and mouth in blue placed over her full body lit with green, while hands and arms of yellow beckoned the young lord from his spot. But, the aura burned brightly and the Buddha was impervious to the temptations of the flesh. Next, we had live male dancers dressed in terrifying Balinese-like masks (made of mylar) with long tusks, attack Gautama in an effort to terrify him but to no avail. Even tarantulas we had filmed at the Museum of Natural History had no effect as they came crawling down the screen to the sound of Tibetan thigh-bone horns.

At this point, the Buddha commences his journey through the mind. Ralph and Steve Ashton projected multiple sequences of slides simultaneously over the entire screen. At first, these were of microscopic organisms, which then dissolved into various insects, and the chirping of thousands of crickets and cicadas could be heard everywhere. Soon the entire screen was covered with images of every animal on Earth blending into one another. In the background, the roar of lions and the trumpeting of elephants competed with the soft traveling music of the sitar and tabla. This vision was replaced by multiple images of men, women, and children from throughout all the countries of the world—their national distinctions blurring into one another. At last, footage of stars and galaxies from planetary observatories dominated the screen as the mind of the Buddha opened inward and outward to the celestial cosmic realms. At the climactic point, a bright strobe light flashed over the audience and, as paper rose petals together with gold and blue glitter fell over the audience, and the following words were heard: "Oh wonder of wonders, all beings are the Buddha!" These are said to be the first words uttered by the Buddha after attaining enlightenment.

Later, there were further psychedelic productions in which our studio got involved. "The Third World" was directed by Professor Bob Lowe, who was teaching graduate students film direction at Columbia and had set up this studio and film school on the Lower East Side. Bob was really my first Teacher. He'd read in all the great spiritual traditions and had studied Sanskrit. Bob taught us that everything we appeared to be doing — like making films or any other form of engagement — was really a front for spiritual transformation. I have tried to keep this in mind every day of my life. At the time we set up the studio, disciples of several Indian spiritual teachers, such as Bhaktivedanta, of the Hare Krishna movement, and Ramana Maharshi, were setting up centers in the area, which we would visit. Maharshi's picture hung at the studio, and we had all read his book of "conversations." He, in fact, represented the state of being we all wished to achieve in this lifetime.

A "be-in" was held on Easter in Central Park. All of the artisans in our area went uptown to celebrate. A few of us donned Indian feathers. There was music. People flew kites. This event was broadcast nationwide, and these celebrants were called by the media, "hippies." It wasn't long before youth from all other parts of America began to pour into New York, dressed the way we were on that Sunday. They began taking psychedelic drugs, and "head shops" sprang up everywhere to accommodate the "look." The art that arose was an attempt to simulate the experience of psychedelic expanded consciousness. Andy Warhol opened up his operation on 8th Street/St. Marks Place — which boasted of the Electric Circus. Inside, tent material was stretched to simulate sinews and, upon this psychedelic light shows were projected. People ate dishes of brown rice with vegetable, miso and sometimes, shrimp. Macrobiotic cooking was in. In what seemed like an instant, what had begun as an effort by intellectuals deeply concerned with the nature of the mind and with finding ways to experience ultimate reality or God, became a popular movement based on love and flower power. It was actually very innocent, though in time, of course, the drug aspect took its toll.

Our studio, which basically made straightforward documentaries, was suddenly asked to do a light show for Janis Joplin at the Cheetah on Broadway. By this time, one could actually buy DayGlo dresses and shoes at Saks Fifth Avenue which looked wonderful in the black light. My father came up from Louisville and, after an evening watching his daughter work at the Cheetah, was very disheartened. Soon, a company called Sandpiper Films visited The Third World and proposed that we write and produce a film of our own choosing, which they would be willing to finance. We decided to do a take-off on the hippies versus the Establishment theme. The hippies would be represented by Indians, whose clothing and teepees would be in day-glo colors. The cowboys, who represented our parents, would be pixilated – for example, we sprayed the boulders in a valley with gold paint and, as these cowboys mechanically moved toward these large stones to embrace them they too turned to gold. The film was shot up at Millbrook and began in the Big House where Timothy Leary lived. I was in charge of makeup and, for the scene with Tim in a dream state, I created a special mask out of dental impression cream that had little hands sticking out of everywhere. Charlie Mingus played the Cisco Kid, and he drove a buckboard painted in chartreuse and lime green. The entire cast and crew lived in the forest in a teepee village, also painted with psychedelic patterns and colors. I cannot tell you how difficult it was to find eighteen small straight trees to be used as the poles for each teepee, and to prepare them by stripping off all the branches. We, of course, slept on deerskins. It was a relief to be out of New York City and to sit in the evening and watch the sun set. In order to do the DayGlo makeup, I studied with Rod Steiger's makeup artist and also, with the Ringling Brothers' people for the horses. Imagine powdering a small herd of horses, in the early dawn, with different color pigments. Appearing in the mist of early morning were actors, dressed in giant Kachina doll costumes we had manufactured with the help of Dalton schoolchildren, riding upon these steeds, holding up torches, and chanting the sacred syllable "OM." Of course, Lord Krishna was included. I had to be very careful with his bright blue body makeup because, at this time, certain models had nearly died from full body makeup. In any case, this was quite something to behold!

As this film production ended, The Third World studio had come to an end. Most of us on the crew felt we could not return to the Lower East Side, the dirty pavements, and the Bowery bums. Some moved to California, including Bob Lowe, who became a healer. Some went to Chicago to join the protests against the Vietnam War in 1968. My new Venezuelan husband, Fyodor, and I boarded a Yugoslavian freighter headed for North Africa with Cairo as our final destination. He had read a great deal about the living saints of North Africa, and we thought we needed to check that out. After all, all we had ever wanted, from the beginning, was sanctification and to somehow reach that state of divine presence which we could see in the eyes of Ramana Maharshi.

Dr. Richard Alpert – aka Baba Ram Dass, 1973

Part 5

Concluding Reflections

Dr. Ralph Metzner, 1979

GB At the end of the Millbrook scene you each went your separate ways, dropped psychedelics and went on with your spiritual journey. Do you have any final comments on the Millbrook experiments on transcending personality and your interactions with Tim Leary?

RD We all had our own personality stuff – we didn't get rid of that with all those experiments. We made do, for who we were.

RM I agree, we didn't get rid of personality patterns. But I do feel we all changed. I certainly did. I learned new ways of relating to others, gained new self-understanding. You want to have a personality that is true to your essence.

RD I felt the bumping of personality with Tim. Because of his personality, he had this thing about reacting to authority. I used to think, that's the Irish in him. But the way he did it, was much too paranoid. "They're out to get him."

RM I didn't pick up the paranoia; I picked up on provocative. Like the slogan – turn on, tune in, drop out. You and I knew what he meant, and in his writings he'd spell it out. It meant drop out of your commitment, your ideological commitment to the social consensus reality, and tune in to deeper reality. It didn't necessarily mean to go live in the woods or something and take drugs all the time. But he would let that ambiguity ride or even exploit it for the sake of stirring things up, or to jolt people out of old ways of thinking, it seems to me. I remember I had one turning point conversation with him, in the later post-Millbrook phase, in California: I said I thought we should add a fourth phrase to the slogan, so it would be: turn on, tune in, drop out and come back. He looked at me like I was crazed. He said, "Well, that's your trip," with this condescending smile. I thought, but the other one is your trip. But they are a little different.

RD There we have it.

Tim, San Luis Obisbo, CA 1973

GB   With regard to Leary's paranoia – is it paranoid if it's true? Tim was the focal point of a lot of projection by the culture. They did "have it in" for him. They wanted to bust him. He was called "the most dangerous man in America" by President Nixon.

RM   Did you feel his attitude was dangerous?

RD   Dangerous? No. But it was something we had to deal with.

RM   But you didn't like the way he dealt with it or rather you felt the way he dealt with it was dangerous.

RD   Yes, yes! Because he was aggressive toward them. We were concerned he would push public opinion against psychedelics.

RM   He had that sharp, mocking wit and he would use it. And more so, the more he got embroiled in various difficulties with law enforcement. I don't agree with Nixon and others that he was a danger to the culture or to young people in general. I felt he was dangerous for himself, his family and friends who were around him. I was scared to be around him during this later more public and political phase of his life. I felt myself withdrawing from being too close to him. I was very frightened by his numerous arrests and imprisonments. I was involved in the first trial, for the Laredo pot bust as a defense witness and I worked on the media education part of the Leary Defense Fund.

I had what seemed like a very narrow escape, later in 1968, at Christmas time. I and my girlfriend Rebekah were visiting Tim and Rosemary, when they were living on the ranch of the Brotherhood of Eternal Love, in the mountains near Idyllwild. Rebekah and I were going to go back down to Laguna Beach; Tim. Rosemary and his son Jack were also going to go back down to Laguna Beach where The Brotherhood had their main public center, the Mystic Arts Bookstore. We originally planned to go down together but my girlfriend got sick and we left early. That was the time Tim got busted in Orange County, when the cops planted some roaches in his car, and he was handed another ten year sentence on top of several other charges he already had against him. The possibility of going to jail really, really bothered me; much more than it apparently bothered him. I think I'm a more cautious personality. Albert Hofmann has said he thought Tim was reckless in regard to his own person and I would agree with that.

GB   What about the popular perception that Timothy Leary became brain damaged from taking too many drugs?

RM   I don't know many people thought that.

GB   It was a common perception, reinforced by some of the media coverage.

RM   I don't believe he was brain-damaged at all, having seen him in later stages of his life, after hundreds if not thousands of trips. But his recklessness would sometimes extend to taking drugs unwisely, for example while giving a lecture, or trying to. His own theory of set and setting should have told him otherwise. I remember one time (probably in 1968 or '69), I went to hear him talk at the University of Syracuse. He'd taken LSD before the lecture; he was on the stage with Rosemary and he was completely out of it, incapable of saying anything. He was on a bad trip, where you feel paralyzed, can't think, can't talk. He basically just handed it over to the audience. He kept looking at Rosemary for assurance. He described his latest horror trip vision, which was that we were all rats in an experiment, programmed to run in a maze with no way out. Then, he would stop and grin. There were some two thousand people there, mostly college students. He invited people from the audience to come up and say something, anything. People would come up to the mike and rant and rave. A rock group from New York, who called themselves the Motherfuckers, came up on stage and rocked and screamed. It was horrendous. I felt shame and embarrassment for him. It was such a contrast with the early days where he could be the silver-tongued orator who had audiences spell-bound.

RD   He was always seeing how far we could push things. If you could do that with it, maybe you could do this.

RM   Which was a bit of a departure from the social science research idea, the original model for using psychedelics during the Harvard days. Or from the spiritual or religious model espoused by people like Aldous Huxley, Huston Smith, Alan Watts, and ourselves during the days of the *Tibetan Book of the Dead*, the Zihuatanejo program, and the early years at Millbrook. Basically, psychedelics were used in a retreat format: You withdrew from the world for a certain length of time (a day, a week, a month) to devote yourself to inner explorations. I think Tim always agreed with that idea: To get the optimum psychedelic experience, you have to carefully consider the set and the setting. The performance at Syracuse was, I think, an aberration. I'm sure he regretted it. It's almost an addictive pattern: using the same means to alter consciousness too often or inappropriately in relation to the place you are, emphasizing the tool over the process. I think many people in the psychedelic drug "movement," to judge by some of the internet self-reports, seem to be in that same place. They seem to think that just taking a drug is in itself a spiritual practice. And it isn't.

RD   I don't know that it isn't. We very rarely ritualized it to make it a sacrament.

RM   Yes, but isn't that the point? It has to taken with that kind of intention and preparation. The way the shamans in the Amazon do with ayahuasca and the Native American Church folks do with peyote. And just taking the pill without that preparation and intention doesn't do that. The Charles Manson story really brought that point home to me. Here he was, taking LSD and using it to brainwash his followers to be sex slaves and killers. That really brought home the truth of the set and setting principle. After my ten-year experience in the Agni Yoga meditation school, I always have integrated psychedelics with spiritual energy-work. I wouldn't want to do it any other way. And I suspect that you, Ram Dass, wouldn't ever take them either except with a sacramental attitude. But at the time of course, none of us knew any better. We just winged it as best we could, with the limited knowledge and experience at our disposal.

GB   So you think it's a mistake to try to do ordinary functioning activities on psychedelics, such as giving a lecture?

RM   For me, it would be a mistake. I once found myself, inadvertently, having to give a lecture while a low dose of LSD from the night before had not yet dissipated. I was anxious and uncomfortable, though people told me that from outside I appeared and spoke quite normally. On the other hand, I know if an emergency required it, I could function normally. The issue of control versus non-control, or the feeling of not being in control is the big one for most people. A friend of mine, Stephen Foster, an English professor at San Francisco State, in the 1960s, told me he used to take a moderately high dose of LSD and then drive his car around town. I was astonished and asked him why on Earth would you do that? Why didn't you sit down somewhere and enjoy the experience? He said, "I had to prove to myself that I could control it that way."

The West Coast Acid Tests and Ken Kesey

GB   Ram Dass, you said you had some early connections with the West coast culture?

RD   Well, Kesey and I were at Stanford together, and Vic Lovell and all those folks.

GB   Would this have been in the late 1950s, early 1960s?

RD   Yes, I was known as the hip therapist. And Vic Lovell turned me onto pot and I had heard of peyote. Then later, when I was still doing the Math Program at Stanford, I would go to the acid tests. They were wild. I hung out with the Grateful Dead.

GB   What were your impressions of that scene?

RD   It was out of control. Everybody sort of jacked up. I went to a party at Kesey's, a party with the Pranksters and Hell's Angels and it just got way out of control – confrontations, and a lot of crying, gang sex.

GB   Ram Dass, how would you compare the West Coast scene at that time with your previous knowledge of communities centered around the use of psychedelics? You had been at Millbrook; you had known other communities in Newton Center and in Zihuatanejo.

RD   We were serious and they weren't.

GB   OK, say more.

RD   We had desks and offices, (Laugh) and they had the acid tests. I went to the acid tests and they were everybody just being caught up in ecstasy.

GB   Did you feel okay with that scene? Were you grooving with it?

Ginsberg and Leary, 1967

RD   Yeah. Tim didn't, I don't think. But I liked the Grateful Dead. Owsley had already made a lot of good acid, and he was the sound engineer for the Dead. He and his crew would put huge speakers up; he liked doing that and I liked being part of it. They were all younger than I was and I liked that, too, because I would always get enlivened by their shenanigans. I'd met Ken Kesey when I was a faculty member at Stanford, so it goes back that far.

GB   You said that when you were with Kesey and the West Coast scene that you thought they were on to something, doing something right and you approved of it. And yet, you said also that you were disillusioned with the psychedelic scene in general. Could you expand on that?

RD   There were so many egos. So many egos like Tim and Owsley and all these different egos would come out of the woodwork because of LSD. And if they recommended LSD, it was not something I wanted, you know.

GB   So you didn't see the leaders of the movement as people to emulate, or having wisdom, spiritual wisdom? You felt there was a lack of depth in their understanding?

RD   Yes. And in my own understanding. They were much deeper than I thought at the time. My interpretations were very, very shallow.

GB   Ralph, could you comment on the Merry Pranksters and the acid tests?

RM   After attending several of these acid tests and dances in San Francisco where Owsley was passing out his little pills with 300 to 500 micrograms, and getting totally blasted – plastered against the wall, so to speak, I stopped taking LSD around that year. I was feeling physically run down and emotionally drained and didn't yet know how to restore my energies. So it was just not a good experience for me to continue taking these drugs. I needed something to balance and restore my energies and started looking into Reichian bioenergetics and similar practices. I later found my way to the Agni Yoga methods taught by Russell Schofield.

RD   With Kesey and the Kool-Aid acid tests, it was very loose, no controls at all. You could see lots of people freaking out and lots of people having good trips. It's funny because at first I thought Tim was turning the culture against psychedelics by his irresponsibilities. And then later I thought Ken Kesey was going to do it.

RM   I remember being astonished at these scenes with thousands of people all taking acid, in high doses too, and the rock bands playing, The Grateful Dead, Big Brother and the Holding Company with Janis Joplin, The Jefferson Airplane, and people dancing. My prior experience, in the small group work we had done, would have led me to believe this was madness. But, after my initial shock and judgment wore off, I could see it wasn't that bad: there were people sometimes hunkering on the floor, clearly out of it, but then others would take care of them. I never saw any violence or obnoxious aggressive behavior at these events, as you might see at a similar gathering with alcohol. I think the music and dancing helped to hold it together, functioned as a kind of safe container.

Leary and the Prohibition of LSD Research

GB   What's your view of the opinion among many medical-psychiatric researchers that Tim was responsible, through his irresponsible attitude and statements, for psychedelic research being stopped?

RM   Yes, I've had a public disagreement with my friend Myron Stolaroff about this point – although I think now we no longer disagree. He was working with the Menlo Park creativity research project and they were told their license for psychedelic research would not be renewed because of Tim Leary. In one of his letters to me in India, Tim told about a meeting with Myron and the group, in which they asked him to tone down his rhetoric. I'm sure that's true – that the FDA used Tim's behavior as a rationale for their denial. But whether they would have permitted research on psychedelics to continue if Tim hadn't been so public in his enthusiasm is another question. After all, his influence has long been officially denigrated, and he's long gone, and the amount of officially sponsored research is pathetically small compared to what it was in the 1960s.

There were six alcoholism treatment programs with LSD in North America in the late 1960s! I think it was the spread of the drug into the general public, out of the control of the medical-psychiatric establishment, which freaked them out. Our group was not responsible for that, especially since the IFIF project never really took off. If you're going to blame anyone for the spread to the masses, it would be more the Kesey group and the electric Kool-Aid acid tests. In any event, there's no need to blame anyone – it was a complex kind of cultural revolution, a revolution in collective consciousness, with many different factors playing into it, that had its own momentum, and with long-term effects that we're still pondering. Our approach was always small groups of people, like twelve or so at a time. The set and setting was psychological, spiritual, and creative. The purpose was personality change and transformation, though not necessarily exclusively as an adjunct to psychotherapy as in the psycholytic model.

RD   We were contacting the psychiatrists with a new model, a new approach.

RM   Yes, and they wanted to control it their way, within the psychiatric mental health model that was current at the time, which was very biological, just like now: A disease model where you find a drug that will knock out the disease. Psychedelic substances don't fit that model very well, although people did try. I used to go to these talks at colleges where they'd put me on a program with Sidney Cohen, the psychiatric expert who had given LSD to Cary Grant and Henry Luce and several other Hollywood celebrities in the 1950s. I would be featured as being for these drugs and he'd be the cautious expert worrying and warning about dangers and so forth. And I felt that was a false dichotomy right there. I was not a drug advocate. I said these are things we've discovered, here are methods that can be used. I wasn't saying everybody or anybody should do it. I was saying think for yourself, look for yourself, become informed. I felt as if I was trapped into this duality. Very strange polarizing. But that's the way the system goes: Action and reaction. And whether things would have been any different if Tim had been more circumspect, who knows? Somehow, I don't think so.

GB   Ram Dass, you also had interactions with Sidney Cohen. In fact, didn't you write a book with him, called *LSD* (published 1966) and how did that come about?

RD   There was a photographer named Larry Schiller, who had pictures of LSD trips and he wanted to do a book with his pictures. He set it up it so that Sidney Cohen was the good guy and I was the bad guy. I was the junior bad guy, because Tim wouldn't do it, but I agreed. We worked at Larry Schiller's place in Hollywood and we each selected and commented on the pictures. The pictures Sidney selected were mostly negative pictures, people cowering or writhing. And I commented that they were negative. The one picture we both selected was of a guy on a trip, lying on the floor, looking at a spilled coke bottle. Sidney took that as an example of how people under LSD were doing nothing important with their time. And I said, maybe he was contemplating the infinite in the mundane – so I liked that picture.

GB   Do you see any parallels between the way LSD prohibition came about and the campaign against MDMA in the 1980s?

RM   Yes, the sequence of events was echoed almost exactly twenty years later with MDMA. At first it was a tool for psychotherapists doing accelerated, intensified psychotherapy. Then, many people wanted the experience and didn't want to become somebody's patient to get it. So, entrepreneurs appeared and manufactured it; they saw a need and met it. It became widely and inexpensively available, started to be used at dances, raves. Then the authorities crack down. Not because people were harmed or alarmed but because the authorities were alarmed. The dangers are exaggerated or even fabricated. The retractions of misleading research are ignored. The drug war and prohibition control mentality take over. The people that are dancing at raves or at the sixties' acid tests aren't necessarily getting therapeutic or spiritual insight – that's not their set and their setting. But if they're not hurting anyone or themselves, I don't knock it. So what's wrong with that, what's wrong with dancing?

RD   That's a good title: "What's Wrong with Dancing."

RM   They may not be thinking deep thoughts, but what the heck? What business is it of the government?

GB   Did you feel you were advancing psychology and science?

RD   I didn't feel that. Although at Harvard before we became infamous, we were developing new methods in psychology.

RM   I definitely thought that we were contributing to psychology and science, especially in the early days; really searching for new approaches, expanded perspectives and theories. I always identified with the role of the explorer and I think Tim did too.

RD   Explorers, yes, I identify with that role.

RM   And inventors too, inventing new forms of research, new forms of therapy, new forms of enhancing creativity, new forms of spiritual practice, new cultural forms. These were tools that could be helpful to the culture. And then at Millbrook, experimenting with new social forms and new ways of being together. This was parallel to and happened at the same time as the human potential movement that flourished in places like Esalen in California. A great deal of that movement was inspired by psychedelic experiences.

The Role of Psychedelics in the Cultural Revolutions of the Sixties

RM   Looking at it from a larger point of view, I would say the mission of our project at Harvard and Millbrook was to find a way to introduce these tools into the middle class professions – the psychological, medical, religious, artistic, innovative practitioners of the culture; to try to find some way to make maximum effective use of these tools. That was kind of our assignment. And, I'd say, Tim realized pretty soon that those old models were going to be insufficient, that the whole thing was going to have to expand beyond them. Not that he was opposed to research; at Harvard, he worked within that model, we all did. And, he wasn't opposed to other people doing research afterwards.

RD   I think Tim tuned into a cultural malaise and he showed the way the culture was moving. And that malaise led to the 1960's.

RM   Yes, I completely agree. There was a malaise motivating all the various movements of cultural transformation, the "counterculture" (to use Ted Roszak's phrase) of the 1960s. The environmental movement, the women's liberation movement, the anti-war, the civil rights, the sexual liberation, the new artistic styles, that all took off during the 1960s.

RD   And they all seemed to have psychedelics in them.

RM   Well, they had that quality of consciousness expansion, even if only a very small number of the people involved in these movements knew about the drugs. Rachel Carson's book, *Silent Spring,* that's considered the beginning of the American environmental movement, was published in 1963. She was saying the birds are not singing anymore, due to the kind of chemicals we've been pouring into our air and water. That's an expansion of awareness, becoming more conscious, noticing what you didn't notice before. And then you think, no, I don't want to be doing this. So that leads to taking responsibility, to making changes.

RD   People being more compassionate, more conscious, more loving.

RM   And so while we were carrying out that assignment, infiltrating psychedelics into the professional middle class, mostly on the East Coast, unbeknownst to us, Ken Kesey and his friends on the West Coast, were following a totally different assignment, which apparently was to get as many people turned on as possible, by whatever means possible. It's not that one way was better; it was like the assignment was different. I don't know to what extent consciousness expansion, in the psychological and spiritual fields, was his philosophy or not. It seems this is a school of thought that says – bring these heightened energies of psychedelics into artistic expression. It's not so much educational, psychological or spiritual in its orientation; although I don't want to make any value judgments here.

RD   Comparing the creative model or the educational and spiritual growth approach, I find the creative one has an awful lot of ego connected with it. Because, it's *I'm* doing the creative expression.

RM   The Prankster's motto, which they wrote on their famous cross-country bus, was FURTHER. Just go further, more far out. The creative one is definitely more fun. It's more fun oriented.

RD   Then you're identifying with your creations,

RM   I know what you mean: you identify with your creations and with the creative process itself. There's an idealizing of the creative process. There is perhaps less interest in helping to bring about change in your fellow human beings. I'm just going to do this thing. It's what I think is a cool thing to do. And I don't care if you like it or not. I'll find some friends to do it with me, and we'll have fun in the process of doing it. Kesey's novels are awesome: *One Flew over the Cuckoo's Nest* – celebrating that drive for freedom, liberation from the system. In that way, Leary and Kesey were very much alike.

GB   Sounds like the Burning Man philosophy. A community with creativity based on psychedelics. It seems a good model of responsibility. There's recycling, everything is burned or removed.

RM   Burning Man is like a further evolution of the acid test model. You take responsibility for your well-being, your house, and the environment, things like that.

Leary, Psychedelics, Spirituality and Religion

GB   What about Tim's attitude towards religion and spirituality?

RM   Early on, while still at Harvard, Tim recognized the spiritual-religious dimensions of psychedelic experience. He wrote a key essay on "The Religious Experience – Its Production and Interpretation." He supported the Good Friday study; he adapted the *Tibetan Book of the Dead*, and the *Tao Te Ching*. On the other hand, he seemed to despise Catholicism, no doubt due to his upbringing by two devout Catholic women, his mother and his aunt. And he didn't much care for the Indian guru trip, and poked fun at Ram Dass for becoming one.

His attitude toward religion as a form of social organization was that we should use it, for our own purposes. That's why he incorporated The League for Spiritual Discovery as a church, I think in 1966, while at Millbrook, after the bust in Laredo. There were several small groups using psychedelics in those days that incorporated themselves as churches, to provide themselves with a kind of legal umbrella, emulating the Native American Church. He wrote a little booklet about it how to do it: *Start Your Own Religion*. His attitude was, if we have to have a religious organization to get state protection, then start your own religion. I didn't think it was going to fly; plus I thought the acronym was too obvious, too provocative. But he didn't seem to really care about that. It was still the influence of game theory: okay, let's play the religion game in society. And whether people were going to take him seriously or not, he really didn't care.

Much later, after his release from Folsom, for a brief time he was talking of running for governor of California. I don't think he ever gathered any real support but he got John Lennon to write his campaign song: "Come Together." I met him and said, "Tim this could be wonderful, you should really do it, people look to you for inspiration and positive change." He wouldn't have any of it: He said, "Don't be silly, I'm not interested in being serious. We just want to have a party. Come and join our party." I suppose his endless legal and prison hassles had taken away any enthusiasm for serious political work.

GB   Ram Dass, you worked for Tim in his campaign for governor? What did you think of that at the time?

RD   That's what Tim wanted.

GB   Did you take it seriously?

RD   No, no. I sort of did.

RM   You made public statements on behalf of it?

RD   No, I was handling the money and such.

RM: You were fund raising for him?

RD   Yes.

RM   For Tim, it seems it was always about having fun and promoting pleasure, at least in the later years. In his autobiography he said that he went and talked to Marshall McLuhan, the Canadian media philosopher, when LSD was starting to explode in the media. McLuhan advised him

Tim Leary, 1967, Summer of Love

that if you're going to be an advocate for this new approach, you have to be unrelentingly positive and smiling whenever you talk with the media. I think Tim took that to heart and practiced it, flashing that smile even when he didn't feel it, when he was tired and would probably rather have gone and lived somewhere privately. So he put on a good act. Even when he was dying – he was determined to program a good dying experience for himself. But I think in his heart of hearts, he really was devoted to the process of consciousness expansion and encouraging people to take responsibility for their own brain functions and consciousness, regardless of drugs or no drugs, and regardless of the formal belief system that you adhere to.

RD   Yes he was.

RM   Tim was a true seeker. He continued to develop models and theories of consciousness evolution right up to his dying days. When imprisoned, he read science voraciously and wrote several books with pencils on paper. Many people, like Robert Anton Wilson, think very highly of his theory of the eight circuits of the brain. I think it definitely deserves to be taken seriously, as an attempt to formulate a theory of the evolution of consciousness. He called himself a cheerleader for the evolution of human consciousness. But he also intellectually got into space migration, virtual reality and similar high-tech speculations, which is a direction that left me completely cold. It seems he had this fanatical idealization of technology. I was totally uninterested in space migration. I love Earth and want to do all I can to preserve it. He seemed attached to the idea, almost obsessed, that technology was going to solve our problems, overlooking the fact that the misuse of technology has gotten us into many of these problems. But then he was also quite capable of moving on as he did with the cryonics folks about freezing his brain at death, which he dropped abruptly when the time came.

GB   Ram Dass, in the early days, were you totally swept away by Tim Leary and his vision, or did you have doubts as it was happening?

RD   I was totally swept up. It was "damn the torpedoes, full speed ahead," I suppose. As long as Tim needed me, that was my reason for being. I defined myself as someone who's not creative, but helping creative people. He was the first creative person I'd come across, and by far the most creative.

GB   I think you were described somewhere as his loyal lieutenant. Would you say that's accurate?

RD   Yes. That 'servant to Tim's creativity' is ironic because now I'm in the Hanuman role of service to others. And Hanuman's creativity is godly.

GB   Another metaphor that Tim uses is that you two were Tom Sawyer and Huckleberry Finn, having adventures together.

RM   I liked that comparison, it's an American classic. You were Tom, the more normal boy, and Tim was Huck, the wild Irish guy. And Peggy Hitchcock was like Becky Thatcher. I like the adventure image: my first book on psychedelic experiences was called *The Ecstatic Adventure*.

RD   Having adventures was a very big part of it. I remember Tim and I were on the stage at Carnegie Hall both wearing red socks and sneakers and we were just being bad boys. I felt our life together was "bad boys trying this and trying that." We were adventurers – that's what we were.

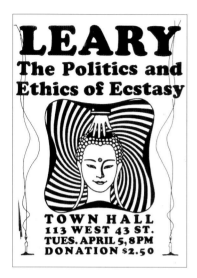

That was more of our mindset, rather than that of scientists, or of servants to humanity, being compassionate and so forth. We were astral adventurers.

RM   Well, I agree that the adventure mindset was a big part. But for Tim and me, the scientist explorer attitude was also present.

RD   Yes. I graduated from the adventurer school and now, I'm on this spiritual quest. The spiritual quest is compassionate; it means I can offer my fellow human beings more of what they need.

GB   It's focused on serving others.

RD   Yes, serving others.

GB   Any final comments or reflections?

RD   From Harvard, to Mexico, to the Caribbean islands – we were all in this wave. It was relentless. There was no way to really step off.

RM   That's right. I remember Haight Street in 1967-68. Tens of thousands of people, the street absolutely packed, people walking around in colored shirts, white robes, flowers in their hair and flowers in their hands, smiling and smelling of patchouli and hugging, singing, dancing, music all over the place. It was amazing to me; a flowering of culture and innovation in the arts. The Beatles would come out with a new song and it would immediately be number one on the charts, before it was even out. People just knew they would love it. There was (and is) a core sort of process or energy source at the center of our world that emanates love, creative and constructive love. The Beatles just seemed to tune into it, and it came out in their songs. Everybody recognized it, felt it. "All You Need Is Love." Then after a while they lost the current. They no longer had instant hits, but still good songs.

RD   We were a step in the process. Haight-Ashbury was a step in a process. We thought we were pioneers. We were pioneers. Tim had a strong sense of history in our work.

RM   And yet his history is so different from yours and mine. The way we each came to that wave, that movement, was different. People shared a common interest, common values and aspirations. In the 1960's many,

many people felt that, much more than usually, I think. But also each person comes to it in a unique way. Your background is completely different from Tim's. And mine is different from either one of yours. We were an unlikely combination in many ways. On the other hand, it's not that uncommon that professors and graduate students continue to work together after meeting at a University.

I like to look for reincarnational echoes; I'm just kind of open to it. I ask myself, did we collaborate before? A psychic, I don't remember who, said that in a past life I was Marco Polo. So, I looked into that story, which I didn't know anything about, other than that he'd traveled in the East, What I found out was suggestive. Marco Polo's famous journey to the East, to the court of the Mongolian emperor Kublai Khan, was actually done in the company of his father Niccolo and Uncle Raffeo. The Polo brothers were Venetian merchants in the thirteenth century, who had already traveled once to China when Marco was a young boy. They took Venetian cloth and jewelry and Christian books to China and brought back spices, silk, herbs, maybe opium and hashish. They went on a second trip when young Marco was seventeen. The journey of over 7,000 miles took three years; and then they stayed at the court of Kublai Khan for over twenty years, returning via Sumatra and India through various dangerous adventures. Marco wrote his famous travelogue after he returned and was in prison for being with the wrong political party.

We don't really know what the three did when they lived in the East for almost twenty-five years. We can presume they liked it there. But they brought back knowledge from another world, virtually unknown to their world in Europe. That knowledge provided a considerable stimulus to the age of explorations which began shortly thereafter, including that other well-known Italian sailor, from Genoa. So, that's what I mean by a kind of reincarnational echo: They were three travelers and explorers, related by family, who traveled to the East, bringing back cultural artifacts, but more importantly, knowledge of the wonders of as yet undiscovered worlds.

Ram Dass and Ralph Metzner, California Institute of Integral Studies commencement event, 1989

Author Biographies

RICHARD ALPERT/RAM DASS

In 1967 Richard Alpert traveled to India, where he met his Guru, Neem Karoli Baba, and received the name Ram Dass, which means "servant of God." Since 1968 he has pursued a variety of spiritual practices, including guru kripa; devotional yoga focused on the Hindu spiritual figure Hanuman; meditation in the Theravadin, Tibetan Mahayana and Zen Buddhist schools; karma yoga; and Sufi and Jewish studies. In 1974, Ram Dass created the Hanuman Foundation, which developed the Prison Ashram Project, designed to help prison inmates grow spiritually during their incarceration, and the Dying Project, conceived as a spiritual support structure for conscious dying. These projects are now directed under independent auspices. Information on Ram Dass' schedule and teachings can be found at www.ramdass.org.

Ram Dass' books include *LSD* (co-written with Sidney Cohen and Lawrence Schiller), *Be Here Now* (over one million copies sold), *The Only Dance There Is*, *Grist for the Mill* (with Stephen Levine), *Journey of Awakening*, *Miracle of Love: Stories of Neem Karoli Baba*, *How Can I Help?* (with Paul Gorman), *Compassion in Action: Setting Out on the Path of Service* (with Mirabai Bush), *Still Here: Embracing Aging, Changing and Dying*, *One-Liners: A Mini-Manual for a Spiritual Life*, and *Paths to God: Living the Bhagavad Gita*. Ram Dass is a co-founder and advisory board member of the Seva Foundation ("seva" means "spiritual service" in Sanskrit), an international service organization. Seva supports programs designed to help wipe out curable blindness in India and Nepal, restore the agricultural life of impoverished villagers in Guatemala, assist in primary health care for American Indians, and to bring attention to the issues of homelessness and environmental degradation in the United States, along with other nations.

In 1997, Ram Dass experienced a stroke which left him with expressive aphasia and partial paralysis, but after a time he resumed speaking and teaching on the nature of consciousness, meditation and service as spiritual practice. In 2001 he became the subject of the widely distributed documentary film *Fierce Grace*, made by Mickey Lemle. In 2004, following a life threatening infection, Ram Dass was forced to curtail travel and focus on recovering his health. He now resides on Maui, where he shares satsang, kirtan, and where he can amplify the healing process in the air and waters of Hawaii. His work continues to be a path of teaching and inspiration to so many. www.ramdass.org

RALPH METZNER

Ralph Metzner, PhD, after leaving Millbrook, continued to edit the *Psychedelic Review* for a few more years, and edited a collection of psychedelic accounts called *The Ecstatic Adventure*. He moved to California, worked for a while at Mendocino State Hospital, at the Stanford University Counseling Center, for Kaiser Permanente in Hayward, and Fairview State Hospital in Costa Mesa. He studied and taught for the School of Actualism, an Agni Yoga group founded by Russell Paul Schofield, during the 1970s; and wrote *Maps of Consciousness*, and *Know Your Type*. He then joined the faculty of the California Institute of Asian Studies, in San Francisco, which later changed its name to California Institute of Integral Studies, where he was the Academic Dean during the 1980s, and where he is now Professor Emeritus. He is founder and president of the Green Earth Foundation, a non-profit educational foundation dedicated to the healing and harmonizing of the relations between humanity and the Earth. He wrote *The Unfolding Self* (1986), *The Well of Remembrance* (1994), and *Green Psychology* (1999). He also published edited collections on the science and phenomenology of MDMA (*Through the Gateway of the Heart*, 1985); ayahuasca (*Sacred Vine of Spirits*, 2006); and the psilocybin mushrooms (*Sacred Mushroom of Visions*, 2005). He continues to practice psychotherapy, and presently teaches workshops nationally and internationally on Alchemical Divination. He lives in Northern California, with his wife Cathy and daughter Sophia. Most recently, he has begun writing and publishing a new series of seven (short) books, with the general title *The Ecology of Consciousness*. The first three titles are: *The Expansion of Consciousness* (2008), *The Roots of War and Domination* (2008) and *Alchemical Divination* (2009). www.greenearthfound.org

Gary Bravo, MD, graduated from Harvard University with a degree in biology and did his medical and psychiatric training at the University of California at Irvine, California College of Medicine. While serving there on the clinical faculty he did research on the subjective effects of MDMA (Ecstasy), and helped Dr. Charles Grob develop the first government approved research protocol on the clinical effects of MDMA. He has published papers and lectured internationally on psychedelics and transpersonal psychiatry. He currently is Chief Psychiatrist of Sonoma County Mental Health in Santa Rosa, California.

Ram Dass with Gary Bravo, 2006

CLOCKWISE FROM LEFT: *Richard Katz, George Litwin, Ram Dass, Ralph Metzner, Paul Lee (with hat) and Gunther Weil surround Tim Leary giving thumbs up at the reunion of the Harvard Project participants, March 1996 (two months before Leary's death)*

Contributors' Biographies

PEGGY HITCHCOCK. Moved to Tucson, Arizona, in 1968. There she married Walter Bowart, a founder of the *East Village Other* (an underground newspaper in NY in the sixties). She had two daughters with him. She is currently president of Arizona Friends of Tibet, which she founded in 1981. She was happily remarried to Allan Bayer, a semi-retired psychiatrist, until his death in early 2007.

SUSAN HOMER METZNER. After departing Millbrook in the winter of 1965, lived in NYC, Cambridge, and Warwick, New York, before settling in New Mexico in 1969 where she still lives. She was a student of Willem Nyland (a direct student of Gurdjieff) until his death in 1975. Susan has one son in California. She is a Buddhist, a student of Reginald and Lee Ray, lineage holders of Chogyam Trungpa Rinpoche.

ELSA VON ECKARTSBERG, PhD. Taught German Literature at Harvard after finishing her graduate studies there in 1962. She also taught for several years a very popular course on Hermann Hesse at the University of Pittsburgh. In 1994 she published a book of essays on the culture of love in pre-Hitler Germany as *Sternstunden der Liebe*. In 2004 she published the novel *Christa Astralis – Eine Amerika Odyssee* in Germany. It is the portrayal of a "psychedelic-ecological" superreligion lived by a group of people in the Eighties in California. She has also self-published a book of her psychedelic poetry, called *Liquid Light – A Celebration of Inner & Outer Space*.

ROLF VON ECKARTSBERG, PhD. Professor at Duquesne University for twenty-nine years after finishing his graduate studies at Harvard. He established a pioneering and influential graduate program in existential-phenomenological psychology and wrote the book *Life-World Experience: Existential-Phenomenological Research Approaches in Psychology* (1986). He also co-edited a book on *The Metaphors of Consciousness*, and wrote several of the book's essays on existential-phenomenological psychology. Rolf passed away in 1993.

Rolf Van Eckartsburg, UCSF, 1966

GEORGE LITWIN, PhD. Completed his doctorate at Harvard under the direction of David McClelland and went on to teach Organizational Behavior at the Harvard Business School, where he created a science of organizational climate. He later became a founder and officer of Forum Corporation, a company that designed organizational training and development for clients worldwide. As a management consultant in organizational climate, he works with automotive factories in Michigan, Indiana and Kentucky, helping workers understand that their life can be better, and that they can have a chance to take pride in their work. He spent two years studying vipassana meditation practices at the Rajneesh ashram in India. He writes "I discovered that there is a way to become high, to live in the present and feel good with yourself, without drugs. It just takes a lot longer. I wouldn't have moved toward meditation if I hadn't taken psychedelics first and discovered the possibilities."

MICHAEL KAHN, PhD. Taught at Harvard, Yale, the University of Texas, and the University of California – Santa Cruz, where he is Professor Emeritus of Psychology. He now teaches at the California Institute of Integral Studies, where he is Professor of Integral Counseling. He is the author of *Between Therapist* and *Client, The Tao of Conversation, and Basic Freud.*

Paul Lee (left) and Allen Ginsberg (right) at the Chanting Celebration, UCSF, 1970

PAUL LEE, PhD. After leaving Harvard and MIT, taught philosophy and religion at UC Santa Cruz, where he was instrumental in bringing the biodynamic farming methods of Alan Chadwick to California, thus sparking the organic movement. He was the Executive Director of the Herb Trade Association and created an herbal education foundation called The Platonic Academy. He was co-director, with Page Smith, of the William James Association and participated in the founding of the California Conservation Corps, under Governor Jerry Brown. He and Page also opened the first Homeless Shelter in Santa Cruz in 1985 which prompted an industry on behalf of the homeless.

FRANK FERGUSON. Involved with computer technology work since 1966, beginning with Office of Economic Opportunity anti-poverty projects in the mid 60's, and with self-owned companies, developing and marketing interactive multimedia software for which he has received several patents. He is currently also doing political research for a program on WPFW, a local Pacifica radio station.

LORA FERGUSON. An orchestral and chamber music clarinetist. She has been a member of the Kennedy Center Opera House Orchestra since 1980. She also teaches in the music departments at George Washington and George Mason Universities and at other schools. Frank and Lora Ferguson have two sons and six grandchildren.

LISA FERGUSON. A writer and documentary filmmaker, living in Los Angeles. She has made a film called *Children of The Revolution: Tune Back In* and written a book about the making of that film. She is working on another documentary—about growing up with her famous father and how his gift for music became the vehicle for her and her family's continued self-actualization and outrageous adventures across the world stage.

Twenty years after Millbrook, Lisa, Maynard and Flo Ferguson Ojai, California

DOROTHY FADIMAN. An OSCAR-nominated, EMMY-winning filmmaker whose subjects range from the light of Spirit in every faith (*Radiance – The Experience of Light*) to progressive education (*Why Do These Kids Love School?*) to the moving story of a woman with spinal cord injury (*Moment by Moment: The Healing Journey of Molly Hale*). Her work includes a series on reproductive rights *From the Back Alleys to the Supreme Court & Beyond,* and a series on AIDS in Ethiopia. Her current focus is on election integrity, beginning with *Stealing America: Vote by Vote.* She is currently writing a book: *Producing with Passion: Making Films that Make a Difference.*

GRAY HENRY. Studied Arabic and Sufism in Cairo (1969-79), then co-founded the Islamic Texts Society in Cambridge, England, where her two children were educated. Since returning in 1991 to her home in Kentucky, she has founded and continues to act as director of Fons Vitae and Quinta Essentia publishing houses devoted to world spirituality, art and symbolism. A founding member of the Thomas Merton Institute for Contemplative Living, she organizes annual interfaith conferences in which the Dalai Lama has twice played a key role.

JEAN McCREEDY. A graduate of the Nyingma Institute training program for Tibetan Buddhist psychology, transpersonal studies, and individual and family counseling. She completed three years of clinical outpatient training and worked as a counselor for eighteen years in the Pima County social services and mental health system in Tucson, Arizona. During this time, she designed and directed an award winning residential program for the mentally ill. Jean has had a private practice in the US and Mexico, specializing in guided regression, individual and family counseling, and Japanese acupressure.

GUNTHER WEIL, PhD. Received his doctorate from Harvard University in 1965, was a Fulbright Scholar in Europe and subsequently was recruited by Abraham Maslow to teach at Brandeis University. He has also served on the teaching faculties of Brandeis University, Boston College and the University of Massachusetts. He is an internationally recognized organizational consultant, psychologist and educator who has for many years provided guidance to executives and their organizations in the areas of leadership, innovation, team building, strategic planning, and executive wellness. Dr. Weil served for 10 years as the CEO of Intermedia Recording Corporation and senior vice president of Intermedia Systems Corporation, a publicly held media production and consulting firm. Dr. Weil is also a recognized veteran internal martial arts practitioner and teacher who has studied and taught with a number of leading masters and direct lineage holders in Tai Chi Chuan and Qigong as well as the spiritual traditions of Gurdjieff, Taoism, Buddhism and Advaita. He was the founding Chairman of the National Qigong Association (NQA-USA) and in 2001 he was invited by Eckhart Tolle, author of the best selling spiritual classic, *The Power of Now* to teach and facilitate the Practice of Presence.

Panel of experts at UCSF conference on LSD, organized by Richard Baker, 1966.
Leary far left, Rolf Von Eckartsberg third from left; Joel Fort far right.

Photo Credits

Three principle archives provided the photographs appearing in this book: Dr. Timothy Leary Futique Trust, and the private collections of Ralph Metzner and Ram Dass.

Photographers include: Richard Bastian: 212; Tor Eigeland: 46, 94, 95; Peter Gould: 106, 107, 110; Robert "Rio" Hahn: 239; Michael Hollingshead: 211, originally published in *High Times*, 1979; Mario Jurrin: 167; Georgios Kollidas, Panther Media, front cover illustration; Lisa Law: 216, 224; Ralph Metzner: 61, 67, 98, 105, 110, 112, 117; Lawrence Schiller © Polaris Communications, Inc.: 196-197; Don Snyder: 163, 164, 182, 185, 187, 207.

Other photographs provided courtesy of: City Lights Books: 21; Joi Ito: photo of John Perry Barlow, in the foreword; Dorothy Fadiman: 134; Lisa Ferguson: 198, 235; Volume 1, *Psychedelic Review* from the Collection of Mark McCloud: 37; Paul Lee: 71, 233, 234, 236; Pennebaker Hegedus Films, Inc.: 109, 128, 141, 142, 154, 156, 157. We were unable to identify photographers of some images. Our apologies if your credit was missed, please contact the publisher.

Publisher's Acknowledgements

It has been an amazing trip to work on this book. I wish to thank some people in particular for their support of this effort: Denis Berry, for being there at the helm of Dr. Leary's Futique Trust and entrusting us with its treasures; Lisa Rein, Digital Librarian for the Futique, who going beyond the calls of duty to dig deep brought some of these rare images to the surface.

Thanks to John Perry Barlow for his powerful historic overview of the decade in his foreword. To this book's editor, Linda Sperling, we are grateful for her unique knowledge and precise care in bringing these words into print; and to our gifted book designer, Arlyn Nathan, whose skill continues to enhance the content of our cutting-edge books.

And to Marion Wasserman at Elemental Design who helped bring new beauty to these archival images; to Lisa Law, for her iconic images and ideas; to Gay Dillingham, CNS Communications, who shared perspectives from her documentary work on the life of Dr. Leary; to Joanna Harcourt-Smith for her key insights; to Peter Ellzey for cheerful assistance in resolving digital mysteries; to Jessica Evans, whose assistance has been invaluable; and to so many other friends who have contributed their energy and support to this book along the way.

Finally, my deep appreciation to Ram Dass, Ralph Metzner, and Gary Bravo for sharing their memoir with us, expanding our understanding of this transformative era.

And, to Tim Leary, who inspired me to think for myself.

Deborah Parrish Snyder

Select Bibliography

Timothy Leary in his Los Angeles home, 1994

Forte, Robert (ed) *Timothy Leary: Outside Looking In.* Rochester, VT: Inner Traditions International, 1999.

Greenfield, Robert. *Timothy Leary – A Biography.* Orlando, FL: Harvest Books, Harcourt, Inc., 2006.

Higgs, John. *I Have America Surrounded – The Life of Timothy Leary.* London: Friday Books, 2006.

Hollingshead, Michael, *The Man Who Turned on the World.* New York: Abelard-Schuman, 1974.

Kesey, Ken, *One Flew Over the Cuckoo's Nest.* New York: Viking Press and Signet Books, 1962.

Leary, Timothy. *High Priest.* New York: New World Publishing Co., 1968

Leary, Timothy, *Flashbacks – An Autobiography.* Los Angeles: Jeremy P. Tarcher, 1983.

Leary, Timothy, Metzner, Ralph and Alpert, Richard. *The Psychedelic Experience – A Manual Based on the Tibetan Book of the Dead.* New Hyde Park, NY: University Books, 1964.

Leary, Timothy, *Psychedelic Prayers – After the Tao Te Ching.* Berkeley, CA: Ronin Publishing, 1966/1997.

Metzner, Ralph (ed), *The Ecstatic Adventure,* (New York: Macmillan, 1968).

Ouspensky, P.D., *In Search of the Miraculous.* New York: Harcourt, Brace & World, 1949.

Ram Dass, *Be Here Now*, San Cristobal, NM: Lama Foundation & Crown Publishing Group, New York. 1971.

Ram Dass, *Paths to God: Living the Bhagavad Gita*, Harmony Books, 2004.

Roszak, Theodore, *The Making of a Counterculture.* New York: Anchor Books, Doubleday Publishing, 1970.

Smith, Huston, *Cleansing the Doors of Perception,* New York: Jeremy P. Tarcher/Putnam, 2000,

Stevens, Jay, "Storming Heaven – LSD and the American Dream," New York: *The Atlantic Monthly Press,* 1987.

Wolfe, Tom, *The Electric Kool-Aid Acid Test,* New York: Farrar, Strauss & Giroux, 1968.

To learn more about our other Books for Comprehensive Minds, please visit www.synergeticpress.com